Related Books of Interest

Implementing ITIL Configuration Management
by Larry Klosterboer
ISBN: 0-13-242593-9

The IT Infrastructure Library® (ITIL®) helps you make better technology choices, manages IT more effectively, and drives greater business value from all your IT investments. The core of ITIL is configuration management: the discipline of identifying, tracking, and controlling your IT environment's diverse components to gain accurate and timely information for better decision-making.

Now, there's a practical, start-to-finish guide to ITIL configuration management for every IT leader, manager, and practitioner. ITIL-certified architect and solutions provider Larry Klosterboer helps you establish a clear roadmap for success, customize standard processes to your unique needs, and avoid the pitfalls that stand in your way. You'll learn how to plan your implementation, deploy tools and processes, administer ongoing configuration management tasks, refine ITIL information, and leverage it for competitive advantage. Throughout, Klosterboer demystifies ITIL's jargon and illuminates each technique with real-world advice and examples.

 Listen to the author's podcast at: ibmpressbooks.com/podcasts

Understanding DB2
Learning Visually with Examples, Second Edition
by Raul F. Chong, Xiaomei Wang, Michael Dang, and Dwaine R. Snow
ISBN: 0-13-158018-3

IBM® DB2® 9 and DB2 9.5 provide breakthrough capabilities for providing Information on Demand, implementing Web services and Service Oriented Architecture, and streamlining information management. *Understanding DB2: Learning Visually with Examples, Second Edition*, is the easiest way to master the latest versions of DB2 and apply their full power to your business challenges.

Written by four IBM DB2 experts, this book introduces key concepts with dozens of examples drawn from the authors' experience working with DB2 in enterprise environments. Thoroughly updated for DB2 9.5, it covers new innovations ranging from manageability to performance and XML support to API integration. Each concept is presented with easy-to-understand screenshots, diagrams, charts, and tables. This book is for everyone who works with DB2: database administrators, system administrators, developers, and consultants. With hundreds of well-designed review questions and answers, it will also help professionals prepare for the IBM DB2 Certification Exams 730, 731, or 736.

 Listen to the author's podcast at: ibmpressbooks.com/podcasts

Sign up for the monthly IBM Press newsletter at
ibmpressbooks/newsletters

Related Books of Interest

A Practical Guide to Trusted Computing

by David Challener, Kent Yoder, Ryan Catherman, David Safford, and Leendert Van Doorn
ISBN: 0-13-239842-7

Every year, computer security threats become more severe. Software alone can no longer adequately defend against them: what's needed is secure hardware. The Trusted Platform Module (TPM) makes that possible by providing a complete, open industry standard for implementing trusted computing hardware subsystems in PCs. Already available from virtually every leading PC manufacturer, TPM gives software professionals powerful new ways to protect their customers. Now, there's a start-to-finish guide for every software professional and security specialist who wants to utilize this breakthrough security technology.

Authored by innovators who helped create TPM and implement its leading-edge products, this practical book covers all facets of TPM technology: what it can achieve, how it works, and how to write applications for it. The authors offer deep, real-world insights into both TPM and the Trusted Computing Group (TCG) Software Stack. Then, to demonstrate how TPM can solve many of today's most challenging security problems, they present four start-to-finish case studies, each with extensive C-based code examples.

RFID Sourcebook

by Sandip Lahiri
ISBN: 0-13-185137-3

Approaching crucial decisions about Radio Frequency Identification (RFID) technology? This book will help you make choices that maximize the business value of RFID technology and minimize its risks. IBM's Sandip Lahiri, an experienced RFID solution architect, presents up-to-the-minute insight for evaluating RFID; defining optimal strategies, blueprints, and timetables; and deploying systems that deliver what they promise.

Drawing on his experience, Lahiri offers candid assessments of RFID's potential advantages, its technical capabilities and limitations, and its business process implications. He identifies pitfalls that have tripped up early adopters, and shows how to overcome or work around them. This must-have resource can also act as a reference guide to any nontechnical person who wants to know about the technology.

From building business cases to testing tags, this book shares powerful insights into virtually every issue you're likely to face. Whatever your role in RFID strategy, planning, or execution, have Sandip Lahiri's experience and knowledge on your side: You'll dramatically improve your odds of success.

IBM Press

Visit ibmpressbooks.com for all product information

Related Books of Interest

Mainframe Basics for Security Professionals
Getting Started with RACF

by Ori Pomerantz, Barbara Vander Weele, Mark Nelson, and Tim Hahn
ISBN: 0-13-173856-9

For over 40 years, the IBM mainframe has been the backbone of the world's largest enterprises. If you're coming to the IBM System z® mainframe platform from UNIX®, Linux®, or Windows®, you need practical guidance on leveraging its unique security capabilities. Now, IBM experts have written the first authoritative book on mainframe security specifically designed to build on your experience in other environments.

The authors illuminate the mainframe's security model and call special attention to z/OS® security techniques that differ from UNIX, Linux, and Windows. They thoroughly introduce IBM's powerful Resource Access Control Facility (RACF®) security subsystem and demonstrate how mainframe security integrates into your enterprise-wide IT security infrastructure. If you're an experienced system administrator or security professional, there's no faster way to extend your expertise into "big iron" environments.

Lotus Notes Developer's Toolbox
Elliott
ISBN: 0-13-221448-2

IBM Rational Unified Process Reference and Certification Guide
Shuja, Krebs
ISBN: 0-13-156292-4

WebSphere Business Integration Primer
Iyengar, Jessani, Chilanti
ISBN: 0-13-224831-X

Understanding DB2 9 Security
Bond, See, Wong, Chan
ISBN: 0-13-134590-7

Mining the Talk
Spangler, Kreulen
ISBN: 0-13-233953-6

Service-Oriented Architecture (SOA) Compass
Bieberstein, Bose, Fiammante, Jones, Shah
ISBN: 0-13-187002-5

Persistence in the Enterprise
Barcia, Hambrick, Brown, Peterson, Bhogal
ISBN: 0-13-158756-0

Sign up for the monthly IBM Press newsletter at
ibmpressbooks/newsletters

Implementing ITIL Change and Release Management

Implementing ITIL Change and Release Management

Larry Klosterboer

IBM Press
Pearson plc
Upper Saddle River, NJ • Boston • Indianapolis • San Francisco
New York • Toronto • Montreal • London • Munich • Paris • Madrid
Cape Town • Sydney • Tokyo • Singapore • Mexico City

ibmpressbooks.com

The author and publisher have taken care in the preparation of this book, but they make no express or implied warranty of any kind and assume no responsibility for errors or omissions. No liability is assumed for incidental or consequential damages in connection with or arising from the use of the information or programs contained herein.

© Copyright 2009 by International Business Machines Corporation. All rights reserved.

Note to U.S. Government Users: Documentation related to restricted right. Use, duplication, or disclosure is subject to restrictions set forth in GSA ADP Schedule Contract with IBM Corporation.

IBM Press Program Managers: Tara Woodman, Ellice Uffer

Cover design: IBM Corporation

Associate Publisher: Greg Wiegand
Marketing Manager: Kourtnaye Sturgeon
Acquisitions Editor: Katherine Bull
Publicist: Heather Fox
Development Editor: Julie Bess
Managing Editor: Kristy Hart
Designer: Alan Clements
Project Editor: Jovana San Nicolas-Shirley
Copy Editor: Gayle Johnson
Indexer: Lisa Stumpf
Compositor: TnT Design
Proofreader: Water Crest Publishing
Manufacturing Buyer: Dan Uhrig

Published by Pearson plc

Publishing as IBM Press

IBM Press offers excellent discounts on this book when ordered in quantity for bulk purchases or special sales, which may include electronic versions and/or custom covers and content particular to your business, training goals, marketing focus, and branding interests. For more information, please contact:

   U.S. Corporate and Government Sales
   1-800-382-3419
   corpsales@pearsontechgroup.com

For sales outside the U.S., please contact:

   International Sales
   international@pearsoned.com

The following terms are trademarks or registered trademarks of International Business Machines Corporation in the United States, other countries, or both: IBM, the IBM logo, IBM Press, Lotus Notes, and Tivoli.

Microsoft, Windows, Windows NT, and the Windows logo are trademarks of Microsoft Corporation in the United States, other countries, or both. UNIX is a registered trademark of The Open Group in the United States and other countries. ITIL is a registered trademark, and a registered community trademark of the Office of Government Commerce, and is registered in the U.S. Patent and Trademark Office. IT Infrastructure Library is a registered trademark of the Central Computer and Telecommunications Agency, which is now part of the Office of Government Commerce. Other company, product, or service names may be trademarks or service marks of others.

Library of Congress Cataloging-in-Publication Data
Klosterboer, Larry.
  Implementing ITIL change and release management / Larry Klosterboer.
    p. cm.
  ISBN 978-0-13-815041-9
  1. Configuration management. 2. Information technology—Management. I. Title. II. Title: Implementing Information Technology Infrastructure Library change and release management.

  QA76.76.C69K65 2008
  004.068'8—dc22

                    2008040421

All rights reserved. This publication is protected by copyright, and permission must be obtained from the publisher prior to any prohibited reproduction, storage in a retrieval system, or transmission in any form or by any means, electronic, mechanical, photocopying, recording, or likewise. For information regarding permissions, write to:

   Pearson Education, Inc.
   Rights and Contracts Department
   501 Boylston Street, Suite 900
   Boston, MA 02116
   Fax (617) 671 3447

ISBN-13: 978-0-13-815041-9
ISBN-10:   0-13-815041-9

Text printed in the United States on recycled paper at R.R. Donnelley in Crawfordsville, Indiana.

Second Printing of May 2011

This book is dedicated to my sons, Kevin and Brian.

I am amazed by the things you do, but even more by the men you have become.

You are my pride and joy!

Contents

	Acknowledgments	xv
	About the Author	xvi
Part I	**Planning**	**1**
Chapter 1	**Change and Release Management: Better Together**	**3**
	Introducing ITIL	3
	The Overall Library	3
	The Service Management Life Cycle	4
	Service Transition	5
	Service Operation	6
	Change and Release Management	6
	Why Change and Release Belong Together	6
	The Focus of Release Management	7
	The Focus of Change Management	9
	Business Benefits of Implementing ITIL Change and Release Management	9
	Control	10
	Consistency	11
	Collaboration	11
	Confidence	12
	Looking Ahead	12
Chapter 2	**Discovering and Managing Requirements**	**13**
	Uncovering Requirements	13
	The Need for Requirements	13
	Types of Requirements	15
	Discovering Requirements	17
	Deriving Additional Requirements	19

Prioritizing and Managing Requirements	21
Creating a Requirements Document	21
Defining and Using Requirement Priorities	22
Allocating Requirements to Projects	23
Balancing Development Requirements and Operations Requirements	25
Looking Ahead	25

Chapter 3   Defining Change and Release Management Processes   27

How to Define a Process	27
Start with Process Flow	28
Identify Needed Policies	29
Create Procedures	30
Document Work Instructions Where Needed	30
Standard ITIL Process Activities	31
Change Management	31
Release and Deployment Management	32
Change Management and Operations	33
The First Policy	33
Documenting the Request for Change (RFC)	34
Reviews and Impact Assessment	35
Approval, Authorization, or Both	35
Post-Implementation Review	36
Release Management and the Project Life Cycle	37
Release Unit Identification	37
Release Policies	38
Releases or Bundled Changes	38
Support and the End-of-Life Cycle	39
Looking Ahead	40

Chapter 4   Building Logical Work Flows   41

Work Flows by Change Category	41
Data Center Changes	42
Workstation Changes	43
Data Changes	44
Documentation or Administrative Changes	45
Work Flows by Change Urgency	45
Emergency Change	45
Urgent Change	46
Normal Change	47
Long, Complex Change	47
Work Flows for Release Management	48
Software Development Flow	48
Infrastructure Release Flow	49
Integration Project Release	49
Looking Ahead	50

Chapter 5   Completing the Implementation Plan — 51

- Planning to Meet Requirements — 51
  - Turning Requirements into Tasks — 51
  - Estimating Task Sizes — 53
  - Building Dependencies — 53
  - Completing the First Draft — 54
- Planning for Data Migration — 56
  - Tasks for Data Migration — 56
  - Tasks for Data Consolidation — 58
  - Adding Data Tasks to the Plan — 58
- Planning to Implement Tools — 59
  - Tasks for Planning — 59
  - Tasks for Acquisition — 59
  - Tasks for Customization — 60
  - Tasks for Training — 61
- Building a Complete Project Plan — 62
- Looking Ahead — 63

Part II   Implementing — 65

Chapter 6   Choosing the Tools — 67

- Tools for Change Management — 67
  - Integrated Service Management Tools — 68
  - Dedicated Change Management Tools — 69
  - Change Detection and Compliance Tools — 69
- Tools for Release Management — 70
  - Work Flow Tools — 71
  - Software Control Tools — 72
  - Promotion and Deployment Tools — 72
  - Patch Management Tools — 73
  - Asset Reuse Repositories — 74
- Integrating Operations and Development — 74
  - Process Integration Points — 74
  - Data Integration Points — 75
  - Tool Integration Points — 76
  - The Ideal Tool — 76
- Features to Look For — 77
  - User Interface — 77
  - Architecture — 78
  - Data Model — 79
  - Work Flow — 79
  - Integration — 80
- Using a Trade Study to Choose Tools — 80
  - Defining Requirements — 81
  - Establishing Weighting — 81

Evaluating Alternatives	81
Scoring and Judging	82
Looking Ahead	83

Chapter 7 Migrating or Consolidating Data — 85

Dealing with Legacy Systems	85
Accessing Legacy Data	86
Adding Values to New Fields	87
Converting Data Values	88
Dealing with Unclosed Records	88
Data Retention Policies	89
Defining and Using Policies	89
Archiving Aged Data	90
Techniques for Consolidating Data	90
Identify Common Keys	91
Reconcile Similar Data Values	92
Form New Data Records	93
Merging Release and Change Data	93
Configuration Items as a Common Denominator	94
Looking Ahead	95

Chapter 8 Bringing the Process to Life — 97

Running a Process Workshop	97
Workshop Participation	98
Agenda and Purpose	98
Expected Workshop Outcomes	100
Building the Right Organization	100
Change Management Roles	101
Release Management Roles	101
Staffing the Roles	102
Training the Team	103
Preparing Training Materials	103
Delivering Training	104
First Steps Toward Success	105
Certify Key Staff	105
Measure Frequently	106
Evaluate and Adjust	107
Looking Ahead	107

Chapter 9 Choosing and Running a Pilot — 109

Reasons to Perform a Pilot	110
Choosing the Right Pilot	112
Measuring the Pilot Project	114
Running an Effective Pilot	115
Evaluating the Pilot	116
What Happens When Pilots Fail	117
Looking Ahead	119

Chapter 10	**Moving from Pilot to Production**	**121**
Determining the Implementation Axis		121
Organizational Implementation		121
Geographic Implementation		123
Technology Implementation		123
Measuring to Show Benefits		124
Change Management Measurements		124
Release Management Measurements		127
Timing and Productivity Measurements		128
Measurement Summary		129
Corrections for Common Implementation Problems		130
Lack of Resources		130
Overwhelming Data		131
Looking Ahead		131
Part III	**Operational Issues**	**133**
Chapter 11	**The Forward Schedule of Change**	**135**
The Basic Contents of the FSC		135
Which Changes to Include		135
What Information to Include for Each Change		137
FSC Timing Issues		138
Assembling a Useful FSC		139
Automating the FSC Creation Process		140
Multilevel FSC for Multilevel CABs		140
Integrating Change and Release Management Schedules		141
Changes Implement Releases		142
The FSC Versus the Release Road Map		142
Looking Ahead		142
Chapter 12	**Building the Definitive Media Library**	**143**
Overview of the DML		143
Physical Aspects of the DML		144
Logical Aspects of the DML		144
Building a Distributed DML		144
How the DML Differs from Other Software-Tracking Tools		146
Purpose of the Definitive Media Library		146
Contents of the Definitive Media Library		146
Uses of the Definitive Media Library		147
Tracking Versions in the DML		147
Acquiring New Software		148
Retiring Software Packages		148
Lending Software from the Library		149
Replacing Lost Media		149
Using the DML to Optimize Change Management		149
Consistency of Deployment		150
Helping the Sunset Problem		150
Improving Audit Posture		151
Looking Ahead		151

Chapter 13 Defining Release Packages ... 153
- Understanding the Software Stack ... 153
  - Application Software ... 154
  - Middleware ... 155
  - Operating Systems ... 156
  - Hardware ... 157
- Guiding Principles for Release Package Design ... 158
  - Design Packages from the Top Down ... 158
  - Keep Packages as Simple as Possible, But No Simpler ... 159
  - Test Each Release from the Bottom Up ... 159
  - Never Count on Vendor Release Schedules ... 160
- Using the Release Packages ... 161
- Looking Ahead ... 161

Chapter 14 Auditing and Compliance Management ... 163
- Control Points ... 164
  - Defining Control Points ... 164
  - Implementing Control Points ... 165
  - Control Point Guidelines ... 165
- Controlling Changes Across Control Points ... 166
- Regulations and Release Management ... 168
- Data Auditing and Process Auditing ... 169
  - Process Audits ... 169
  - Data Audits ... 170
  - Internal and External Audits ... 170
  - Building an Audit Program ... 171
- Looking Ahead ... 172

Part IV Reaping the Benefits ... 173

Chapter 15 Business Impact Analysis ... 175
- Technical Impacts and Business Impacts ... 175
  - Technical Impacts ... 176
  - Business Impacts ... 176
- How to Determine Business Impact ... 177
- Recording Business Impact in a Change Record ... 179
  - Impact Assessments as Text ... 180
  - Impact Assessments as Data Fields ... 180
  - Impact Assessments and Relationships ... 181
- Using Business Impact Analysis in the Change Advisory Board ... 182
  - Scheduling Decisions ... 182
  - Authorization Decisions ... 183
  - Project Decisions ... 183
- Looking Ahead ... 184

Chapter 16 Reports and Service Levels	**185**
Reports About Changes	186
Changes by Implementer	187
Changes by Requester	187
Changes by Component	188
Change Statistics	188
Reports About the Change Management Process	189
Change Aging Report	190
Failed Change Report	190
Changes by Lead Time	191
Reports About Releases	192
System Engineering Reports	193
Project Management Reports	193
Quality Management Reports	194
Reports About the Release Management Process	195
Deployment Reports	195
Planning Reports	196
Looking Ahead	197
Chapter 17 Linking to Other Processes	**199**
Some Other Connections to Consider	199
Process Linkage	200
Data Linkage	201
Benefits of Integration	201
Linking Changes to Incident Management	202
Process Linkage	202
Data Linkage	203
Benefits of Integration	203
Linking Changes to Problem Management	204
Process Linkage	204
Data Linkage	205
Benefits of Integration	205
Linking Release Management and Capacity Management	205
Process Linkage	206
Benefits of Integration	207
Some Other Connections to Consider	207
Looking Ahead	208
Index	**209**

Acknowledgments

Once again the writing process has been made much easier, and probably much more intelligible, by a crew of wonderful reviewers. I want to thank Brian, Jabe, Kristin, and Mike for their thoughtful work, which made this text so much stronger than I could make it alone.

Thank you also to my IBM mentors and managers—Rhonda, Amy, Wally, Ken, and Claudia. They have pushed, cajoled, and guided my career for the past ten years or so, and without their help along the way, I would never have had the world of experiences necessary to write any book.

I appreciate the help and support of my editorial team. They know how much work it is to turn an IT person into an author, and they do it painlessly.

Finally, thank you to the many customers I've had an opportunity to serve. You've consistently entrusted the IBM team with your business success, and although we've made a few mistakes along the way, this book is a testament to the success (and fun) we've had together.

About the Author

Larry Klosterboer is a certified IT architect specializing in systems engineering. He works for IBM's global service delivery team out of Austin, Texas. He has more than twenty years of experience in service delivery, spanning technologies from mainframe to networking to desktop computing. Most of that time has been spent designing and implementing service management solutions. Larry currently works as a lead systems engineer for IBM's large outsourcing customers.

PART I

Planning

Every great project begins with a great plan. A plan consists of a scope, a set of resources, a design, and a schedule. The chapters in this part guide you as you document your requirements to clearly indicate the scope of the project, define your processes to identify the needed resources, establish the work flows that form the foundation of your design, and then bring together all these pieces into a comprehensive schedule.

CHAPTER 1

Change and Release Management: Better Together

A manager of information technology (IT) has no greater worry than an environment that is out of control. When a server is down and the IT manager didn't even know the server was supposed to be in production yet, stress can be high. When a new business application is introduced to production and the infrastructure support team hears about it only when the application takes over half the network capacity, the stress really builds. When users begin installing the latest desktop widget and the service desk doesn't yet know how to support it, the IT manager may start thinking about a career change.

One key to avoiding this kind of stress lies in gaining control over all aspects of the IT environment. This book describes how you can gain that control. Using an international best practice called the Information Technology Infrastructure Library™ (ITIL™), and specifically two disciplines called change management and release management, IT managers can learn how to gain or improve control over the total environment.

Introducing ITIL

Although this book focuses on change and release management, it is difficult to understand these disciplines without at least some background in ITIL. This section is not intended as a substitute for the actual books of the library, but it helps remind you of the salient points about ITIL.

The Overall Library

The IT Infrastructure Library is now in its third version. You can find information about the latest version from the British Office of Government and Commerce. This group provides central administration of the library and offers the latest information about ITIL on its website, www.best-management-practice.com.

Currently the library consists of six books. The first book is an introduction to the entire area of IT service management, and the other five books form the core of the best-practice recommendations. Ultimately that is what ITIL is—a set of recommendations based on thousands of examples and the combined centuries of experience of its many contributors. Because of all that experience and the heavy scrutiny the recommendations have received, none should be taken lightly. On the other hand, it is quite likely that none of those experienced contributors have worked in your exact situation, so they couldn't possibly foresee every nuance and challenge that you will face in implementing service management.

This means that you can't simply take ITIL "out of the box" and implement it. You must adopt it and tailor it to fit your situation and to optimize exactly the services you want to provide to your IT consumers. That is the goal of this book. This book isn't a substitute, but it is a supplement that provides a concrete set of steps that help you tailor the recommendations of ITIL to your needs.

The Service Management Life Cycle

Setting aside the introductory volume, the five core books of the ITIL Version 3 library describe a circle of activities that describe almost all IT projects. The circle, called the service management life cycle, is composed of five segments. The titles of the core books of ITIL describe the segments:

- Service strategy
- Service design
- Service transition
- Service operation
- Continuous-service improvement

As expected, the service strategy volume explores the motivation and challenges of service management to help an organization formulate the policies and strategies that will drive the overall IT direction. It includes great information on the value of services, sound principles that foster best practices, and how to use both technology direction and service management strategies to achieve tighter integration between IT and your business.

The service design volume gets a bit more specific. In addition to dealing with organization and technology issues, it focuses on a set of process areas that proactively manage IT services. These processes include service-level management, capacity management, and IT security management, among others. The focus, of course, is on the design of services using these processes.

The service transition book focuses on disciplines that introduce or retire IT services. Both release management and change management are described in the service transition volume of the library because they focus on introducing and retiring IT components and services.

The service operation book primarily deals with the day-to-day management of services that are in operation. Processes associated with operations include event management, incident management, and access management, among others. Service operation also includes functions such as the service desk that are vital to day-to-day IT operations.

Finally, the ITIL volume on continuous-service improvement describes an overall approach to ensuring the quality of the services delivered. Metrics and reporting on services play an important role and are described in this book.

These five volumes together describe the services life cycle, which is the major innovation found in the third ITIL version. The life cycle is shown in Figure 1.1. It is important to be somewhat familiar with this cycle in order to understand the place of change and release management in relation to the other ITIL processes.

Figure 1.1   The IT Infrastructure Library defines a service life cycle.

Service Transition

Transitions are important in the life of IT services. There are many stories of failed projects in IT, and many of those failed projects can be directly related to inadequate service transition. The service transition volume of ITIL provides guidance on how to implement services successfully. The underlying assumption in the service transition book is that each new service is introduced through a basic IT life cycle.

The cycle assumed by the service transition book includes the following:

- Planning for service implementation
- Implementing the service
- Documenting the service
- Testing the service
- Evaluating the effectiveness of the implementation

This cycle applies to every IT service that can be implemented, including change and release management.

Although planning, implementing, and testing are common to almost every IT endeavor, the notions of documentation and evaluation may be new to some organizations. ITIL reports that best practice is to capture the service as a set of configuration items and/or service assets that can then provide ongoing documentation for anyone who needs to understand how the service is delivered. In addition, evaluating the service by defining and tracking service metrics is described as a best practice.

This book provides additional details on material that is found in the ITIL volume on service transition. That volume does an excellent job of describing the best IT practices, but it isn't detailed enough to allow direct implementation. It highlights seven different processes as part of service transition, but it doesn't focus on any of them. It provides an excellent set of concepts that this book fills in with practical advice.

Service Operation

Although the disciplines of change and release management are described in the service transition book, it is nearly impossible to understand their context without also understanding the processes described in the ITIL service operation book. This is by design. ITIL describes an integrated set of processes that cannot function or be understood in isolation.

The volume on service operation describes what happens in the day-to-day workings of an IT service. Things break, circumstances change, services get degraded, and operational disciplines keep the disruption to a minimum. Like the other books in the ITIL library, service operation does not describe exactly how to keep things running efficiently. However, it does offer a compendium of best practices that you can use to define your own operational practice.

There are many linkages between service transition processes such as change and release management and service operations processes such as incident and problem management. You must account for these linkages when planning how you will implement change and release management, so this book assumes that you have a good understanding of the service operation processes.

Change and Release Management

Release management is like an orchestra conductor, and change management is like the musicians. The conductor sets the overall strategy, direction, and tempo. The orchestra blends an array of skills and emotions to realize the conductor's musical ambitions. A conductor without musicians can hear the music in his head, but he or she can't make it real. Musicians without a conductor can create noise, but not harmony or beauty. This section explores this analogy to see why release management and change management go together like a conductor and an orchestra.

Why Change and Release Belong Together

Change management provides a disciplined approach to implementing IT changes. Decommissioning a service, upgrading an infrastructure component, and adopting a new delivery process are all examples of changes that should be tracked by the change management discipline. Each change is considered in isolation and flows through a set of steps, including identification, documentation, assessment, authorization, execution, and evaluation.

Release management provides a strategic approach to implementing an IT service. Much more will be said about IT services later in this book, but as a working definition, an IT service is a set of components and service assets that work together to provide a unique benefit to the organization. Before ITIL V3, many organizations used the term "IT system" instead of "IT service." "System" places the focus on IT components, whereas "service" emphasizes value to the organization.

The most common example of an IT service is a business application such as payroll. A typical payroll system consists of infrastructure components such as servers and network equipment. It also has software modules and some service assets such as user guides, application logon IDs, operating procedures, and measures of the effectiveness of the payroll service.

Release management is the discipline of managing the interrelationships of all these pieces when a new version of the service is needed. Producing a new version of the payroll system might involve updating software modules, which could spark a need for more memory in servers, higher bandwidth on network lines, and changes in the operating procedures. Like a skilled conductor, the release management process determines which changes play at what time, and how they can be blended harmoniously to produce the desired outcome. Release management and change management are the yin and the yang behind service transitions, as shown in Figure 1.2.

Figure 1.2 Service transition consists of the short-term view of change management and the long-term vision of release management.

The Focus of Release Management

Release management is the domain of big-picture thinking. It is involved in understanding services and coordinating releases of those services. Release management views each service as having a complete life cycle, beginning with planning for that service and ending with the sunset of that service. Ideally the early planning for a service will indicate a release management policy, indicating how frequently new releases will be introduced, how contents of those releases will be determined, and when the final release will be retired from service. In practical experience, most organizations don't have quite this much foresight when introducing new IT services. However, release management is still involved in understanding the components of the new service and determining the impact of a change to one part of the service on all the other parts.

Release management plans may span multiple years. They consider the introduction of new technology at the infrastructure level, new software at the application level, and new business practices at the service asset level. The release management plan considers changes from hardware and software vendors and determines the best time to upgrade components to those new levels.

Release management also looks at the microcosm of IT. In this guise, ITIL speaks of release and deployment management together. The cycle of building something new, testing its suitability to purpose, and then deploying it into the IT environment is release and deployment management. As shown in Figure 1.3, release planning is a strategic discipline, change management is a governing discipline, and release deployment is a tactical discipline.

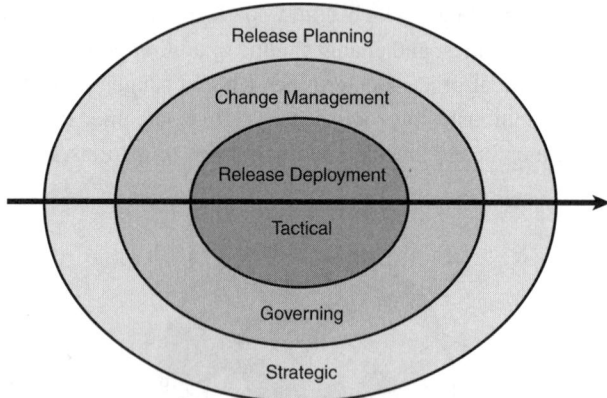

Figure 1.3 Release management encompasses both the strategic planning aspect and the tactical deployment aspect.

As a concrete example, consider again the payroll service described in the preceding section. A complete release management plan would begin with the introduction of the payroll service (or perhaps with the complete revamping of the service from a legacy system). The plan would span several years, taking into account times for refreshing the hardware with newer models, and plans for implementing new versions of operating systems, middleware, and the payroll application as they become available. This entire plan would define periods of change followed by longer periods of stability. It also would give business users a good idea of when to expect new features of the service to be introduced.

Release management is the conductor in the sense that it weaves together the various parts, ensuring that smooth and harmonious service results despite the number of changes needed.

The Focus of Change Management

If release management is the conductor, change management represents the individual musicians. It focuses on details that are necessary to make each change go smoothly, but it cares nothing about the big picture. Just as a musician must accurately produce the correct rhythm, pitch, and intonation, the change manager must determine the schedule, implementation details, and back-out plan for each change. These details are critical to the success of each change, and the focus of the change management process is to see that each detail is understood in advance.

Because it focuses on details, change management is bound to a tactical time frame rather than a strategic one. Most of the changes being managed are scheduled a week or two out, with some exceptionally large or complex changes scheduled months in advance. Normally the change-management process dictates a minimum delay between proposing a change and executing that change, but change management also recognizes that urgent changes sometimes are necessary.

Of all the service transition processes, change management is the most intimately related to service operations. Long before the days of ITIL and formally recognized best practices, every IT operations department had at least some form of change control in place. Every IT person has recognized that the best way to solve problems with permanent resolutions is through organized and controlled change to the environment. Unfortunately, every IT manager has also regretted making a change in which the details weren't examined or controlled closely enough. This book examines this close relationship between change management, problem management, and incident management because it must be considered when implementing ITIL change management.

Change management controls IT execution and release management encompasses the wider vision and deals with the fine details. Release management sets the course and powers the ship, whereas change management stands at the rudder to steer the ship. All these analogies point out why it is critically important to approach change management and release management together.

Many organizations have implemented change management and relegated release management to the same shelf as the IT strategy they hope to define some day. That is a mistake, because those organizations will soon find themselves embroiled in discussions about changes that don't seem to make sense. They don't debate whether a change can be successfully implemented, but whether there will be value from implementing it. In essence, they are having a release management discussion without formally recognizing it or having the foundation necessary to conduct the discussion.

Business Benefits of Implementing ITIL Change and Release Management

Although ITIL makes perfect sense, and is generally a good idea, you need significant funding to implement change and release management, and funding is difficult to obtain without some concrete benefits. Fortunately, the business benefits of change and release management are very real and can be quantified relatively easily. This section describes both the quantitative and qualitative benefits you can reasonably expect; they are summarized in Figure 1.4.

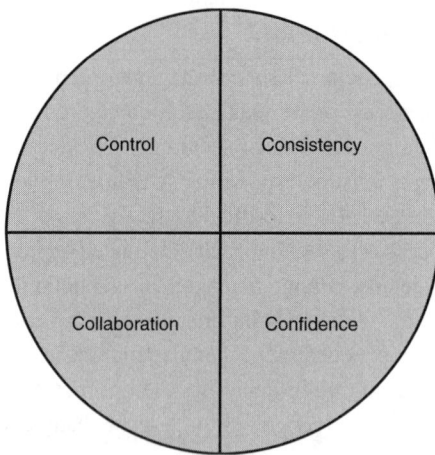

Figure 1.4 An ITIL-aligned change and release management process has tangible business benefits.

Control

The primary reason for implementing change and release management is to gain control over the IT environment. Release planning gives you long-term control by setting the course and speed of technology. It is release management that dictates how quickly your organization will respond to changes by hardware and software vendors. Organizations that desire a slower pace, for example, can have their release management policy dictate that certain operating system versions will be skipped. These same release management policies help control the funding process by indicating which releases can be expected in any given funding cycle. Rather than putting out a general broadcast asking everyone what they want to spend money on, an organization using release management can focus on dividing precious resources between new service proposals and services that are due for a new release. When release management is working well, much of the overall business plan for IT can be constructed several years in advance, giving the organization extensive control over the planning process.

Although release management provides high-level control, change management has daily control over what happens to the IT environment. The central attribute controlled by change management is quality. By insisting that each proposed change be reviewed first, you automatically eliminate many changes that would have failed without review. If you add post-implementation reviews as well, you can incorporate lessons learned from one change into the plans for the next change. This kind of feedback loop will significantly improve the quality of the IT environment. Change management should also insist on reviews of all failed changes, adding another quality checkpoint where you can ask how the organization can improve its future change efforts. A successful deployment of ITIL best practices should show a measurable reduction in the number of failed changes.

By following a structured release deployment method, you enhance control at the tactical level as well. Every organization should have policies regarding the level of testing that is necessary before a release can impact the production environment. That policy gives release deployment the power to stop a change before it can cause service disruptions.

Consistency

Another business benefit of ITIL aligned change and release management is consistency. Although consistency is more difficult to measure, it is important to all IT organizations faced with rapidly changing business demands and technology solutions. Appropriate release management helps create consistency within a single service by providing a high-level vision, a consistent set of goals, and continuity from one release to another within the service. By insisting that the service be treated as a single entity from the time it is conceived until the time it is retired, release managers provide a more consistent view of each IT service than is possible by treating releases as unrelated IT projects. Release management also tends to provide consistency in the development, testing, and deployment of new services, because it promotes the longer-term view associated with systems engineering and portfolio management rather than the more isolated view of project management.

Change management also contributes to consistency in the IT environment. By structuring each request for change (RFC) in the same way, the change management process forces people to think about implementation plans, test plans, and backout plans. Eventually smart IT people realize that the more consistent those plans are, the more easily the RFC will be approved. Although actually copying records from one change to another can promote occasional sloppiness, it certainly promotes consistency in implementation.

Change management also introduces the concept of standard changes. These are tasks that are repeated frequently and accomplished in essentially the same way each time. For example, when a user has forgotten his or her password, the service desk often needs to make a change to the server environment by resetting the lost password. These changes carry such a low risk and happen so frequently that they can be defined as a standard change. Normally standard changes are defined as services in the service catalog and are executed through the service request process.

Collaboration

One of the greatest benefits of a full implementation of change and release management is how it improves communications and collaboration among IT professionals. This increased collaboration begins with better, more consistent planning between groups. As soon as it is accustomed to the discipline of release management, your IT organization will begin building plans around projected release dates. For example, imagine that your release management process has determined that the next release of your marketing promotions application will be available in the third quarter of next year. Armed with this information, the server administrators can determine when they'll need more capacity to respond to new promotions that are made possible by the new application. The network team can gear up to provide the necessary bandwidth. The application support team can schedule their vacations earlier in the year to be on hand to support the new application. This kind of collaboration simply isn't possible without the foresight provided by active release management plans.

Release planning no doubt improves long-range goal planning, but ITIL change and release management helps daily communications as well. The main purpose of change management is to facilitate communications before changes adversely impact the environment. The change requester needs to work with the team implementing the change to agree on the details of what needs to be accomplished. The change approvers need to communicate with the technical team to be sure they really understand the technical and business impacts of a change. When change management is implemented and working well, the volume and quality of communications increase dramatically. This communication may initially be seen as bureaucratic, but it is really a significant business advantage.

A nexus for this communication is the change advisory board (CAB) meeting. This meeting typically goes through all the important changes happening in the environment. It exists primarily to allow the many different parts of the IT organization to communicate with one another. Chapter 11, "The Forward Schedule of Change," has much more to say about the CAB, but essentially it serves as one place where all factions of IT can discuss the potential impact of changes before they are made, and then review the success of changes after they are implemented. In fact, it is almost impossible to find an organization that doesn't have some kind of centralized communications mechanism for dealing with impending changes. Formalizing this mechanism as a CAB based on the ITIL framework makes it even more effective.

Confidence

Ultimately, implementing reliable release and change management processes will give your IT organization confidence. Although it is difficult to quantify confidence as a business benefit, there is no mistaking an organization that has it. Confident organizations plan more accurately and more thoroughly. Organizations with greater confidence execute more successfully. Better planning and execution in turn result in more confidence. Ultimately a confident IT organization results in every IT manager knowing with certainty that his or her environment is under control. This is the ultimate protection against any kind of audit, whether internal or external.

Looking Ahead

You have had a whirlwind introduction to ITIL and an overview of change and release management. You've learned that release management is both the micro-level discipline of deploying a single new thing and the macro-level discipline of planning across a broad horizon. Change management is the controlling discipline that helps govern the ongoing changes in the IT environment. Working together, change and release managements will provide control, consistency, and collaboration for your IT environment, and ultimately give you confidence that your IT organization can handle whatever course the larger organization chooses to pursue.

With this background behind you, the next chapter helps you make a plan to implement change and release management for your organization.

CHAPTER 2

Discovering and Managing Requirements

"Managing requirements" is the technical term for knowing what your project is doing. Whether they are documented or simply exist in someone's head, requirements are part of every project. This chapter describes the benefits of formally documenting and managing requirements. Then it gives you detailed information about working with requirements for your implementation of change and release management.

Much of what you'll find here is common to all IT projects. The techniques described have indeed been used to develop software, implement business applications, improve IT processes, and define IT services. If your organization is already familiar with the rigor of requirements management, much of what is covered here might be a review. On the other hand, if you think you can implement change and release management without ever writing down your requirements, you should read this chapter very carefully.

Uncovering Requirements

Requirements aren't created out of thin air. Instead, they are uncovered by careful detective work. If you hope to discover the correct requirements for your project, you need to know where and how to look for them. This section provides some motivation for finding requirements, and then it covers the techniques you can adopt to uncover the requirements lurking in your own organization.

The Need for Requirements

Before you start an all-out search for requirements, you need to understand the value you expect to gain. Like everything else in IT, requirements can be justified by the value they produce. The single best reason for taking the time to discover and document requirements is that they define the scope of the project. IT projects that have vague or undefined scope are like black holes that suck in time, effort, and resources and never give anything back. If you have ever been involved with a vague project, you know that having a clearly defined scope saves time in initial planning and saves even more time and effort in rework as your project sponsors and stakeholders later try to clarify what they wanted in the first place. Clearly defined requirements prevent your project from suffering through the endless churn of a fuzzy scope.

Requirements also drive the quality of any project. All IT projects measure quality by testing the project's output. If the requirements are unknown or unclear, these tests are much more difficult and expensive to perform. Here's a simple example. Imagine you are implementing change management, and you choose not to document requirements. If your only goal is to manage changes, you might decide to install a whiteboard in a shared area and have everyone write down anything they will change. You could even create procedures for when to erase the whiteboard and how to use different colors of markers for different types of changes. But is this a successful implementation of change management? You could imagine testing to see that the whiteboard could be read by others, and that all the markers work. Maybe you could even test to see if people actually wrote down what they did and did what they wrote down. But have you really achieved the goal? You cannot know, because you never specified the goal with any certainty in the beginning. Projects that want to finish with a quality outcome must have well-defined requirements.

So requirements are important, but do you really need to make the effort to write them down? Perhaps your organization is small and simple, with few people in IT. Writing down requirements takes effort, and time for reviews and rework, but it is always worth the effort. Even if only two people are working on a project, they will differ in some details on what the requirements are. The discipline of documentation highlights these differences early on, while they can still be ironed out with a minimum of difficulty. Committing thoughts to paper provides a mechanism to clarify those thoughts and allows others to better understand them. The documentation process itself is critical for the same reasons that having requirements is critical—it prevents fuzzy scope and lets you test for project quality.

Unfortunately, requirements, like thoughts, are dynamic rather than static. As your project moves forward and begins to accomplish its goals, some of those requirements will change. This should be expected, and each of those changes should drive you back to the documented requirements. Update the documents as necessary, and be sure that all project stakeholders have access to the updates. It seems simple when someone suggests an additional report that needs to be created by the project. However, when you're rushing to meet the committed schedule, that simple thought will get lost or interpreted to mean something less than it originally did. Taking the time to update the requirements documents and get concurrence on the change requirements will save time and effort later in the project.

So requirements need to be discovered, documented, and maintained throughout the life of the project. This is the first key to a successful implementation of ITIL aligned change and release management.

Types of Requirements

To discover requirements, you need to know what you are looking for. There are many different ways to classify requirements into different types. This section presents a simple classification that is appropriate for implementing an IT service such as change or release management. This simple classification is shown in Figure 2.1.

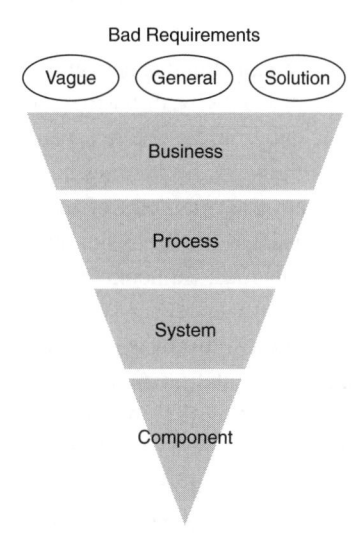

Figure 2.1 A good requirements set includes different requirement types.

The first kind of requirement to look out for is bad requirements. Unfortunately, this is the most common requirement you will uncover, and you need to sort through them to get to the good requirements. Bad requirements come in lots of shapes and sizes. Unclear or vague desires such as "We need to allow for auditing" are bad requirements because they don't help clarify and sharpen the scope of your project. On the other hand, declarations of a solution such as "The release management tool shall be IBM Tivoli® Service Request Manager" make bad requirements because they don't leave room for the project team to make a trade-off and create a good design. Bad requirements might also be so high-level as to be almost meaningless, such as "We need to control changes."

Several great books can help you distinguish between good and bad requirements. If you are new to discovering and managing requirements, it would be well worth your effort to find and read one or more of them. Requirements definition is a skill that requires training and experience to develop.

As soon as the bad requirements are out of the way, you can begin to discover the good requirements that will help shape the scope of the change and release management project. Normally you should start this effort at the top of the requirements hierarchy by identifying the business requirements. Business requirements are those that describe at the highest level what the project should accomplish. Because business requirements have a higher scope than other types, it's often tempting to make them vague. It is important to be specific even with these higher-level requirements. Rather than saying "Change management shall help us pass audits," state a specific requirement like "The change management project shall improve our audit success rate by 12% within the first year of completion." The scope is still very large, but the desired outcome is much more specific.

Business requirements typically deal with business entities. Requirements concerning cost, revenue, business quality, employee productivity, or business unit efficiency are business requirements. Requests for IT process efficiency, infrastructure capacity, end-user features, or documentation updates are not business requirements. Sometimes business requirements can be difficult for IT people to discover because they are often part of basic assumptions rather than specific requirements. When defining your business requirements for a change and release management project, never be afraid to state the obvious. Someone else may find that requirement far less obvious.

Another type of requirement you will discover is process requirements. If your IT organization typically does development or implantation of business applications, process requirements might be foreign to you. When implementing ITIL best practices, however, it is easy to see that process requirements will be your most common type. Process requirements help define characteristics of the process and procedures. They give you guidance as you begin to actually define the process. Here are some examples of process requirements that others have used when implementing release management:

- A policy shall be defined indicating which IT components and service assets form a release.
- A procedure shall be documented to describe inspection of release test plans.
- The release management process shall include a measurement of the cycle time from planning to deployment of a release package.
- The release manager shall review and update release policies at least semiannually.

All these process requirements help define the scope of the release management process and put constraints on the team fully documenting the process as part of the ongoing implementation project.

The next set of requirements to consider is probably the most familiar. These are system requirements, which are sometimes known as tool requirements. This is where you start to uncover what people want the release and change management systems to do and be. System requirements are further split into functional requirements and nonfunctional requirements. As their names imply, functional requirements describe how people can interact with the system and what the system can accomplish. Nonfunctional requirements describe capacity, performance, serviceability, and other IT characteristics of the system.

The system requirements necessarily focus on the software used to automate the change and release management processes. You should be careful, therefore, that your system requirements don't conflict with the process requirements. If the process requirements say that two approvals are sufficient for any change, don't document system requirements that say the tools must support ten or more approvals. That would be unnecessarily restrictive and would end up skewing your tools decision later in favor of a technology you won't even be using.

The most detailed requirements are called component requirements. Typically these are used only to define a specific part of the overall system that might be understood in different ways even after the system requirements are complete. You can think of component requirements as directives to the design team about which design choices they should make. Normally this is a rare case, and you can probably create a very good set of requirements for your change and release management project without ever worrying about component requirements. If you do find yourself in a situation where your system requirements don't seem to capture enough detail, you can use component requirements as needed.

Discovering Requirements

Now that you understand the different types of requirements, it is time to actually start discovering the requirements for your project. There are literally hundreds of ways to go about finding the best requirements, but they generally can be broken into only a few categories.

Experience shows that the fastest way to get a large block of requirements is to hold a requirements workshop. This is a meeting of the project stakeholders specifically for the purpose of understanding what they want the project to accomplish. It is best if this meeting can bring everyone together face to face, typically for two or three days. The face-to-face aspect helps people understand not only the verbal but also the nonverbal communications, which can be just as important. Having a meeting span several days gives people time to leave the meeting and reflect on some of the decisions being made. Nonverbal communication and opportunity for reflection enhance the creative process and help your stakeholders better visualize the desired end results of the project. Ultimately the set of requirements is nothing more than a description of the end state.

After you get concurrence to bring together a group of people for a multiday meeting, you don't want to waste their time. Table 2.1 shows some of the activities you might consider as part of a complete requirements workshop.

Table 2.1 Potential Activities for a Requirements Workshop

Activity	Duration	Benefit
Introductions	30 minutes	People who know each other collaborate better.
Review ITIL documentation	3 hours	Understanding the ITIL recommendations helps everyone keep the goal in mind.
Discussion of current shortcomings	2 hours	Current dissatisfactions are a rich source of future requirements.
Demonstration of tool(s)	2 hours per tool	The requirements workshop provides a great forum for vendors to demonstrate potential tools, or for IT to demonstrate a selected tool.
Discussion of business benefits	1 hour	Talking about expected business benefits helps you find business requirements.
Policy discussion	1 hour	A discussion of current and potential policies helps create process requirements.
Tools discussion	2 hours	Understand existing tool strengths and weaknesses, and determine whether new tools will be implemented as part of the project.
Review time	2 hours	Review progress at the end of each day to help people reflect.

During the requirements workshop, you should assign specific people to be the moderator and the scribe. The moderator must ensure that people stay on task, but also create an atmosphere of collaboration and creation. A workshop full of silent people is certainly not helpful or effective.

The scribe should capture as much of the workshop as possible as raw notes. There will be time after the meeting for the scribe to turn these notes into requirements in the proper form, so don't worry about the format during the meeting. Some groups find it helpful to have more than one scribe to prevent the loss of critical ideas and to enable larger groups to split into multiple smaller groups during discussion time. If you choose to split the group, the role of the scribe is to report on the discussions when the group comes back together.

Follow up quickly to help maximize the value of the requirements workshop. You should quickly scrub through the notes and publish them for all the participants for review and comment. That way you can keep the stakeholders engaged while the team is sorting and translating the notes into good requirements. This quick response to the workshop shows that the project is making forward momentum and shows the stakeholders that you value their opinions. Keeping the stakeholders involved benefits your implementation in many different ways.

Another technique that is frequently used to discover requirements is the interview. An interview is simply a small discussion about requirements. Typically, interviews are used for key stakeholders who cannot participate in a requirements workshop, but it is also possible to use interviews exclusively if your organization is small enough.

A very useful technique when gathering requirements via interview is to share the results of interviews with other stakeholders. In this way, you get some of the benefits of a requirements workshop as the interviewees build on each others' thoughts. It is important to take good notes during interviews, because you certainly don't want to lose out on the insights of these key stakeholders. Those notes can be shared as a follow-up activity, just as you would do with the notes from a workshop.

Another great place to discover requirements is by looking at legacy projects to see what they did. For example, perhaps you have access to someone who remembers the deployment of the current change management tools, or the definition of the current release management process. You can use the interview technique to understand what requirements they sought to achieve in that previous project. Often you will find that previous projects wanted to do more but were stymied by cost or schedule pressures and thus didn't accomplish everything they wanted to. Take advantage of this situation to turn those unimplemented features into requirements for your project.

If your project will scrap some of the work of the previous project, you should also look carefully at the requirements that were implemented in the past. If you plan to replace the current process with an ITIL aligned process defined from scratch, you will certainly want to understand the motivations and requirements for the previous process. If you're replacing the legacy service management tools with new ones, you should be sure that the new tools are not perceived as a having less function than the previous ones. Legacy requirements are often assumed at workshops and interviews, so sometimes careful consideration of what got built in a previous project is the only way you'll be sure that your project isn't viewed as a giant step backwards.

Finally, if someone else has taken care of part of the work for you, don't forget to take advantage of this. Sometimes you can find existing requirements statements already documented. Process documents are especially fruitful, because many process designers tend to document the requirements for the process as they go. If you can find existing release or change management process documents, they are likely to contain some requirements. Similarly, tools documentation often contains statements that can be easily turned into requirements. Check both documentation on tools that are already installed and any documents you receive from the vendor on tools that are being proposed for your environment. Of course, any requirements you find documented will have to be tested to ensure that they are not duplicates of those you've already documented from workshops, interviews, or other sources.

Deriving Additional Requirements

Some requirements need to be uncovered, and others need to be created. In the technical jargon of systems engineering, discovered requirements are called *elicited*, and requirements created by the project team are called *derived*. The difference between these two means of documenting requirements is fairly important.

Defining requirements is a top-down process. The first step is to discover or elicit requirements using any of the techniques already described. After requirements are discovered, they need to be clarified. Normally this is done by distributing workshop or interview notes and getting feedback to ensure that thoughts have been captured accurately. After requirements are clarified, the project team derives additional requirements to bridge the gap between stakeholder understanding and exactly what the project team needs to do. This drives the requirements to the lowest level.

The requirements cycle is then turned on its head for review. The most detailed requirements are reviewed first by the project team to ensure that they are complete, accurate, and consistent. Next, the project stakeholders review the midlevel requirements as a means of understanding and validating the project scope. Finally, the project sponsors review the top-level business requirements to ensure that the project fits with the overall IT strategy. This entire cycle is shown in Figure 2.2.

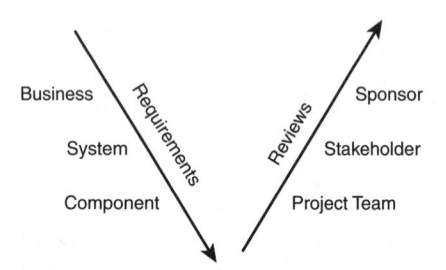

Figure 2.2   Gathering and reviewing requirements follows a natural cycle.

One important point in deriving additional requirements is to allow room for the judgment of your technical team. Tension naturally occurs between the business people, who are likely to be your stakeholders, and the technical people, who make up your project team. The stakeholders won't know enough to provide detailed requirements, but the project team won't always understand enough to make sure that the technical requirements align with the business. The business people and the technical people need to communicate with one another to resolve this tension. The process of gathering and defining requirements provides the perfect opportunity for this communication. This is the purpose of the reviews shown in Figure 2.2.

A simple example illustrates the importance of derived requirements. Suppose one of the requirements coming out of your workshop says "A report shall be created to track unauthorized changes on a month-to-month basis." This is one of dozens of requirements specified for reports at the requirements workshop, and the stakeholders believe it is fairly specific. When the technical team gets hold of it and starts thinking about actually creating that report, however, they are left with dozens of questions and design decisions. Should the report use a graphic such as a bar chart or line graph? What exactly makes a change unauthorized, and what query can pull exactly that information out of the change management tool? What do we mean by a "month-to-month basis"? Does that mean the current and previous month, or perhaps the past thirteen months to include a full calendar year?

All these questions could be asked of one or more stakeholders, but the answers would likely come back with some questions of their own. The stakeholders don't know how difficult it would be to create a bar graph instead of simple numbers. They may want to know the extra cost of thirteen months compared to just two months. Rather than get into a back-and-forth set of questions that can take an inordinate amount of time to resolve, best practice says that we let the project team derive additional detail requirements. They make assumptions about what the stakeholders are likely to want and then document those assumptions as derived requirements.

The challenge with deriving requirements is in knowing when to stop. Following our example, the project team would never create individual detailed requirements specifying the column headings, the font size of the text, or any such specific details on the report. They would, however, create requirements around exactly what data to get from the database and the general layout of that data on the report. The rule of thumb when deriving requirements is to use enough detail that the stakeholders won't be surprised at the project's eventual outcome, but to also leave room for a competent design person to make some choices about how the requirements are fulfilled.

Prioritizing and Managing Requirements

When you have finished gathering requirements, it is time to do something productive with them. You need to sort these requirements statements and put them into a format that will make them accessible for the rest of the project. The best way to sort requirements is by assigning them a priority based on the needs and ambitions of your stakeholders. This section describes some techniques for organizing and managing requirements.

Creating a Requirements Document

Because requirements are natural-language descriptions of the project, they belong in document form. Your requirements might also be in spreadsheets, a database, or even a requirements management tool, but the best way to review requirements is a document, so that is what you will ultimately end up producing. Because requirements determine the scope of a project, your set of requirements should end up being part of the scope document for your change and release management implementation project.

But requirements are only part of a scope document. You will also want to add some other elements to create a complete scope document. Many organizations already have a standard template for defining the scope of an IT project, and you should certainly use that template if it's available. If you don't have a template available, the elements you will probably want to include in your scope document include the following:

- Business context of the project
- List of project sponsors
- List of project stakeholders
- High-level description of the end state (sometimes called the operational concept)
- Approvals page

Of course, the bulk of your scope document will still be your requirements. Sometimes you may even have so many requirements that it seems you are bogging down the scope document with too much detail. When this is the case, you can split the requirements into two separate documents. The business requirements would still belong in the scope document, but the more technical process, system, and component requirements can go into a separate document called a "service requirements specification." Two documents are especially useful if your approach will be to have the sponsors approve the higher-level requirements and the project team and technical stakeholders review the lower levels. Thus, each document could be reviewed and approved separately.

Whichever format you use to document the requirements, one important technique is to maintain those requirements over the entire life of the project. Changes happen to all IT projects, and your implementation of change and release management is no exception. Hopefully you already have a strong procedure for dealing with project changes, and that procedure will include updating the changed requirements. After each requirements change, you should revisit the approval of the requirements documents just to be sure all stakeholders still agree with the scope of your project.

As changes happen and the project progresses, you will definitely see benefit from a requirements management tool. If your organization has a good tool to use, be sure you take advantage of it. If you do not have a tool, you might want to see if you can carve off a piece of the project budget to invest in a good requirements management system. Experience shows that it will pay for itself if your project has more than sixty requirements or so.

Defining and Using Requirement Priorities

As soon as you have all the requirements documented and approved, you need to select a system for choosing which requirements will be accomplished first. In other words, you need to prioritize the requirements. These priorities will be used in several ways. Together with an estimate of work needed to fulfill the requirement, the priorities determine whether you implement change and release management as a single project or as several smaller projects. The priorities also will be used toward the end of the project when the schedule is tight and something needs to give in order to finish the project on time and with the allowed resources. Finally, the simple act of putting the requirements into a priority order helps the stakeholders really communicate with one another and the project team. Nothing is better for clarifying your thoughts than setting priorities.

Best practice shows that you should set requirements priorities in two steps. In the first step, simply set up some categories and assign each requirement to one of the categories. The top category should be named something that denotes an essential requirement. This category is reserved for requirements that, if not included, would invalidate the entire project. The bottom category should be reserved for requirements that could be left out of the project without serious consequences to your overall success. Between the critical and the disposable, you set up three other categories for high-, medium-, and low-priority requirements. These three categories should get almost all the requirements assigned to them.

After you put all the requirements into one of the five categories, it is time for the second pass. This time you can safely ignore the requirements in the top category, because you know they will get done anyway. You can also ignore those in the bottom category, because they shouldn't be taking much of your attention at this point. Next you should rank the remaining requirements within each category. For example, if you have forty-five requirements with a high priority, you should determine which ones are in the top ten, second ten, third ten, fourth ten, and bottom five. You don't have to assign each a unique place, but at least understand whether each requirement is relatively toward the top or bottom of the within that category.

Prioritization works only within a single level of the requirement set. It makes no sense to prioritize business requirements against system requirements, for example, because many of the system requirements will simply be a more specific version of the same business requirements. Because of this relationship between requirements at different levels (which systems engineers call *traceability*), you should start prioritizing with the business requirements. If a business requirement is prioritized at the top of your list, all the process, system, and component requirements that make it possible to achieve that business requirement must also have a high priority. This makes perfect sense, because it lets the business priorities rather than the technical priorities drive the project's importance.

Sometimes requirements prioritization sparks a heated debate. Different stakeholders or even sponsors may have significantly differing views of the priorities. Be sure to plan for this situation, and be pleasantly surprised if you don't need it. The best approach normally is to establish an escalation path that indicates who can settle this kind of disagreement. This might be the standard management hierarchy, or it may be a special hierarchy set up to govern IT projects. Either way, get agreement on the best way to settle disagreements before they come up.

Allocating Requirements to Projects

One of the primary reasons to prioritize requirements is to determine whether you can accomplish all the requirements in a single project. In some cases, it is possible to implement all change and release management in a single project. For many organizations, however, multiple projects are needed to reach the final desired end state. To understand which situation you are in, you need to assign a size to each of the requirements.

Estimating work to be accomplished is a fairly standard activity for most IT organizations. It is surprising, therefore, how often our estimates turn out to be poor. Fortunately, you don't need a high degree of accuracy to be able to allocate your requirements to projects. If you simply assign each requirement an estimated number of weeks to be completed, you will have enough information to determine your project boundaries. Simply add up the number of weeks for all the requirements, and find out how much effort will be needed for a complete implementation. The odds are good that you will find more weeks of work than you expected.

The problem with very large projects lasting dozens or even hundreds of weeks is that they either completely succeed or totally fail, and you won't know which one will happen until you've invested a good amount of that time. Because of this simple principle, most organizations choose to split the implementation of change and release management into multiple projects. This allows a separate value proposition for each project, which means that you can gain some value for less than the total effort, and even if one of the projects fails, you can still get value from the others.

The number of projects you should use is directly related to the specific incremental values you can identify. If you see four separate groups of functionality, each of which provides significant value to your sponsors and stakeholders, you should run four projects or phases of the implementation. The key is getting agreement that each of the phases provides significant value, and balancing that value. If you gain most of the benefits from the first phase of the implementation, you will be challenged to explain why you should do the following phases. On the other hand, if you delay most of the value until the third or fourth project, you will spend lots of time explaining why you did the first two phases.

After you have identified all the phases or projects you will use, it is time to assign requirements to each phase. This is primarily driven by the benefits expected from each phase, but it is also driven by a realistic estimate of how long each requirement will take to accomplish. At this stage, you will most likely need a more detailed estimate than you did to just determine the phases. Most organizations use a high-level estimate early on and a more detailed estimate when actually allocating requirements. This lower level of detail helps you balance the different phases so that they will all require approximately the same effort. This is also the stage at which smaller requirements might get pulled into a phase even though they have a lower priority than the larger requirements.

Allocating requirements to phases or projects is much like filling a series of buckets with stones, as shown in Figure 2.3. The larger stones or requirements need to go in first, but then you have room to add smaller stones, pebbles, and even some sand before each bucket is full. In the requirements world this equates to requirements with differing sizes, from weeks down to days or even hours.

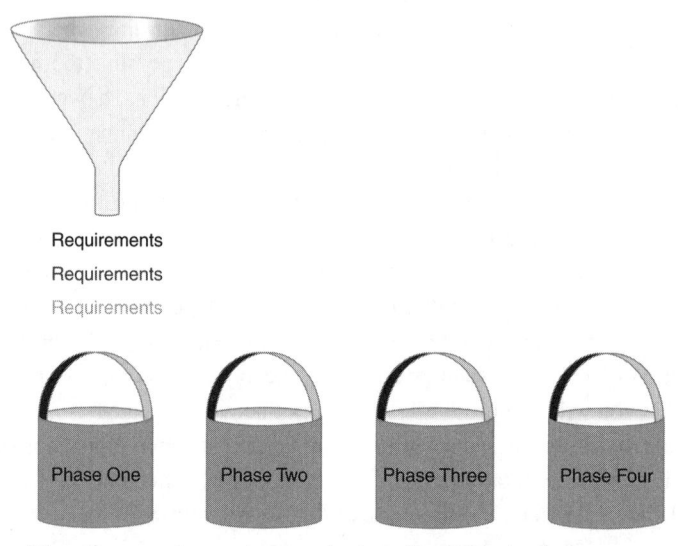

Figure 2.3 Allocating requirements to projects is like filling buckets.

Balancing Development Requirements and Operations Requirements

A very common problem with sets of requirements for change and release management projects is a lack of balance. Organizations tend to focus too much effort on requirements in one area and not enough in another area. The most common mistake is putting too much focus on requirements for the tool set. The second mistake is ignoring the tool set and putting too much focus on the processes. This section takes looks at these two common mistakes and offers some ideas on how to avoid them.

When an organization becomes enthralled with tools and begins to ignore the process that the tools are supposed to automate, bad things happen. Although it is seldom stated clearly, many IT organizations believe that if they can simply install the right software, it will solve all their problems. This focus on development efforts often manifests itself in a strong and deep set of requirements around the tools but hardly any requirements involved with the process or the operational aspects of change and release management.

Look at your requirements set. If there are twice as many system requirements as process requirements, or if hundreds of detailed component requirements deal with tools but hardly any deal with process, you know a problem exists. You have an unbalanced requirements set, and you need to spend more energy on understanding the process and organization.

On the other hand, some organizations focus very little on the tools and believe they can implement change and release management as a process while keeping their legacy tool set in place. IT processes normally are automated by some tool set, and if you ignore the tools, you will end up with a process that is automated incorrectly. You need to make at least some changes to the tool set if you really want to align your processes with the best practices defined by ITIL. This means that you should have some requirements that focus on what the tool needs to do.

The best way to balance your requirements to ensure that you have adequate focus on both development and operations is to get a wider audience involved in your requirements workshop up front. If you have people from the operational side as well as some people who deal with tools, it is much more likely that requirements for both tools and processes will be raised. After the workshop, you can get operations people involved in creating lower-level requirements even while development people are deriving lower-level tool requirements. Keeping both sides in balance will help you achieve a more complete and successful implementation project.

Looking Ahead

Requirements elicitation and management is a complex topic covered by many excellent books. This chapter has touched on the basics and explained how they apply to your deployment of change and release management. You've learned how to discover the requirements that already exist, and then to manage them in a way that produces a useful project scope.

These requirements form the beginning of a project plan. In the next several chapters, you will learn about other essential elements that go into your project plan, and then how to pull together the complete plan.

CHAPTER 3

Defining Change and Release Management Processes

The heart of ITIL is in processes and the disciplines surrounding them. Thus, it should be no surprise that early in the planning for change and release management, you need to begin defining processes. Although version 3 of the IT Infrastructure Library defines the processes in more detail than any previous version, it still doesn't describe exactly which process every organization should use. This is because one of the best practices is that each organization should define its process somewhat differently.

This chapter starts with a generic description of how to define any process at four levels. After you understand the basics, the ITIL suggested high-level processes are introduced, followed by specific suggestions about how to customize your own change and release management processes.

How to Define a Process

Like most specialties, process engineering uses its own vocabulary. The words aren't complex or difficult, but they are used in a specific context and must be understood that way. To work effectively with process engineers, you must know this vocabulary. This section introduces the important terms and concepts used to define a process. Figure 3.1 shows the steps required to build out a process.

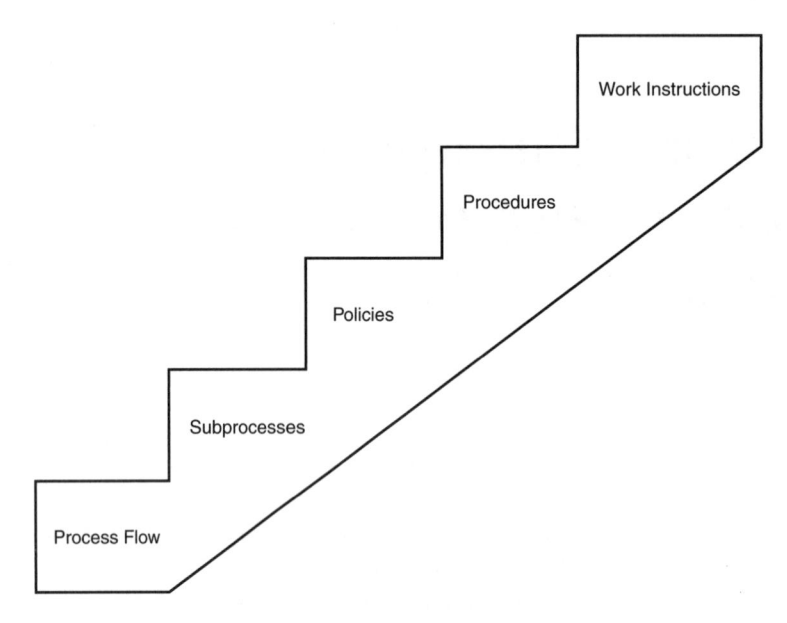

Figure 3.1   Five basic steps are needed to create a process.

Start with Process Flow

At the onset of defining your process, you need to grapple with what is meant by a *process*. Although more technical definitions are available, the working definition of a process is a sequence of defined actions that produces a measurable and desirable outcome. Because a process is a sequence, the place to start with definition normally is a flow diagram of some sort. Whether you favor a "line of visibility" diagram that delineates the different roles in the process or a simple flowchart that captures only the steps, your organization should adopt a standard way of defining a process flow. Look around for other process documents, and copy whatever style is in use for your organization.

Creating a workable process flow requires a solid starting point. Fortunately, the ITIL service transition book provides a solid start. In Chapter 4 of that book, you'll find some excellent sample process flows that can serve as a starting point. If your organization already has change management and/or release management processes documented, those can also serve as good reference points.

After establishing a starting point flow, the next step is to look back at the requirements you documented. Look very closely at the process requirements, and see if any of them dictate that you change your starting flow in specific ways. It would be unlikely at this high level, but occasionally a requirement will cause you to add a step to an overall flow.

Be sure not to get too detailed in your high-level flow. A good rule of thumb is that the top level should fit on a single page. Most of the process requirements will be around the details rather than the high-level process. Those details will be worked out eventually, but you have the greatest chance of success if you start with a single sheet that all your stakeholders can agree is the top level of the process.

After you have used existing starting points and your own judgment to define a high-level process flow, it is time to validate it. Take the single sheet to your sponsor, your stakeholders, and the project team. Get their ideas and incorporate them. Be sure to keep everyone aligned with the scope of your project. This is not a second round of requirements gathering, but an attempt to meet the requirements and scope you have already defined. It is important, however, that the high-level flow meets everyone's understanding of the project scope, because you are about to base many hours of work on this single page.

Frequently one or more activities on the high-level flow will be worthy of a separate flow by themselves. In the language of the process engineer, these are subprocesses. Identify these subprocesses as you validate the high-level flow, and work with the stakeholders and project team members to build these flows as well. As before, constrain each to a single sheet of paper, and focus on getting the flow documented in a consistent format. The subprocesses do not need to be especially detailed at this point, but they should provide enough information to allow later definition of the details.

As soon as all the flows are complete, you have the basic outline for all the process work. From these simple flows, you will determine which policies need to be defined, how many procedures will be written, and ultimately how many work instructions need to be documented.

Identify Needed Policies

The next term to understand is *policy*. A policy is an axiom or rule that is always true because your organization says it is true. Change and release management abound with policies, and throughout this chapter, you'll find many examples of policies that you may want to adopt for your process work. For example, many organizations insist on a policy that no IT component or service can change without an authorized change record. Policies are declarative statements about how things should work, and many times these policies result directly from the requirements.

When the high-level process flow and subprocess flows are done, the next step is to read the requirements and determine where policies will be needed. One clue is that policies often are associated with making a decision. Look at the decisions on your process flows, and determine how that decision will be made. Is there a policy statement to be defined? Unless the decision is very simple, you will probably want to provide some guidance in how it is to be made, and that's the perfect reason to create a policy.

Not all policies are large and encompassing. Instead of a single grand policy on change approvals, let the process flow guide you in creating smaller policies on change advisory board (CAB) membership, voting rules, handling of emergencies, and so forth. Try to keep the policies focused on one area at a time, and later you can combine them into a single policy document if that's more convenient to manage.

Create enough policies that no important decision or action is left to the imagination of one person. That is when you know enough policies have been defined.

Create Procedures

Procedures are the meat of the process definition. They are the narrative description of the step-by-step actions that someone will take to follow the process. Although the high-level flow provides a good overview, the procedures are the details of how to actually execute the process.

Procedures should be detailed enough that two people executing the same process step will always get the same result. They do not need to be so detailed that two people following them will use *exactly* the same method to get the desired result. Finding the correct level of detail requires an understanding of your organization and the skill level of the people who will be assuming the change and release management roles.

Procedures normally are documented as a numbered list of the specific steps that need to be taken. Not every activity in the process and subprocess flows will require a procedure to be written, but many of those steps will. If the outcome of an activity on the high-level flow is critical, or if that activity will involve a lengthy set of steps, document that activity with a procedure.

Often procedures are written into the same document as the high-level flows. This is a good format, because it keeps all process documentation in one place and is easier to maintain. On the other hand, if you have many procedures and policies, keeping everything in a single document can result in a very long document that is difficult to review and read. Some organizations choose to keep their process and procedure documentation online in a web page or wiki. That format lends itself much more readily to having each procedure and policy written as a separate short document that can be indexed from a process home page.

Document Work Instructions Where Needed

Sometimes procedures can get too lengthy and cumbersome, or the same set of steps needs to be repeated in multiple procedures. This is where a work instruction can be useful. A work instruction is a very specific bit of guidance on how to achieve a specific task within the process domain. For example, in your change management process, you may have several procedures that start with someone looking for a specific change record in an online tool. If the tool has been in your organization for a while and everyone knows how to look up records, you can probably just include a single step in every procedure that says "Look up the change record." On the other hand, if the tool is new, you might want to document exactly how to look up a record. You could do that in one place in a work instruction and refer to it in your procedures.

Normally, work instructions are tool-specific and procedures are not. This is a good practice, because it allows you to change tools in the future without having to rewrite your procedure documents by simply creating additional work instructions. If this is important to your organization, you will have general procedures with many more work instructions.

Keep the work instructions at a higher level than a tool user guide, however. They should be used only to describe specific uses of a tool where many options might be available. For example, your release management tool might support a variety of approaches to documenting a release policy. You could write a work instruction that directs people to always follow a very specific method. This ensures that people within your release management team always use the tool in the same way regardless of the latitude offered by the software publisher.

Standard ITIL Process Activities

Now that you understand how to define and document a process, it is time to think specifically about change and release management. As stated in Chapter 1, "Change and Release Management: Better Together," these processes are intimately linked. We will consider them separately here because in all likelihood, you will be defining them separately, but throughout this section as well as the rest of the book, examples will point out the linkages between these process areas.

Change Management

Almost every organization has a change management process in place already, whether or not it is aligned with ITIL best practices. Surprisingly, most change management processes are similar at the highest level. This happens because there is really a basic flow that works for almost everyone, and that is exactly the high level suggested by the service transition volume of ITIL. This basic flow is shown in Figure 3.2.

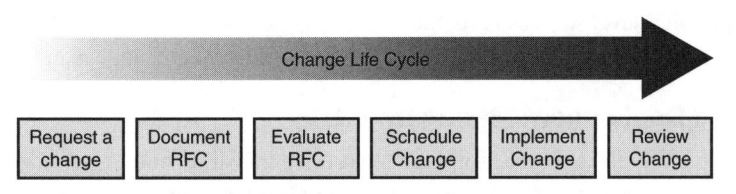

Figure 3.2 Change management follows a standard high-level flow.

The change flow begins with someone proposing a change. This person is called the change requester, and his or her proposal is called a request for change (RFC). The RFC is documented using a set of standard fields, most likely in a change management tool, but sometimes just on paper.

After the RFC has been documented, the evaluation stage begins. Evaluation can be very simple or somewhat elaborate. The most basic form of evaluation is someone looking at the documented RFC and deciding whether it makes sense to proceed with making the proposed change. Some organizations split this decision into a technical evaluation, aimed at making sure the change is technically feasible, and a business evaluation, designed to assess the business risks versus the potential rewards of the change. Throughout this book, you'll learn much more about ways to evaluate RFCs to determine whether to enact the changes they propose.

Assuming the evaluation is positive, the change gets woven into the operational schedule. This can be a complex task, depending on the size of the environment and the number of changes happening near the same time. You must consider the urgency of making the change, any available maintenance windows for the environment being changed, other business activities needing the resources that are being changed, and several other factors. The change is eventually placed into the operational schedule, known in ITIL terms as the forward schedule of change (FSC). Normally a change is scheduled with a specific start date and time, as well as a specific end date and time, so that others will know exactly when the change will be finished.

After scheduling, the next major step in the process flow is implementation. Some preparation activities may take place before the start date and time, but normally implementation starts when the schedule indicates that it should. A change may be implemented successfully, or the implementation may fail. Failed changes may be retried, or perhaps the change may be backed out to restore the environment to its state before the change was attempted. Besides the actual change itself, the status of the change as either successful or failed is the most important aspect of implementation.

After implementation is complete, the process concludes with a review of the change. If the change is successful, this review may be very brief. For failed changes, the review normally includes much more detail, including a recovery plan to indicate how the change will be retried later with a greater likelihood of success.

Based on their needs, different organizations will emphasize different aspects of this basic cycle. I've worked with organizations that separated evaluation into separate steps of evaluation and then approval. I've seen organizations that did hardly any review, even of failed changes. Frequently the request and documentation are combined into a single step. It isn't necessary that you have the same number of high-level steps as ITIL, but it is very important that you think through each part of this high-level flow and determine how they will be handled by your change management process.

Release and Deployment Management

The official name for release management in the service transition book gives some indication of the emphasis of the process—it is called "Release and Deployment Management." The emphasis is very much on the rollout of new or significantly modified services into the environment.

You should be aware of two levels of activity when thinking of the release management high-level flow. One set of activities occurs once per service and makes high-level plans for the entire life cycle of the service. This macro-level planning involves determining the overall business goals of the service, managing risks associated with the service, and evolving the architecture and design for the services. Some of the key issues settled at the higher level include how many releases or projects will be used to initially deploy the service, how often the service will be enhanced with new features, what cost model will be used to fund the service, and when to retire the service. This higher level involves strategic thinking and long-range planning.

At the same time, each service will be broken into a series of individual projects called releases. Each release adds incremental function to the overall service and represents a separately deployed part of the service. At the lower level, release management is about orchestrating these releases through a cycle that includes planning, building, testing, and deploying the necessary components. Normally each release is a project, involving a project team, a scope, a design, and a project plan of its own.

ITIL would say that the top level is called "service design" and is described in the book by that name, and that the lower level is properly called "release and deployment management." For the purposes of your implementation, however, it is almost impossible to achieve the lower level without a solid understanding of the higher level, so you should plan to include both in your release management process document, as shown in Figure 3.3.

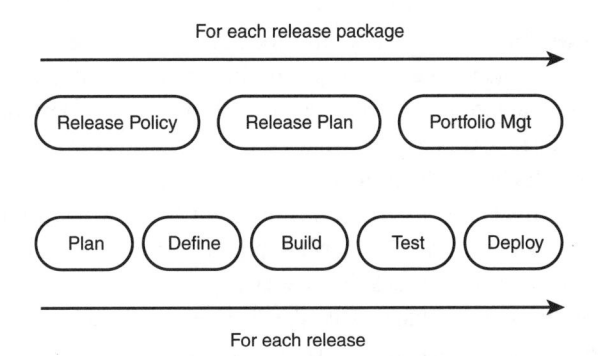

Figure 3.3 Release management spans both service design and service transition.

At the lower level, release management is much like traditional IT project planning. Actually, many organizations leverage the same process for both project management and deployment management because they are so similar. If your project management process covers a full life cycle, including planning, designing, building, testing, deployment, early support, and transition to full support, you can also use it for the lower-level process of release management.

Change Management and Operations

Now that you understand the basics of creating a process and what the standard ITIL documents offer, it is time to look more deeply at the change and release management processes. This section covers change management, and the next section discusses release management. The goal is to provide an overview of some of the more interesting process issues that you will undoubtedly face. The issues are not necessarily resolved for you, but at least they are outlined so that you can begin to find the best resolutions for your organization.

The First Policy

When beginning to define change management in a more formal way, every organization struggles with the question of exactly which activities need to be controlled with a change record. After establishing the highest-level flow, you should try to get agreement about the policy of when a change record is needed. This is the first, and perhaps most important, policy to define.

In most organizations, data center changes are already under change control. Moving a server to a new rack, deploying a major business application, modifying firewall rules, and decommissioning a network appliance are all activities that normally are subject to change control. But why does everyone agree that data center activities need to be controlled? It is really because of the potential impact of something going wrong. Perhaps a good policy to use is that if the change could cause a serious negative consequence, it must be controlled through the change-management process.

That is a great working definition, but it is too ambiguous to be of direct use. What seems like a serious negative consequence to one person might seem like a minor inconvenience to another. For example, swapping the 21-inch display attached to my desktop PC with a 14-inch display probably wouldn't seem like it could have serious consequences to the CIO or most of the IT organization. To me, however, the results of even a successful swap would drastically reduce my screen size, and thus my ability to multitask, create illustrations, and monitor events all on the same screen. Therefore, I would interpret this swapping of monitors as having serious negative consequences. So would a change record be necessary?

Consider a weekly batch job that updates data in your customer support database. The same job runs each month, picking up data from several sources and then integrating that data into the database that all your customer support representatives use to respond to customer calls. Certainly if this job fails in such a way that the database is scrambled, you will have serious negative consequences. But the job has run for years now and has never failed. Does your policy call for a change record to control this job? Sometimes data changes require significant controls, and other times they might be considered standard operations and require no additional controls.

Spend some time at the beginning of the change control process considering as many different scenarios as possible and creating a clear, concise, and helpful statement of when a change record is needed and when it is not. This first policy will probably need to be amended from time to time, but making it comprehensive early on will save effort later in the implementation project.

It is worth taking some time to document the scenarios you use in creating this policy. Those scenarios will be valuable when it comes time to validate your policy and to test the change management process flow.

Documenting the Request for Change (RFC)

The content of a request for change (RFC) is the second issue you will face. Many people assume that whatever tool they choose will determine the contents of the RFC, but this is a mistake. Certainly all tools will come with a comprehensive list of fields that can become part of every RFC, but all good tools also allow you to customize these fields, and you should certainly take advantage of this flexibility.

Most organizations will adopt common basic fields for their RFC content. A number; a title; information about the requester, sponsor, and implementer; scheduled and actual dates and times; and some indication of status are all essential. You will probably also want to have information about the approvals necessary for the change and some implementation information such as an implementation plan, a plan for backing out if necessary, and perhaps a plan to verify that the change is successful.

The best practices contained in ITIL indicate that each change should reference one or more *configuration items*. These are entries from your configuration management database (CMDB), and each change should record exactly how the configuration of your environment will be modified by the change being proposed. If you already have a CMDB with well-structured identifiers for each item, you're in great shape, and you will want to be able to attach one or more of these identifiers to an RFC. On the other hand, if you haven't yet implemented a CMDB, you still need some way to allow the requester to specify which parts of the environment he or she is changing. This will be very important in assessing the technical impact of the change.

Some organizations like to include fields in every RFC to help understand the compliance implications of the change. Often these are simple check boxes or flags that indicate whether the proposed change will affect audit posture. You may also need something more complex, such as pointers to a separate compliance management tool. The requirements you documented will guide how much you need to customize the fields that make up the RFC.

Reviews and Impact Assessment

The number and types of reviews needed is another significant process issue to explore. Some organizations choose a single review that focuses on the question of whether a change should be made. Other organizations like to use separate technical and business reviews to focus on the technical and business risks and implications of the change. Your process definition should consider the number and order of the reviews and should assign appropriate roles for each review. The names of the people reviewing each RFC might change, but the roles should be consistent from review to review.

Part of the review process should involve assessing the impact of each proposed change. Impact assessment consists of two parts—technical analysis followed by risk management. The technical analysis phase determines what components of the overall IT environment might be affected by the proposed change. For example, if the change calls for rebooting a specific server, it would be natural to understand which business applications depend on that server. Those applications could potentially be impacted by the change. The technical analysis would also determine whether those applications could be switched to other servers or whether an outage of the applications would be certain with a reboot of the server. Having a complete and accurate CMDB makes technical assessment of a proposed change much simpler.

The second phase of impact assessment deals with risk analysis. This involves using your imagination and technical understanding to guess what could go wrong with the proposed change. Consider the possible ways the change could fail, and build a two-dimensional matrix. The first axis in the matrix is the likelihood of any potential failure happening, and the second axis is the damage that would result if that failure actually happened. In the server rebooting example, for instance, it is possible that a hard disk failure might keep the server from restarting. Given the reliability of modern disk drives, there is a low likelihood of this happening, but the impact of the server's not restarting might be quite significant. This kind of analysis could be repeated with all the potential failures for the change, and the aggregation of risk data will help assess whether the change should be attempted.

Approval, Authorization, or Both

One of the key questions to be determined in your change management process is to what extent you will require changes to be approved before they are implemented. Many different models for approval exist, and the one you choose should allow sufficient control without undue bureaucracy.

Experience suggests that you might want to use two different kinds of permission—approval and authorization. Approval grants you permission to invest time (and therefore money) to plan a change and is essentially a business approval. For something like a major release of a business application, this might involve a team of programmers or the purchase of a vendor software package. For hardware implementation, approval may be required to purchase a new router or to invest in architect time to define a new SAN layout. Any change that requires investment to get ready for implementation might require an approval to make that investment.

The second kind of permission is authorization. Whereas approval grants permission to expend resources, authorization grants permission to alter the production environment and thus is a technical or IT approval. Consider again the implementation of a major business application. Many months might pass while the developers are working on building and testing the application. Approval was granted to spend money during those months, but there is no guarantee that the results of the effort are safe for deployment. Authorization is an acknowledgment that the testing of the application has been sufficient and that plans for implementation have considered and mitigated the risks involved.

You should spend a significant part of your change management process work on this question of approvals and authorizations. You will probably determine that some changes require only authorization and that others require both authorization and approval. Be sure to define a policy that will help everyone understand which kinds of permission are required for which changes.

Post-Implementation Review

ITIL recommends that you review each change after implementation, and it gives you some general ideas of what to look for in that review. That guidance is sound as far as it goes, but you will certainly need to fill in many details concerning how post-implementation reviews will be conducted for your organization.

The central purpose of reviewing a change is to learn how to improve your future implementations. We learn more from our failures than our successes, and this is also true in change management. The changes that fail have the most to teach us about future success and thus should be thoroughly reviewed. Understanding the reason for a failure can make future changes more successful. This is why each failed change should be reviewed.

Your process definition should include the specifics of how post-implementation reviews will work. Identify the roles to be involved, the potential actions to be taken, and the ways in which discovered information will be fed back into future changes. If these reviews are new to your organization, you need to specify even more closely how they will be conducted to ensure that they provide the maximum value.

There are many more topics to understand when documenting change management. The topics common to nearly every implementation are covered throughout this book, but some topics may be more specific, so you need to deal with them on your own. In dealing with any issue in process definition, the best resolution always comes from forming agreements between your stakeholders and sponsors. Introduce the issue, generate lots of communication around it, and then proceed with the resolution that makes the most sense to everyone involved. Remember that policies, procedures, and processes can always be modified later to be even more useful. In the continuous service improvement book, ITIL suggests that each process document be reviewed at least annually to find potential improvements, so don't be too determined to get everything perfect on the first pass.

Release Management and the Project Life Cycle

Almost every organization has a change management process, but very few have a specifically named and defined release management process. Unless your organization does a lot of software development, you may not have given much thought to release management. Whereas many of the issues described earlier for change management are familiar to you, those described here for release management may cover new ground. This doesn't, of course, make the issues any less important. You will soon discover that release management is every bit as important as change management, and that together change and release management form the core of how new services get introduced to your environment. This section covers the highest-level process issues in release management.

Release Unit Identification

Just as change management begins with defining which activities will require a change record, release management begins with documenting which components will be released simultaneously. ITIL defines a release unit as the set of components that get upgraded, installed, or changed all at the same time. As a simple example, often the next version of a business application requires new versions of middleware software products. This means that the application and the middleware form a release unit, because they are deployed at the same time.

There are many reasons to form a release unit. Vendor prerequisites might determine release units, as in the business application example. Sometimes purchasing considerations define a release unit, such as when new PCs come with a new operating system already installed. The PC and operating system become a single release unit. Project management often determines release units based on an analysis of the risks versus rewards of implementing multiple parts of a complete project at the same time. In some cases, there are valid architectural reasons to create a release unit out of multiple components. Whatever the reason, when your organization determines that multiple components should be joined for the sake of introducing a new service, you have defined a release unit.

You should try to create release units along consistent lines. Some people find that releases based on business application environments work well. They change out the operating system, middleware, and business application all at the same time as part of the release management process. Others like to create release units based on technology types, creating a desktop PC release consisting of bundled hardware, operating system, and standard software.

It takes a great deal of communication to create a release unit policy. It would be extremely difficult to identify in advance every situation that might cause a release unit to be formed, so you should focus instead on creating some guidelines that help people decide how to best create them. Work with the various deployment teams in your organization to understand and document these guidelines. Ultimately, deploying two or more things at once is always more risky than deploying only one component at a time, but most organizations find those risks worth taking in certain circumstances. Understand what those circumstances are, and document them as part of your release unit policy.

Release Policies

As soon as you understand release units, you can begin defining some general policies concerning release management. Most organizations find it useful to define a policy about how many releases should be produced per year. This policy helps in IT planning activities, because the organization can lay out the annual plans based on how many release units are active and how many releases each of those units will go through per the policy.

Of course, the number of releases per year will most likely depend on the number and type of components that make up the release. If a significant component of your release package is a software product, you won't be able to create releases more often than the software publisher produces releases. If you are bundling hardware refresh into your releases, the release cycle will depend on how often you choose to refresh your hardware. This will lead to a release policy that determines the frequency of releases based on the kinds of components that will make up the release unit.

An alternative to defining numbers of releases is to constrain the size of releases. You can constrain the size by either project budget or hours expended. For example, your policy might say that each release will require less than 2,000 hours of planning, testing, and deployment. This kind of policy ensures that your organization doesn't attempt huge projects that have correspondingly large risks. Limits of this kind will force projects to break their desired results into multiple releases and allow your organization to stop those releases if the cost or risk of achieving all the benefits appears too high.

Regardless of how you choose to define release policies, they are worthwhile to define. Release policies help create consistency in your organization and tend to create deployment projects that are roughly the same scope or size. This consistency helps you better evaluate successful and failed projects, and you can tune your release policies to optimize the size and scope of the projects for your organization. By creating fewer, larger releases, you will get larger projects that run longer, consume more resources, and return more value. By optimizing toward smaller releases, you wind up with small projects that generally return value more quickly.

Releases or Bundled Changes

Somewhere in your definition of the release management process, confusion is likely to arise about the difference between a release and a set of bundled changes. Although these may seem similar on the surface, they are really quite different.

Normally changes are bundled as a scheduling tool. There might be three different activities that all require the mainframe to be restarted, so rather than restarting the mainframe three separate times, these changes are bundled. All three things are done, the mainframe is restarted, and the changes are marked as complete. This is a convenient grouping of changes that happens one time because the schedule works out that way.

A release, on the other hand, is determined by a set of permanent policies that define release units and release frequency. The components of the release are related to one another by technology or business purpose, and the relationship is permanent rather than transitory.

A release might be deployed as a single change, or as a group of changes that are related to one another. For example, if the release includes an operating system and a middleware product, these might be deployed through two changes that take place on consecutive weekends. If the first change fails, the second change cannot happen, because the release control process ties the two together into a single release, and the release cannot be only partially deployed. In other words, a release can result in a group of bundled changes, but there are perfectly legitimate reasons to bundle changes that have nothing to do with release management.

Support and the End-of-Life Cycle

One of the key benefits of release management is that it causes an organization to think about the entire life cycle of a release unit. Many organizations have no policies or, at best, ineffective policies, around the end of support. I've been involved with companies that had six or even seven separate versions of an application all being supported because they just didn't know how to sunset that application. A key part of the release management process definition should be a policy surrounding the end of life for your releases.

Normally a release reaches end of life because a newer release replaces it. It might take some time to fully deploy the new release, and during this time both releases will be part of the supported environment. Your policies should take this situation into account and define how long the older versions will be supported. Your policy might insist that each release deployment project include the costs of supporting and then removing the old release.

In addition to the end of any specific release, your policy should consider how to define the end of a release unit. For example, imagine that your release unit consists of a payroll application, web server, database middleware, and common server operating system. You can define new releases as the middleware changes or new versions of the application become available, and each release retires the previous release. But you should also consider when you will move to a new payroll application that requires different infrastructure and thus creates a new release unit. If you make it an organizational policy to include this kind of long-range planning in release management, you will be able to forecast the large number of resources required to actually launch such a large project. This kind of complete life-cycle thinking is one of the hallmarks of a mature release management process.

Looking Ahead

Process definition is at the heart of ITIL. It is impossible to achieve best practices without documenting what those practices will look like in your organization and training your people to use them. In this chapter, you've learned about the different parts of a solid process document and how to assemble them. Using this knowledge, you can now read the ITIL books and begin to build your own implementation of change and release management. In the next chapter, this idea is extended to included logical work flows, which are repeatable procedures that cover a variety of common situations.

CHAPTER 4

Building Logical Work Flows

Process documentation is great for understanding the overall process, but it often falls short of explaining exactly what needs to be accomplished in every situation. Most modern change and release management tools support work flow implementations. So in addition to understanding the overall processes, you need to consider some concrete work flows that your organization will use to accomplish change and release management.

A work flow is a discrete set of steps that can be captured and then automated in a tool. A process describes every possible situation and outcome. Work flows, on the other hand, are used to describe and capture the most common scenarios that people follow to get through the process. Automating these work flows is a very efficient way for your organization to ensure consistency in change and release management.

This chapter describes some of the more common work flows. Like the previous chapter, it does not prescribe exactly how you must implement these scenarios, but it does give solid examples of work flows that have been effective for other organizations. You might need to add more work flows, or you may not need all of those described here. The goal of this chapter is to help you plan the work flows that will help your organization build the most consistent change and release management practices.

Work Flows by Change Category

There are many different ways to classify the work flows you might define. One very common way to think of work flows is to consider the type of change for which each work flow might be used. Given that a work flow is a specific path through the change management process, it makes sense to organize work flows around each of the most common sets of changes. This section provides sample work flows for some of the common change management categories.

Data Center Changes

Because almost every organization already has a well-understood way of dealing with data center changes, it is the easiest work flow to understand and define. Fortunately, data center changes also encompass most of the elements that are common to other work flows, so defining this flow first also makes sense from the standpoint of the change management implementation project.

A data center change is anything that impacts the servers, networks, facilities, or business applications of your data center. Because all these components are shared between many users, changes to them can significantly impact the productivity of your organization. Because of this characteristic, data center changes normally have a more rigorous work flow than changes with less impact. Figure 4.1 shows the steps for a typical data center change.

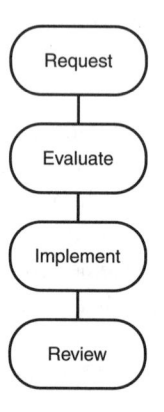

```
Request
   |
Evaluate
   |
Implement
   |
Review
```

Figure 4.1   A data center change goes through all change management phases.

Typically, data center changes form the bulk of the workload for your change advisory board (CAB). A typical CAB meeting should spend 80 to 90 percent of its time focused on data center changes and determining the impacts and dependencies among those changes. The work flow for a data center change ideally would include approvals from several different organizations. The server or network administrators who manage the affected infrastructure should be on the approval list. In addition, the designated owners of any impacted business applications should be on the approval list. Finally, it is usually desirable to also have a representative from impact business or user communities on the approval list. When the business, application team, and infrastructure team all agree that a change should go forward, you can be fairly certain that the appropriate amount of diligence has been shown.

Most change management tools allow you to define a series of tasks that are generated automatically when a change record is created. If you define these tasks based on the category of the change, you can save time for everyone who later needs to create these tasks for each new change they make. This is a great tool, but unfortunately it won't help very much with data center changes. There simply is no set of standard tasks that need to be accomplished each time. Deploying software to a set of servers involves significantly different steps than updating the rule set for a firewall. For data center changes, the tasks must be created each time by someone with knowledge of exactly what will be required to implement the requested change.

Workstation Changes

Workstation changes stand in sharp contrast to data center changes, so the work flow describing them is dramatically different. Whereas there is no doubt that data center changes should always be managed through change control, many organizations will choose not to view changes to workstations as within the scope of change control. Many organizations instead create a completely separate process discipline called Install, Move, Add, and Change (IMAC). Although this might be useful from an operational standpoint, workstation changes are really just a subset of the overall change management process with a different work flow.

Changes to workstations normally don't have any impact on your overall production environment. By definition, a workstation impacts only the one person assigned to use it, so these changes do not pose a high risk. Approvals are necessary only if your organization wants to exercise greater control over the costs of workstation changes. If that is your desire, you'll want to have an approval from the manager of the person making the request. If cost controls are not important, you can eliminate approvals from the workstation change work flow. Figure 4.2 shows a work flow with approval included.

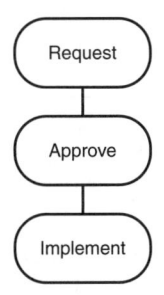

Figure 4.2   Workstation changes do not need evaluation or review.

Whether or not you consider workstation changes part of the scope of the formal change management process, you should use the change management tool to implement them. Your change management tool's ability to create standard tasks will really pay off for workstation changes. Each change to a workstation will have standard tasks to review the site (to determine power and network requirements), implement the change, get sign-off from the user, and update the asset database. Your template in the tool for workstation changes should include these tasks so that they can be generated automatically with each new RFC.

The greatest challenges with workstation changes are that they are so easy to make that they don't always go through your IT people. It is extremely simple for a user to download and install new software without IT ever being involved. Increasingly users can also purchase and install new hardware from a local office superstore. Your organization should define policies to encourage the right behaviors to help make your workstations more manageable.

Data Changes

Another type of change that often warrants its own work flow is a data change. These are changes to business data or control files without any alterations to the infrastructure, software, or environment. As with workstation changes, some organizations will question whether data changes even need to flow through the change management process. If you consider the potential impact of these changes, and the difficulty of discovering them if they aren't recorded by change management, you will quickly understand why ITIL recommends that they be included in your change management scope. A very small change to a key data element might impact how your entire organization can record transactions. Without change control, it would be very difficult to understand who made that initial modification and why.

Normally changes to data are required and are not complex. These characteristics lead most organizations to remove the approval phase for data changes. This isn't to say that the changes won't be evaluated and the impacts will be well understood. Evaluation should be performed by the business owners of the data, but approval from the IT infrastructure team is not a necessary step in the work flow.

The good news is that changes to data are the most standard kinds of changes. Because of this, it should be quite easy to define the steps you want the organization to go through as standard tasks that can be automatically generated for every data change. These steps typically include evaluating the data, planning for the update, making the update, and verifying that the update was successful. Figure 4.3 shows the high-level work flow for a data-only change.

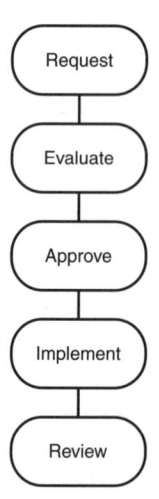

Request → Evaluate → Approve → Implement → Review

Figure 4.3 Data changes can safely skip the approval phase.

Like workstation changes, data changes are hard to detect and often are done without the controls imposed by the change management process. You need to document and demonstrate the value of change management to encourage your organization to start making changes to data through the process rather than going around the process.

Documentation or Administrative Changes

The vaguest category of changes is known as documentation or administrative changes. These are changes to artifacts such as process documents or operations "run books" that are used only indirectly to support your environment. Although many organizations discount these changes and believe they hardly need the rigor of change control, there is a very good reason to include them as part of an ITIL aligned change management process. You need them to maintain the configuration management database (CMDB). If you are following the ITIL suggestions for configuration management, you will quickly learn that documents are a critical part of your environment and should be maintained as configuration items. After you take that step, you will quickly understand that without documentation change control, you have no way to keep the CMDB updated. Thus, documentation and administrative changes should be considered a part of change control.

Although documentation changes often need authorization as part of a project, they have no need for operational approval in most circumstances. You normally put the change record in place simply to reflect an already accomplished fact in your environment. The person implementing the change normally is the owner or author of the document, so asking for his or her approval doesn't make sense either. Thus, the work flow for documentation changes does not include approvals.

Administrative or documentation changes are so simple that they probably do not need tasks, whether automatically generated or entered manually. In this sense, it is misleading to talk about a work flow for this category of changes. In essence, the work flow is simply a matter of asking for the change and then making it, as shown in Figure 4.4.

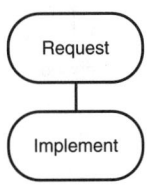

Figure 4.4 Administrative or documentation changes have the simplest work flow of all.

Work Flows by Change Urgency

Another factor that can influence work flow design is how urgently the change must be made. From time to time, every organization encounters situations that demand that a change be made to the environment very urgently. This section provides some suggestions on how to tailor your work flows to handle changes based on the time available to implement the change.

Emergency Change

When your IT services are completely disrupted because of a failure of one or more components, you don't want to wait for a normal change approval cycle to get them restarted. Incident management often requires a change to IT components to fulfill its mission of quickly restoring service. When changes simply cannot wait, an emergency change might be appropriate.

Emergency changes normally are approved by a manager who is responsible for the resolution of an ongoing incident. Sometimes this person is called the critical situation manager or availability manager. For the duration of the incident, this person has purview over all IT functions needed to resolve that incident and get service restored. Part of that purview is approval of any change activity needed. Because this manager is likely to already be on the phone communicating with both business and technical people, there is no delay in having him or her approve the change.

Some organizations prefer to handle emergency changes more formally by creating an emergency CAB. Typically this is a very small group of senior IT managers who will be aware of ongoing service disruptions and can be reached to make an approval decision about an emergency change record. Rather than have the availability manager for the incident make the decision, the emergency CAB can be convened very quickly to provide an impartial view of the necessity of the change and the risk of implementing it as an emergency.

At first glance, emergency changes might appear similar to uncontrolled changes. They are implemented very quickly, and the request is often recorded in the change tool only after the implementation is complete. The key difference is that the organization has agreed (normally by a predefined policy) that the situation is an emergency and warrants special handling. The typical work flow for an emergency change includes approval followed by implementation, with the request made later. This work flow is shown in Figure 4.5.

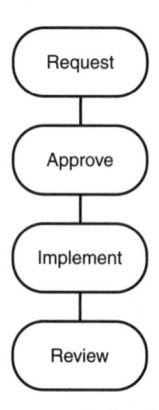

Figure 4.5 Emergency changes are recorded only after implementation.

Emergency changes should have a close association with incidents. Many organizations create a policy statement that an emergency change cannot be approved or implemented without being related to a high-severity incident. This policy helps avoid the tendency to put a change into the emergency category simply because someone forgot to record it before it was implemented.

Urgent Change

Urgent changes are changes that are not emergencies but that cannot wait for the normal cycle to play out. To understand an urgent change, you must first understand how most organizations handle routine change approvals. Typically RFCs are held until a weekly CAB meeting in which they are all approved or rejected. Those that are approved can then be executed, but only after the CAB approves them. Because the typical CAB meets only once per week, situations arise in which someone wants to implement a change before the next CAB meeting. Clearly if the situation is urgent, the emergency change work flow could be used, but sometimes the situation allows for three or four days but not the full week that would be required to wait for the next CAB. This is where the urgent change work flow comes into play.

You have two different options for approving urgent changes. The most common option is to institute an emergency CAB. This is a subset of the full CAB, who can hold ad hoc meetings whenever one or more urgent changes need to be considered. As members of the full CAB, these people are very familiar with evaluating and approving changes and have a good understanding of the other changes that might interfere with the urgent change being considered.

The other option for approving urgent changes is to route the change record electronically to approvers. Rather than wait for a CAB meeting, the approvers can take action immediately. When all approvals have been granted, the net result will be the same as if the CAB actually met, although the opportunity for discussion between approvers is eliminated.

Other than having a shortened approval cycle, the work flow steps for an urgent change are exactly the same as those for a nonurgent change. Refer to Figure 4.1 for this complete set of steps.

One issue with urgent changes is that their use must be closely controlled. Lack of planning should not be tolerated as an excuse to make all changes urgent. Normally no more than 3 to 4 percent of the changes in your organization should be marked urgent. If you are seeing a higher percentage, you need to strengthen your policy regarding urgent changes and ask that approvers reject changes they believe should not have been marked urgent.

Normal Change

A normal change is simply one that satisfies your standard approval and lead times. Most organizations use a normal change as the baseline or default length of change and follow the work flow defined by the change category as described earlier in "Workflows by Change Category."

Long, Complex Change

Some changes take so long that the lead time is measured in months or even years rather than days or weeks. When software needs to be purchased or developed, or a major project is involved in creating a service, the change cycle may be very long. Immature change management processes tend to ignore these long-running changes and simply ask that the project managers put a task into their plan to invoke change control when the project is almost ready to deploy. This approach seems like a wasted opportunity.

These long, complex changes are most likely releases in disguise. The full release management work flows described in the next section can be used to track the entire project, with a change management record being submitted directly from the release work flow. This blending of release and change management is exactly what ITIL suggests as the best practice that should be implemented.

Work Flows for Release Management

Release management is very work flow-oriented, just like change management. Actually, it is often difficult to separate the work flows of release management from those of project management. The steps are very similar, and in some senses release management is really the ITIL term for what most organizations have called project management for a very long time.

The difference between project management and release management is one of focus more than procedure. Project management focuses on cost and schedule, trying to optimize the available resources to meet the established project schedule. Release management instead focuses on quality and interrelationships between releases, attempting to minimize operational risk while improving the quality of the releases. Of course, quality and risk management are important to project management, and schedule and cost are important to release management. Ultimately release management has a bigger focus than project management because it governs release units across a whole series of individual projects or releases.

Software Development Flow

Anyone who has written code knows that the flow of software development can be the most unpredictable. Despite the best efforts of the IT industry, developing and testing new code simply takes as long as it takes. Estimating practices and the disciplines involved with software development are getting better. But in general, planning for a release that includes development of one or more significant components is the least certain of any release or change management work flows.

The software development work flow reflects your adopted development method. If your organization uses agile development, the flow will be dramatically different than if you are using an iterative approach or the traditional waterfall approach. Somewhere in the overall set of steps you will have requirements elicitation, system architecture, code design, development, several types of testing, deployment, and support. Those steps may happen for each time-boxed iteration or once for the entire project. If your organization uses multiple methods, you need to develop separate work flows for each of them. Figure 4.6 shows a typical work flow for a waterfall method.

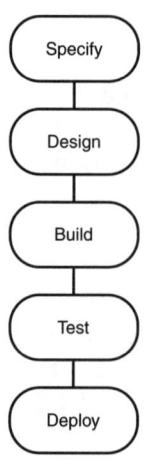

Figure 4.6 A complete release management work flow can be built for the waterfall development method.

Infrastructure Release Flow

Although many people associate release management with the introduction of new business applications into the IT environment, it is quite possible to define a release package that consists exclusively of infrastructure components. When you deploy infrastructure as a release, the work flow takes on a different shape than when you develop or deploy software.

The key feature of an infrastructure release is the acquisition of the components to be deployed. Hardware can have an especially long lead time, and acquiring infrastructure components normally involves the IT asset management process. However, the work flow is straightforward, as shown in Figure 4.7.

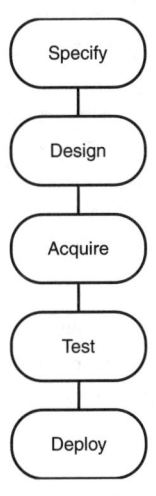

Figure 4.7 An infrastructure-only release involves acquiring the components.

Integration Project Release

As a final example, consider a release that mixes infrastructure with commercial software components to create or update an IT service. This is by far the most common type of release in most organizations, and it is called an integration project. The goal is to deploy a single solution consisting of the individually acquired parts.

Because almost all commercial software products allow customization to some degree, the work flow for an integration project release contains elements of both software development and infrastructure releases. Development activities will be required to tailor the software to your specific needs, and infrastructure activities will be needed to acquire and deploy the hardware and software. Figure 4.8 shows an integration project work flow for release management.

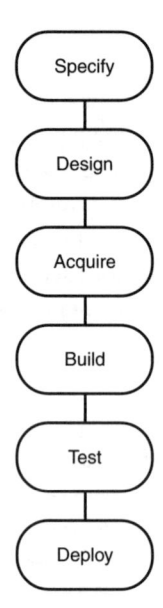

Figure 4.8 A complete release management work flow can be built for the waterfall development method.

These work flows for both change and release management should give you enough details to create the correct flows for your organization. You will want to build specific work flows for categories that will occur frequently so that your organization can standardize and optimize the accomplishment of those frequent activities.

Looking Ahead

Process documentation describes each role and each action that is possible within change and release management. When that process meets the reality of an automated tool, however, it becomes clear that several paths are followed much more frequently than others, and those paths are easier to automate. Those paths have been introduced in this chapter as work flow, and examples were given that span both change and release management. If you take the time to consider the work flows carefully, you can add significant value to your implementation by automating the activities your IT community will need to perform most often.

In the next chapter, the last of Part I, you will learn how to blend requirements, process documentation, and work flow design into a cohesive and realistic project plan.

CHAPTER 5

Completing the Implementation Plan

Requirements, processes, and work flow are necessary ingredients in planning for change and release management. They are the cornerstones of any successful implementation plan, but like cornerstones, they are insignificant without the rest of the structure around them.

Building a complete implementation plan requires some deep thinking and specific actions. This chapter describes the elements of a complete plan. It ties together the previous chapters to put the capstone on the subject of planning your change and release management implementation.

Planning to Meet Requirements

The goal of any project is to meet the scope defined by the requirements. The foundation of every successful project plan is a set of tasks defined to meet the requirements that are in scope. The requirements should be formulated as tasks to be accomplished, complete with both duration and an assignment. Those tasks are then assembled into a project plan.

Turning Requirements into Tasks

The first objective should be to get each requirement assigned to an individual. A project architect or system engineer with a good understanding of the requirements set should allocate the requirements by function to people on the project team. Table 5.1 shows a typical project breakdown, with the requirements areas and the role that those requirements would be assigned to.

Table 5.1 Assigning Requirements to the Proper Roles

Requirements Domain	Role to Assign
Process design	Process architect
Tool customization	Tools support
Policy creation	IT management
Communication	Project manager
Organization structure	IT management

If a single domain has many requirements, assign more than one person to the role, and split the requirements evenly. Don't worry too much about getting exactly the right person early on, because there will be time later to change the assignments. What is important is that every requirement is assigned to exactly one person who can analyze it.

Analysis is the next step. Each requirement should be viewed in light of whether it is a single task, multiple tasks, or perhaps no tasks in the final project plan. This kind of analysis requires experienced people and a bit of time. Ideally the person who estimated the task during requirements analysis should revisit it and determine exactly how he or she would go about satisfying the requirement. Many organizations have a policy indicating that tasks greater than a specific number of hours should be broken into multiple tasks. If you don't have such an organization-wide policy, you should at least establish one for this implementation project. Giving the assignees a specific number of hours per task helps bring consistency to your final project plan. It will be much easier to create a plan and level resources if you don't have any tasks running for twenty or more hours. On the other hand, the plan will be much easier to manage if you don't have a multitude of tasks that last just one hour.

Analyzing requirements includes understanding current capabilities. It is fairly common to find requirements that already have been met because of the tool selected or existing process definitions. Don't eliminate requirements that already have been met, but also don't include time in the project plan to create unnecessary deliverables.

Part of this deep requirement analysis involves clarifying requirements and shifting assignments. Inevitably some of the requirements will need people from more than one role to complete. For example, you might have a requirement that states "A monthly report shall be created to indicate the number of failed changes as a percentage of all changes." After some analysis, that requirement becomes a task to update the tool to allow a status of "complete-failed," a task to modify the work instruction around closing changes to indicate when the new status should be used, and a third task to actually create the report. Those three separate tasks might be given to three different people for further analysis to understand if they are individual tasks or might expand into more than the initial three.

Figure 5.1 highlights the steps required to assign requirements as tasks in the project plan.

Assign
Analyze
Align

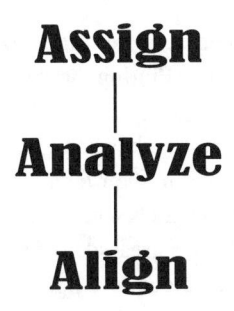

Figure 5.1 Requirements are assigned, analyzed, and aligned to become tasks in the project plan.

Estimating Task Sizes

As soon as the requirements are properly aligned and the assignments are accurate, the newly defined tasks in the project plan can be filled in with more details. Confirm with each person assigned to a task that the task is understood and complete. It is surprising how often a project team member can be assigned a specific task in the plan without completely understanding how to complete that task. Be sure each assignee has reviewed the tasks and understands the work required.

This understanding should include dependencies between tasks and any dependencies that are not reflected in tasks currently in the plan. A solid project plan is based on good dependencies between tasks. The technical team is in the best position to really examine those dependencies.

Next, final estimates need to be created for each task. These estimates should have much more precision than those done when the requirements were simply being sized for possible inclusion in the project. All the tasks at this point are scheduled to be accomplished, and the estimates will be put into the plan to determine the final schedule. The assignee of each task should make this estimate, because no one else can really say how long it will take that person to accomplish this particular piece of work. The estimates should all be provided to the project manager in a common unit, usually hours. This will simplify tracking and resource leveling later.

Although task assignees are in the best position to create estimates, they are not always experienced enough to create accurate estimates. You will want to have other members of the project team review the estimates to see if they look reasonable. This does not need to be a formal review, but unless you have very senior people with lots of experience in estimating, you should at least have a peer review for each estimate. This will help avoid unpleasant surprises later when a task takes twice as long as estimated.

Building Dependencies

After tasks are identified, assignments made, and durations filled in, the remaining piece of the initial project schedule is to establish dependencies between the tasks. Not all tasks can be accomplished at the same time, nor do all tasks need to wait until the previous task is finished.

More than anything else, these dependencies determine how long your overall implementation of change and release management will take. Putting the dependencies in place is like assembling a jigsaw puzzle.

Assuming that each project team member has more than one task, start by having these team members identify dependencies within their own set of tasks. Because they participated in defining the tasks from the requirements, and because they have already agreed to the assignment of the task, your project team should have a great idea of the order in which they need to go about the work. This step is like rotating each piece of a jigsaw puzzle so that the top and bottom are aligned like all the other pieces.

As soon as these initial dependencies are clear, it should be possible to start lining up the segments of the work in order. As a general guideline, process precedes data, data precedes tools, and tools precede training. Using this general order, you should begin to see dependencies between major sections of the project tasks; these dependencies will allow you to see some tasks that were left out. For example, if you have a task to automate a process, but you don't have a task to define the process, now is the time to add one. Looking at the dependencies often allows you to see missing or incomplete tasks just as aligning the edge pieces of a puzzle helps you see how many inside pieces there have to be to solve the puzzle.

After you have worked out the lowest-level dependencies between tasks assigned to one person and the highest-level dependencies between major groups of tasks, the more tedious work begins. This is where each task must be put into the final order and the dependencies between tasks from different assignees are sequenced. Normally this requires an architect or systems engineer who has both a good grasp of the entire project and broad knowledge of all the tasks to be accomplished. Balancing the big picture with the details allows the frame of the puzzle to be finished and each inside piece to be fitted into place.

At this point, you should have a good working outline of a project schedule. You should circulate this outline to the project team to be sure it makes sense to everyone and provides a clear direction for the work. Project reviews and status updates will go much more smoothly if everyone understands the schedule and agrees with how it has been assembled. Figure 5.2 shows how following these steps can help you assemble the whole puzzle.

Completing the First Draft

Just two steps remain in creating the complete first draft of the project schedule. The first step is to level resources. This simply involves looking at the tasks to find places where no dependency exists, but the two tasks are done sequentially because the same person is doing both of them. These are opportunities for you to accomplish the same work in a shorter time by adding another person. An average project schedule has many such opportunities, although it will also have many tasks that can be accomplished by only a single person. Your knowledge of the project sponsors and their inclination will help you know how many of these opportunities to take advantage of. A shorter-duration project with more resources added to it will return value more quickly, but it will also create more risks than a longer-duration project. Balance the desire to do it fast against the risks of doing it wrong, and level resources accordingly.

Planning to Meet Requirements

Figure 5.2 Building a project schedule is like assembling a puzzle.

The second step of creating a draft project schedule is to identify independent tasks. These are tasks that have few or no dependencies on other tasks. These tasks represent your opportunity to mitigate risks by spreading them out along the project schedule. If you schedule all independent tasks at the beginning of the project, you might get behind schedule very early on. If they are all at the end of the project, you might be moving along, thinking everything is on schedule, only to find too much work left over for the time allowed. Spreading independent tasks across the project as some of your team members have unallocated time will help the project run more smoothly.

A good rule of thumb is to look for milestones within the overall project plan, and see if they accurately reflect the pace you want to set. If you go weeks without a milestone, your project sponsors will likely get worried. On the other hand, if you have a milestone every other day, they lose importance, and your sponsors won't get the same feeling of accomplishment they could get from more challenging milestones.

Planning for Data Migration

Requirement-oriented tasks provide the basic outline for your project plan, but they are insufficient to complete the entire plan. Regardless of how adept your organization is with requirements, certain details aren't likely to be covered in enough depth.

The first of those details concerns data. Unless you have an information architect on the team, it is highly unlikely that your requirements alone will dictate all the tasks that need to be accomplished to migrate data. If you have an existing change management tool with some history of change records in it, you will want to take that data and move it forward to your new, ITIL aligned process. Even if you are using the same tool, you will most likely add a few fields, and possibly remove or rework some existing fields. All this effort will require data migration.

Release management is even more difficult. Most organizations today lack a single release management tool. Instead, information about software releases is found in a variety of software development tools, such as a source code control system, a software configuration management system, or even a software license metering tool. To begin ITIL aligned release management, you need to consolidate that data from these multiple sources and migrate it to your release management tool.

Tasks for Data Migration

If part of your scope is migrating data from legacy change and release management tools to new tools, you need to include some tasks for data migration in your overall plan. These tasks are not complex, but they can take some time to accomplish. Therefore, if you forget to put them in the project plan, your project will almost certainly exceed your schedule.

The first task you should include is identifying the sources of data. It may seem obvious that migrating data from a legacy system requires that system to be a source. But you need to be a bit more specific in your project plan. Often change management tools are bundled with other service desk tools such as incident ticketing systems or with asset management databases. In identifying your sources, you must specify which tables are to be moved, and which fields of those tables. Eventually someone will need to create a program or customize a utility to choose specific pieces of data that you want to migrate into the new tool set. Identifying the specific data you want to include will take more time than anyone wants it to. So be sure to determine exactly what tasks need to be done, and allocate plenty of time in your project plan for doing them.

After the data is clearly identified, you need to massage that data into the shape you need for the new system. A whole range of things might need to be done to the data to clean it up and make it fit into the new tools. Perhaps your legacy system has gotten a bit untidy and has data values with the same meaning but slightly different values. For example, you might have started with a status code of "Closed" but later revised your process to include "Closed Successful" and "Closed Failed" as status codes. If you haven't cleaned up the old records with "Closed," now is the time to do so.

In addition to cleaning up data, you will often need to translate that data. As a simple example, assume that your legacy system lets you enter changes with priorities of "Low," "Medium," and "High," but in your new system you've decided to use priorities numbered 1 through 5. To make the old change records meaningful in the new system, you need to create a rule that consistently maps the words to the numbers. Anywhere data elements can have a set of discrete values in the legacy system, you might have to translate those values to the new system, unless you have consciously chosen to use the same values.

In understanding which tasks need to be added to your project plan to deal with data consolidation, you must also consider the timing of those tasks. One of the most challenging aspects of any data migration work is determining when to actually perform the migration in preparation for production use of the new tool. This is actually part of a broader timing issue, as discussed in Chapter 10, "Moving from Pilot to Production," but the data part of the issue is worth understanding.

The issue is that you don't want to be without a change and release management tool during the transition from your existing practice to ITIL aligned best practices. One day you'll be using the old tool set, actively opening and working with change records, and the next day the new tool set should be ready with all those same change records, now in their new format. This requires an outage window of some kind, and the goal is to minimize that window as much as possible.

One way to minimize the downtime associated with migrating data is to break your legacy data into parts based on the status of the records. The first division is between records that are in an active or open state and those that are inactive or closed. The inactive records are accessed much less frequently than the active ones, so it makes sense that you can tolerate a much wider outage window without disrupting operations. If you look closely enough, you may find some records that are accessed so infrequently that it doesn't make sense to even have them available in the new tool set. These should be archived in the old tool and excluded from the migration data set.

The records that are inactive but still good candidates for migration should be put into a data set that is separate from the active records. This data set can be processed one week before your "go live" date. Many people actually find this set of records to be useful for training people on the new tool set, so they transfer it even earlier. This leaves your organization in a mixed state, in which active records are still being worked on the legacy tool, but historical, inactive records are now available in the new tool. This mixed state is probably acceptable for a week or two, but you wouldn't want to stay in it any longer than that.

If you choose this approach, you should make a concentrated effort to close change records that can be closed. This doesn't mean that you should circumvent your current process, but any records that can be closed within the process will help the migration go more smoothly.

By migrating the inactive records first, you accomplish two very important things. You minimize the size of the data set that actually needs to be migrated during the outage window, and you test the migration tools and procedures before cutover time. Both of those help the actual cutover time be shorter and have less risk.

All these tasks for archiving very old records, migrating inactive records, and then migrating the active records should become part of your overall implementation project plan.

Tasks for Data Consolidation

In many ways, data consolidation is another type of data migration issue. Rather than simply moving data from one system to another, you combine data from multiple systems first and then move it into your final change and release management tool set. Consolidation is simply more complex than simple migration.

Like migration, consolidation begins with identifying the sources of data. Knowing that you must begin with multiple sources, you should allocate more time in your project plan to determine the structure of the data in each legacy tool. The transformations of data will likely be more complex, so be sure to allow enough time for those as well.

One of the issues with consolidation is the need to identify or create integration points between the data sources. For example, if you are working with a software configuration management system and a source code control system, you need to find a common data element that helps you tie applications to one another. Even if both tools support the same application, you need to be sure it is formatted consistently and that both tools use it in the same way. If the two tools don't share a common identifier for applications, you have no choice but to build a table that manually matches application identifiers from one system to those of the other system. This is long, painstaking work, and it significantly impacts your project schedule.

Another important issue with data consolidation is the merging of similar data. Two legacy systems often contain the same data with different formatting or spelling. The data needs to be merged in a way that represents the schema of the new tool but also keeps the meaning from the legacy systems. This is another issue that has significant impact on your project plan.

Chapter 7, "Migrating or Consolidating Data," describes these issues in much more detail and provides some suggestions for working around them. The impact of these issues to your project plan is significant and important to project planning, and that is why we are introducing the concept in this chapter.

Adding Data Tasks to the Plan

After you have identified and estimated the set of tasks necessary for migrating and consolidating data, it is important that you carefully weave them into your project plan (see Figure 5.3). Do not simply add extra tasks to the bottom of the plan, but carefully consider the dependencies between the data-oriented tasks and the requirements-oriented tasks. Insert the new tasks where the dependencies indicate, and you'll have a much more readable and manageable plan.

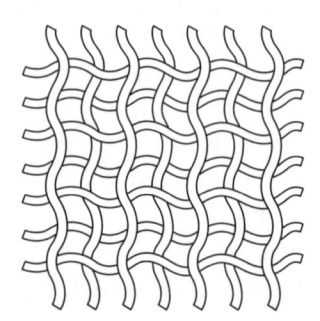

Figure 5.3 Inserting data tasks into an existing project plan is like weaving an intricate design.

Planning to Implement Tools

Tools implementation is a second area where your requirements tasks alone probably don't form a complete picture of the work to be accomplished by your implementation project.

You probably already have a change management tool in place. When aligning your change management process to ITIL, you have two choices. You can either modify your existing tools or replace them with tools designed to handle the ITIL aligned change and release management processes from the beginning. Chapter 6, "Choosing the Tools," helps you better understand the available features of change and release management tools and how to decide which course of action to take. This section helps you complete the project plan by adding tasks related to tools.

Tasks for Planning

The first set of tasks you may need to include in your plan concern choosing the right tools. If you have the luxury of choosing the right tool for the job instead of implementing the tool you've been assigned, you need to define some tasks for choosing the tools. Your requirements serve as the basis of your choice. Depending on the size of your organization and how formally you go about contracting, you might need quite a few detailed steps in your project plan concerning making your final choice of tools.

You will often find that the requirements that were adequate for making a project plan are inadequate for differentiating between the many change and release management tools on the market. If this is the case, you need to define more detailed component-level requirements and have those requirements agreed to in a project team review. These requirements might even split the tools into their various components, such as data model, user interface, reporting capabilities, and architecture, so you can be sure to find a tool set that satisfies the needs of your IT community. A change management tool is a large and long-lasting investment, so the decision should be made with as much thought as possible.

But that time for thinking won't be available unless you put it into your project plan. How much is enough? Experience shows that the most formal process involves three weeks for defining detailed requirements and two weeks for matching tools against those requirements to get to a short list of candidates. You then will want to invite those vendors in to provide a live demonstration of their capabilities, during which your key stakeholders should be prepared to ask questions. Schedule all the vendors in a single week so that you can more readily compare them to one another. After the vendor demonstrations, you will probably need an additional two weeks for analysis and to reach a decision. Following this formal procurement method adds five or six weeks to the overall schedule. If your method is less formal, you may be able to trim this time. For many more details on choosing the appropriate tools, see Chapter 6.

Tasks for Acquisition

After the decision is made, you need some time to actually acquire the software. Your contracts or procurement organization needs detailed specifications of exactly which versions and modules are to be purchased. This information can be obtained from the vendor in the form of a formal price quote. Procurement needs to create the purchase order, which the tool vendor will respond to in its own time.

Be sure to add the detailed project tasks concerning establishing the licensing with the software vendor and setting up access to that vendor's support capabilities. This usually involves either a web page registration or a phone call to the support manager. You will look like a genius if this is all set up before the issue arises with the software, and it is easy to do, so put a reminder task in the project plan to take care of it.

It is even better if you can begin the procurement process if just two or three vendors are left in the short list. This allows procurement and contracts to at least get an idea (on each side) about how long it may take to close out the transaction. You will look like a financial/sales genius if you have the contract nearly in place when you get the decision to move forward with your solution.

Tasks for Customization

After the new software arrives, you need time to customize it to fit your needs. Every change tool allows this kind of customization, because the suppliers recognize that no single process works for everyone. You should make as few customizations as possible, because this will help not only in the first deployment of the tool, but also in subsequent version upgrades. However, you should not be afraid to take advantage of the power the software vendors give you to have the tools work the way your organization works. This section explores some of the customizations you probably will need if you are moving to a new tool.

The first thing to do is to configure the tool's data model. Two areas of customization are possible; whether you do one or both is a matter of preference. The first area is to add in the data elements that are specific to your organization and tweak the names of existing elements to fit your terminology. Almost every organization has some industry- or company-specific terms in its change and release management processes. Using those terms for the data elements greatly simplifies the training effort later. On the other hand, nearly everyone has favorite names and preferred labels for pieces of information, so you shouldn't get carried away by modifying everything in the default database. A good rule of thumb is to modify no more than the key 10 percent of the fields with new names, and to add less than 5 percent new fields to the database.

In addition to adding and modifying, many tools allow you to remove or hide data elements you will never use. This ability should be used with extreme caution. Sometimes key automation features depend on certain fields, and those scripts simply stop functioning if the fields are removed. In other cases, the fields you are not using yet might be part of a great new module that you could buy and deploy in the future. If you remove the fields, that module may never work for you. On the other hand, extraneous fields that the vendor adds to the database confuse users, complicate reporting, and incur some fractional overhead. Remove them if those penalties are important to you; otherwise, simply add new data elements without removing anything.

The second customization type you should use with a new tool is process customizations. This is where you get into the specifics of work flow, approval rules, discrete value lists, and other entries that make the tool really match the process work. At the planning stage, it is difficult to estimate the extent of these customizations, because you have not actually completed the process work. As a rule of thumb, add together all the hours that have been estimated for all process work, down to the work instruction level of detail. Then add 20 percent of that number as the hours required for tool customization to meet that process. As your process work continues, and your team becomes more familiar with the new tool, you can revise this estimate as needed.

One important point is that all customizations to the tool should be documented. To someone familiar with software development, this would be obvious, but often the tools are customized by infrastructure team members. Server administrators and operations people are notoriously bad at documenting, especially simple things like tweaks in the names of data elements. Those simple things can make all the difference, however, when you are working with the tool vendor to resolve an issue. Be sure to know and control all the customizations that happen to your tool set, and do this by including tasks and time for documentation in the project plan.

It is somewhat ironic that a book about change and configuration management needs to explore incorporating good change and configuration management into your own projects and processes. However, without good change and configuration management around your customizations, you will almost guarantee additional time and effort in your testing and quality assurance process as you try to figure out why the system is not working properly.

Tasks for Training

In addition to tasks for planning, acquiring, and customizing the new tool set, you should add a set of tasks for training your teams to use the new tool. Although training is not strictly a tools task, a new tool adds some significant tasks that normally would not be part of the project plan and lengthens the duration of other tasks.

The first part of any training is building a training package. This can be as simple as putting together a set of slides, or as complex as building out training machines with the new software so that users can try out tasks for themselves. Whatever kind of training package you are building will become more complex because you are implementing a new tool. Simple process changes can always be conveyed by slides with adequate diagrams. A new tool is best learned by having the users' hands on the keyboard. If hands-on training is not a possibility, you should at least plan detailed demonstrations of the new tools—possibly different demonstrations for different user communities. The training package tasks will necessarily be more complex because of the new tool.

The logistics of delivering training also are more complex with a new tool simply because the changes affect people more directly. When process changes, people who approve changes or people who review changes might be impacted; when the change tool is different, everybody is affected. More people will need detailed training, resulting in longer sessions and more of them. Coordinating time away from regular duties can become a big logistics problem, so be sure to allow plenty of time in your project schedule for scheduling training.

Like the data migration and consolidation tasks, tasks that you add for tool implementation should be woven into the appropriate places in the project plan based on their dependencies with the tasks already in the plan.

Building a Complete Project Plan

After adding all these tasks and weaving them together to form a network of interdependencies, you should have a very strong project schedule. Now the challenge is building the rest of the project plan around it.

Every project plan should begin with a communications plan. This involves defining the project sponsors, project team, and other stakeholders, and then planning what messages will be delivered to each group. A typical communication plan is expressed as a spreadsheet with two tabs. One documents each stakeholder group and who its members are, and the other documents what messages will be communicated to each group and how those messages will be delivered. The communication plan is an important document to use throughout the project to be sure everyone is well informed.

The overall project plan should also include a scope statement, which includes exactly which requirements will be fulfilled by the project. In addition to the requirements, a scope statement should document the current situation, the business drivers behind the project, and a high-level description of how the project will change the current situation. A project schedule makes no sense without a thoroughly understood scope document behind it.

Finally, every good project plan should include financial information. This may be as simple as a budget showing the estimated human and financial resources the project will need. Or it may be as complex as a business case showing both the expenses of the project and the expected value returned from the project. The financial statement shows the degree to which your organization is committed to the project and should not be skipped.

Most IT organizations use a project management method that dictates the complete contents of a project plan at each phase of the project. That method should dictate what additional pieces go into your project plan, as well as who needs to approve your overall plan before moving on to deployment. This chapter has shown places where that standard method may need to be customized to accommodate an ITIL aligned deployment of change and release management.

Understanding the business factors and business climate are key components of the final project plan. As soon as the plan is completed, it is very important to look at a business calendar and see when the project will take place. For example, if your project is based in Europe and starts during the summer, it is very likely that many of the key people on the project will be unavailable during this time frame because of vacations. Another example is trying to end a project in December for a local or global retailer. Most retailers have hard-code release/project deployment freezes in place from the end of November to January 1 because this is their most important financial quarter of the year.

One thing you can do on projects is to have a "public"-facing project plan and an internal IT project plan. The internal project plan has tighter deadlines and deliverables so that if all goes well, you will deliver the project under time and under budget to the customer based on your customer-facing project plan.

If something is running behind schedule, the gap in time between the internal and external project plan gives you some room for slippage in the schedule while maintaining the promised schedule. This creates a "safety net" for the project while keeping very high customer satisfaction based on setting the right expectations.

Looking Ahead

When it comes to implementing ITIL, planning is more than half the battle. In the previous chapters, you've learned how to define requirements, build a process, and create work flows. Each of these resulted in a set of project tasks, and this chapter has described how to put all those tasks into a complete project plan. Using this information, you should now be able to embark on the actual implementation with much confidence.

Part II of this book describes the actual implementation steps, building more detail into what you've learned. Chapter 6 begins that exploration with a discussion of change and release management tools.

PART II

Implementing

The strength of any plan is determined by the quality of the implementation it enables. Moving from plans to the real world is a difficult but important step. The chapters in this part take you through the various pieces of implementation, including tool deployment, data migration, process implementation, pilot execution, and turnover to production. Careful progress will result in a strong and sustainable change and release management implementation for your organization.

CHAPTER 6

Choosing the Tools

Not every implementation of change and release management requires the purchase and deployment of new tools. In many cases, the current tool set can be extended or customized to accommodate your ITIL aligned process work. Often a significant investment has already been made in service management tools, and this investment cannot be ignored. But whether you are purchasing a new tool, modifying an existing one to better fit the process, or working with what you've been given, you need to understand the capabilities and drawbacks of the available tools.

This chapter provides a broad overview of tools that help with the change and release management processes. Then it dives deeper into specific features that you may want to consider. No specific tool is best for every organization or circumstance, so rather than recommending a specific set of tools, this chapter describes a method you can use to find the best tool for you.

Tools for Change Management

Traditional change management tools have grown alongside service desk tools. This makes for a fairly mature market and some very robust capabilities. These mature tools are essentially ticketing systems with work flow capabilities added so that change records can be routed through a series of different statuses. These tools are extremely good at automating the cycle of request, review, and approval. The tools can also facilitate reviews as long as change implementers update the record with accurate details of what happened during implementation. Some of these tools have been in production use for many years.

Recently, however, change management has become more complex. Trends such as risk analysis, compliance management, and ITIL alignment have emphasized new aspects of change management, and new categories of tools have been developed to automate these new procedures. These new tools have revitalized the market, and new players are emerging to challenge the traditional vendors.

This section introduces the traditional change management tools and some of the new technologies that are emerging in this space. Figure 6.1 shows the high-level options available in the change management tool space.

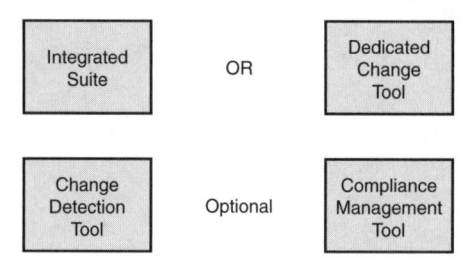

```
┌────────────┐              ┌────────────┐
│ Integrated │              │ Dedicated  │
│   Suite    │     OR       │  Change    │
│            │              │   Tool     │
└────────────┘              └────────────┘

┌────────────┐              ┌────────────┐
│  Change    │              │ Compliance │
│ Detection  │   Optional   │ Management │
│   Tool     │              │   Tool     │
└────────────┘              └────────────┘
```

Figure 6.1 The change management tools landscape is very simple.

Integrated Service Management Tools

The change management tool in place in most organizations is part of an integrated service management tool set. These large, bundled suites of tools normally cover incident, problem, and change management, and they often have modules for configuration management, knowledge management, and sometimes IT asset management. The three leading vendors in this space are BMC with its Remedy product line, HP with the product set acquired from Peregrine, and IBM with its product set acquired from MRO. These suites are intended to provide most of the IT service management capabilities an organization could need.

The huge benefit of a bundled suite is that the necessary integration between components is provided out of the box. When working on an incident record in one of these tools, you can typically click a button to create the change request for the change that will resolve the incident. Likewise, you can frequently do a lookup of configuration items while you are preparing a request for change. Purchasing this integration ready-made is a strong influencing factor, because building that level of integration between independent tools is costly and error-prone.

Of course, the downside of service management suites is that they are adequate in all disciplines but don't really shine in any specific area. One suite may be very good at integrating incident management with knowledge databases, a critical function for the service desk, but be very weak at configuration management. Another suite might automatically build a detailed, useful forward schedule of change report, but be difficult to use for documenting the root cause and corrective actions for a problem. In all cases, the set of features in a bundled suite lags behind the dedicated change management tools. The big suites need to add value in all modules to be worth the tremendous expense involved with migrating from one version to the next.

The bundled suite approach is a great direction for an organization that is basically conservative and wants to place a safe bet on tools. The functions are perfectly adequate today and are being improved by some of the major players in the software business on a very regular schedule. The vendors protect your investment by providing both solid migration tools and a broad base of experts who can help with migrations from version to version. The integrations are already built and tested by thousands of customers who use these tools, so no risky development or integration work is needed. These are compelling reasons for most organizations to use an integration service management suite as their primary change record tracking tool.

Dedicated Change Management Tools

For those who need more functions than an integrated suite provides, or who want to customize their own integration so that it can more closely align with their process and policies, a new breed of dedicated change management tools is being published. These tools often come with a configuration database of some kind. Occasionally they come with a discovery tool that can be used to detect configuration data both before and after a change

The significant advantage of a dedicated change management tool is features. These are tools that don't try to be everything to every process, but focus on change management and do it very well. When the field advances, the vendors of dedicated change management tools are poised not only to adapt, but to push the envelope a bit further. Rather than focus on integration with incident and problem management tools, dedicated change management tools can focus on integration with compliance managers and deployment management tools. As more organizations look to integrate change management with release management, look to the publishers of dedicated change management tools to be the first to automate the linkages.

The disadvantages of dedicated change management tools highlight the advantages of the suites. If you purchase dedicated tools, you have significant integration work to do. You need to define and build the appropriate levels of integration to incident management systems, service request systems, configuration management databases, and many other service management tools. Another significant disadvantage of the dedicated tools is that ultimately you end up paying more than you would with a suite. Certainly the change tool alone will most likely cost less, but by the time you purchase a dedicated incident ticketing system, a stand-alone knowledge management database, a dedicated configuration management system, and a service-level reporting tool, you will have far surpassed the cost of an integrated suite that could do all these things.

The dedicated tools are for organizations that have very special, specific needs. For example, a government organization with its unique information security and compliance issues might need a more robust change management tool than a suite could offer. Dedicated tools generally are used by those who can accommodate the expense and extra risk that these tools deliver.

Change Detection and Compliance Tools

Organizations are beginning to realize that effective change controls consist of more than simply managing a change record from request through approval and review. Many people resist the IT change management process and modify the production environment without going through change control. Over time, these modifications reduce the accuracy of the configuration management database (CMDB) and undermine the compliance posture that IT tries to maintain. Fortunately, we are beginning to see tools from vendors such as Tripwire, Configuresoft, and Solidcore that detect certain kinds of changes in the environment and match those changes against existing change requests to find unauthorized changes.

These change detection tools operate much like discovery tools in the asset or configuration management domains. They scan aspects of the production environment and compare the results of the scans against an existing configuration database. When a discrepancy is found, it is flagged as a questionable change. Someone then investigates all questionable changes to find areas that really have been changed without authorization. Normally the tool provides a mechanism to track these questionable changes and how the discrepancies are resolved. Rather than automate the actual change management process, change detection tools help enforce the policies that are part of that process.

Compliance management has become a hot topic ever since the U.S. introduced the Sarbanes-Oxley (SOX) legislation in 2002. It caused all publicly held companies to become regulated like pharmaceutical and financial companies had been for years. Tools that help document regulations and track compliance to those regulations are becoming more standard in many organizations, and those tools are increasingly being seen as an adjunct to the change management process. When changes are requested, a compliance management application can be consulted to find out how the proposed change will affect the organization's ability to comply with the various regulations. If compliance will be affected, the update can be made in the compliance management system so that documentation will be ready when the auditors need it.

Change detection tools and integrated compliance management tools currently are not part of the mainstream of change management. Certain organizations need them because they are part of heavily regulated industries or because they have trouble with policy enforcement. Other organizations will want to start thinking about them because the trend toward regulation and policy enforcement shows no sign of abating. These tools are not inexpensive, but when the alternative is being caught out of compliance with key regulations in your industry, there really is no choice. You can read much more about managing compliance in Chapter 14, "Auditing and Compliance Management."

Tools for Release Management

Although change management tools are reasonably easy to define and recognize, literally dozens of different tools claim to help with release management. Change management is a very mature space with some recent innovation, whereas release management is a very immature space with almost no de facto standards. This confusion is reflected in the diverse kinds of tools described in this section. Figure 6.2 shows which tools pertain to which parts of the total release management life cycle.

Tools for Release Management

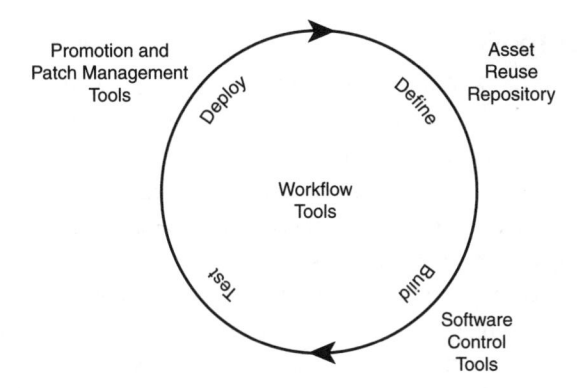

Figure 6.2 Different classes of tools help with parts of the release management cycle.

Work Flow Tools

Release management is the kind of process that naturally invites work flow tools. Each release flows through a well-defined series of steps, and those steps can be automated just as the change management steps can. Many software publishers have introduced release management modules as part of integrated suites of IT service management tools. These modules generally add some work flows to the existing change management modules to accommodate the specifics of release management.

The benefit of using a work flow-based tool for release management is that you can gather statistics and build dashboards to show the status of all release activity at a glance. In other words, you can look across multiple individual projects to see an aggregate picture of how your release management process is functioning. Rather than traditional status meetings, in which each release project has a stoplight chart to show whether it is on schedule (green), at risk (yellow), or lagging (red), release management work flow tools can generate a simple report to indicate which projects are having problems. The meeting can then focus on the exceptions rather than wading through all the projects.

Unfortunately, many of the work flow tools available for release management today have limited functionality and integration. They provide a great deal of flexibility, mostly because the software vendors don't have a very clear idea of what a "standard" release management work flow should be. The tools do a good job of tracking a record through a set of statuses, but they do not have a built-in data structure that supports the concept of a single release package with lots of individual releases or versions of that package being shipped over time. Instead, these tools see each release as a separate record and don't do a very good job of relating releases of the same package to one another. As the thinking of the IT industry concerning release management matures, the software publishers will most likely mature their tools to better support the hierarchical nature of relationships between releases.

Software Control Tools

When many people first think of managing a release, they concern themselves with breaking a software application into modules, Java archive files, or other segments that can be separately tracked and developed. Tools that deal with software releases at this level are called source code control systems. They allow individual components of a larger application to be checked out, modified, and checked back in. They also supervise the versions of each of these different modules that will ultimately comprise the final business application.

Software control tools help in release management by controlling the contents of various release packages and by keeping track of which contents should be part of which package. They help with both the planning and the build part of the cycle and are used extensively during the test cycle to rapidly incorporate changes to components that failed in testing. Often the software control tool automates the actual build of the finished application by integrating with the build utility in the software development environment.

Unfortunately, software control tools cannot be easily adopted for release types that do not include a typical software development cycle. Purchased components normally do not break down into modules at a fine-enough grain to capture into one of these tools, and hardware components do not fit at all. Some organizations have experimented with creating a record for each hardware component, operating system, and middleware component and thus building a complete release inside a software control tool. Of course, some people also have tried pounding a nail with a screwdriver. Although some progress is possible, it makes much more sense to use a different tool for the job.

If your organization does traditional software development, you will undoubtedly already have a source control library of some type. That tool will work well for releases that are completely composed of software you develop. However, as you'll see in Chapter 13, "Defining Release Packages," it is generally a good idea to bundle application code and middleware into a single release. For this reason, you should not extend your source code control system to become a complete release management solution. Instead, adopt a tool that can support all kinds of releases, including hardware refresh, and then integrate the source code control system with your release management tools to automate the inclusion of developed software components into release packages.

Promotion and Deployment Tools

A second category of tools related to release management are deployment or promotion tools, often called provisioning tools. These tools rapidly install software release packages by following policies established in advance. These tools can work in conjunction with a software control tool to automate the build of the software before deployment. They also can handle purchases of software products such as operating systems or middleware components. Initially many of these tools began as desktop software distribution tools. But the class has evolved with many features needed to deploy complete release packages and even install operating systems on servers that don't have any existing software. In addition to simple deployment, these tools normally offer integration with the configuration management database, and sometimes they even serve as a change detection tool for the software they have deployed.

Software deployment tools save significant labor within the release management process by automating the most manual operations. Although this saves significant cost, these tools do not really automate very much of the complete release management process. They have a strong role in deployment, but only a limited role in testing (due to their error-checking process) and no role at all in planning, building, or support. Because software tools cannot deliver hardware, deployment tools also are limited to release packages that contain only software. If your release management policy has indicated that hardware and software are part of the same release package, a software deployment tool will be unable to handle the complete job.

Provisioning tools appeal to organizations that have standardized many layers of the release package. If you are deploying exactly the same operating system and middleware components to thousands of servers, the effort of packaging those pieces and building a release schedule for the tool will be well worth the labor savings you can achieve. But suppose your IT environment tolerates significant configuration differences between servers and deployed instances of a package. You will be doing so much customizing of a deployment tool that it might be easier to simply put CDs in the drives and install the software manually. Of course, if you want to become more standardized, deploying one of these tools gradually is a great way to get there over time.

Patch Management Tools

Patch management tools are very similar to deployment tools. Their key additional feature is the ability to consult a database to see where patches are needed. Patch management tools have been created in response to the flood of operating system patches that need to be deployed across large numbers of desktop or server systems. Like deployment or promotion tools, they install software very quickly to reduce the cost of installation labor. Patch management tools tend to focus on security patches, but they often can be used to deploy any type of software or data file rapidly.

Like deployment tools, patch management tools focus exclusively on the deploy part of the release management cycle. They focus primarily on patches to operating systems and middleware components, as evidenced by the fact that Microsoft™ is a major player in the patch management tool market. In many cases, patches represent vulnerabilities to the software on systems. Often patch management can be viewed as an emergency release management work flow, just as there is a separate work flow for emergency change management.

Every IT organization needs patch management tools, but only the more progressive organizations integrate the patch management tools with the release management process. Frequently patch management is seen as a reactive, operational problem rather than a well-planned activity that fits into an overall release management process. For organizations that do see the correlation, however, there can be significant benefits to treating software patches as miniature release packages. Some benefits include forward planning, more visibility to the patch releases, and the ability to leverage existing release management processes rather than creating a new patch management process.

Asset Reuse Repositories

A different type of release management tool is the asset reuse repository. This is a collection point for software assets that might be used by other parts of the organization. As the name implies, these tools are intended as holding tanks to allow people to quickly find software assets so that they won't have to reinvent them. Of course, this is part of the purpose of the Definitive Media Library (DML) as defined by ITIL. The asset reuse repository normally provides an indexing scheme and a search ability so that assets can be located quickly. In some cases, that asset reuse repository is used as a source of data for the CMDB, where the CMDB holds higher-level data and the asset reuse repository holds details of software applications.

An asset repository can be very useful in the planning phase of release management. When you organize assets according to their release packages, it's very easy to start a new version when it is time for a later release. The repository can also hold metadata about the application, such as key user communities, likely project sponsors, infrastructure contacts, and much more data that will be important to the release manager. As indicated, an asset reuse repository can become a CMDB for your business applications.

Organizations that have large numbers of business applications and no standard way to catalog them should strongly consider implementing an asset reuse repository tool. The repository can serve as a starting point for release planning and as an authoritative data source for the enterprise CMDB. If your organization has few business applications, or already has a good application inventory system, an asset reuse tool will not add significant value.

Integrating Operations and Development

The brief survey of change and release tools in this chapter should give you the impression that change and release management tools are completely separate classes. Unfortunately, this is an accurate picture. Most change management tools are heavily influenced by operational concerns dealing with IT infrastructure. Most release management tools are strongly influenced by application development processes and concerns. Very few tools actually integrate these spheres in the way that ITIL suggests they should be integrated. This section takes a brief detour to describe an ideal change and release management tool that doesn't really exist yet.

Process Integration Points

To build the perfect change and release management tool, it is important to think about the integration points between the change and release management processes. As described in Chapter 1, "Change and Release Management: Better Together," release management divides the operational environment into related groups called release packages. A release package provides a single IT service to the organization, so in many ways a release package can be thought of as the set of all things needed to deliver that IT service. For example, your organization probably has a human resources (HR) application. Assume that an application runs across one database server, two application servers, and one web server. Each of those servers has an operating system, the database server runs a database management software package, the application server runs the

Integrating Operations and Development

code from your HR application vendor, and the web servers run web server middleware. The total release package for the HR application service consists of the following:

- HR application software
- Database management software
- Web server middleware software
- Application server 1 hardware
- Application server 2 hardware
- Database server hardware
- Web server hardware

Over time, you may want to add new features or capabilities to the HR service, which means new versions of one or more of the components in the release package. Imagine that the new features come as a new version of the HR application software, which requires a new version of the database management server, which in turn requires additional memory on the database server. The individual changes to the application, the database software, and the database server are bundled into a single release because they all impact the same release package and they all work together to add the new capabilities.

Thus, the process of release management defines the release package, which in turn determines how many changes can be bundled into a single release. Very tight process integration exists between the release management and change management processes.

Data Integration Points

The data structures within the tools must support the integration between the processes. Continuing the example of the HR application, there must be some way to describe the HR release package and its contents. A natural inclination is to use the configuration management database, but note that release packages are *not* configuration items. They are only conceptual entities that become real only when a specific release is deployed. Although it is possible to use the CMDB to define release packages, it is preferable to have the change and release management tool define its own release package structure. Figure 6.3 shows the structure discussed in this section.

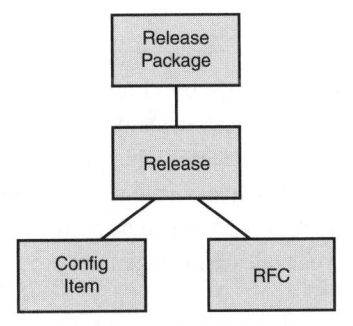

Figure 6.3 Data for release management should integrate with change records.

The release package record should allow attributes such as the name of the package, the IT service it provides, and the general policies related to this release package. The release package should also allow for relationships to specific releases. The release record should also allow for attributes such as the release number, test status, and deployment date. Just like a release package record, the release record is an abstract entity and does not reflect actual deployed items in the environment.

The release record can be related to two different record types. The first is configuration items in the CMDB. Each release consists of one or more specific deployed configuration items, so it is natural that the release record from release management should be able to point to these. The second type of record that can be related to a release record is a change record. Because the release will be deployed in the environment, change records should be created and related back to the release. The entire structure, from release package down to configuration items and change records, helps integrate data across change and release management.

Tool Integration Points

In addition to process and data integration, change and release management should be integrated at the tool level. Tool integration implies that a user of the tool should be able to accomplish release and change management activities seamlessly without having to copy or re-create data between multiple tools. Using the data hierarchy described earlier, several integrations are logical.

A user should be able to focus on a specific release and see all change records related to that release. Navigating from the release to the changes and back again would allow a release manager to understand whether all the appropriate change records were scheduled for the deployment phase of their release, for example.

Another area where tool integration really helps a release manager is defect prediction. At the onset of each release, the release manager should predict how many defects will be introduced in the release and how many will be left when the release is deployed into production. There are some predictive ways to do this, but by far the most reliable way to predict future defects is to look at incident records against previous releases. If the incident tool is integrated with the release management tool, the release manager could look at each past release and quickly see a list of incidents that were reported against that release. This would help predict defects for the next release.

The Ideal Tool

The ideal release management tool would support all three of these integration types. It would automate fully integrated configuration, change, incident, and release processes. It would support a data model in which release packages, releases, changes, and configuration items were all integrated. It would allow a user to seamlessly navigate across related records to see any aspect of a release or release package. Of course, it would also be highly configurable to support all the customizations you have done with your release management process.

Unfortunately, that ideal release management tool doesn't exist—but that isn't the fault of the software vendors. Too few organizations have sufficient maturity in their release management processes to use such a tool, even if it existed. As organizations mature, the vendors will undoubtedly introduce more sophisticated tools that get closer to the ideal.

Features to Look For

Even though you cannot purchase the ideal tool, some very good tools for change and release management are on the market. To find the ones that are right for your organization, you need to understand which capabilities to look for. This section describes some of the features of change and release management tools so that you can determine which features are most important for your purposes. The features are broken into five separate areas, as shown in Figure 6.4.

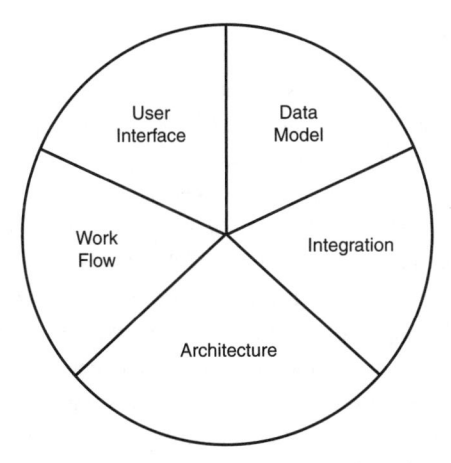

Figure 6.4 Consider features from all five areas when choosing new tools.

User Interface

One of the first concerns with any tool set should be how easily your team can use the tool. Change and release management has many different roles. You should consider all of them when thinking of the user interface for the tools. A release manager will probably spend a significant amount of time working with release records and change records and will need a tool that responds quickly. A change approver, on the other hand, may not have any need to use the tools other than to indicate approvals for records, so he or she might prefer a user interface that allows approvals to be done from e-mails rather than directly in the tool. If you think of each role and how they will access and use the tools, you will have one of the criteria in selecting the right tool for your organization.

Another important user interface characteristic is the ability to find information. Almost every tool allows you to search by record number or by the title on a record, but users need much more than these simple searches. Some tools allow searches on partial titles, or on implementation dates, or even on any field within the change or release record. These capabilities can significantly improve your team's productivity, because they allow people to work in a way that makes them comfortable, rather than in the way the tool demands.

Also look for relational searches—finding records based on their relationship to other records. If the tool allows you to find all changes for a particular configuration item, or all release records for a particular configuration item, you will be much more successful in automating the integrated change, release, and configuration management processes.

A very useful feature of many tools is the ability to customize the user interface. From small tweaks like adding a logo or changing background colors, to very large customizations like rearranging fields and tabs, these user interface changes can help better match the screens to your process. These changes can take only a few hours at the beginning of a project, but they will return many hours of labor savings over the life of the tool. Many organizations put a customizable user interface near the top of their wish list when shopping for change and release management tools.

Architecture

As soon as your change and release management tools are in place, you will want them to remain useful for a long time. The best way to guarantee a long life for a tool set is to make sure the architecture behind it is strong. Nonfunctional attributes such as scalability, capacity, and maintainability will become more important as the tool set gets heavier use and time passes.

Start by understanding which platforms the tool requires, especially for users. If the tool requires you to install some piece of code on every desktop machine, it will inherently be more difficult to maintain. On the other hand, if the tool is accessed by standard web browsers, it can easily be changed without having to reach every user's workstation. Look for web-based tools, or at least tools that support operation without dedicated client code.

Another important aspect of architecture is the data storage mechanism. Most change and release management tools store data about changes, release packages, and releases in a standard database. You will certainly want to choose tools that support the database management system (DBMS) your organization routinely uses. Dealing with a new DBMS just for the sake of a change and release tool requires different administrative skills and will end up costing much more over the life of the tool. This same principle applies to web servers and any other middleware components the system may need. If most of your business applications use WebSphere Application Server, you will want to avoid a change management tool that requires a different web server engine.

Another key architectural aspect to consider when purchasing a tool is scalability. Many people think of scalability in terms of how large a system can grow. But in most organizations, the change and release management functions are not high-growth areas. Given a clear preference, many would like to have these functions accomplished with fewer people, so also consider whether the tool you choose can scale downward for smaller sizes. For example, can you run the database server and web server on a single virtual operating system image? This downward scalability can also help when you are creating development or training environments and you don't want to duplicate all the capacity of the production environment.

Because software vendors typically support only the most recent versions, software upgrades will become an issue if you hope to use tools for a long time. As part of the decision criteria, you should find out how the tool supports version upgrades. If you plan to significantly customize the tools, be sure you understand how those customizations will move forward to newer versions. The longer you have a tool set installed, the greater the percentage of the overall cost you will need to allocate to version upgrades.

Data Model

After the user interface and the overall architecture, the most important aspect of a change or release management tool is the data model underlying it. Every tool comes with some assumptions about how you will want to record changes, approvals, release packages, deployment plans, and the many other artifacts surrounding the ITIL change and release management processes. You will need to live with many of the assumptions that the tool vendor has made on your behalf, so be sure to examine what they are.

The first thing to check is how flexible the model is. Some tools allow you to add as many new fields as you like and support a wide variety of field types. Other tools simply give you a fixed number of character, date, number, and text slots that you can rename as your own data fields. Either kind might be suitable, depending on how well the original model fits your needs. You might also want to check on whether you can remove fields or data elements that are not important to your organization. Extraneous data fields can cause confusion or even errors, and even if you can hide them from the input screens, they may still complicate reporting or data queries.

Be sure the data model is robust enough to satisfy both current and future needs. You may not want to track the financial aspects of every change record right now, but when you implement the rest of the ITIL process set and get to financial management, you'll be glad for the ability. The best tools are those that provide a strong data model but allow you to hide fields until they are needed. Then a later administrative action can make the field available and fully integrated into the model.

Work Flow

Change and release management are systematic processes in which each change or release follows a discrete set of steps, and each step is marked by a change in the record's status. Processes with these characteristics should always be automated by work flow tools, so in looking for a change and release management tool set, work flow is very important.

Like the data model, most change management tools come with a predefined work flow. You will certainly need the ability to modify this work flow, and you probably will want to be able to create entirely new work flows. Carefully consider how much flexibility the work flow gives you versus the difficulty of managing it. Some tools are quite flexible but almost need a programmer to use all that power. Other tools are quite simple but fall short of automating all the nuances of the work flows your organization might define.

Work flow gives you another opportunity to consider what happens to customizations during version upgrades of the tools. If you have to re-create your work flows with every version change, you will be doing rework that makes each upgrade more expensive. A good tool should preserve your work flows through version upgrades.

Integration

In ITIL terms, there is no such thing as a stand-alone tool. Just as every process discipline is integrated with others and bound together in the common services life cycle, so every tool needs to be integrated with other tools to automate the processes. You should think about the integration capabilities of any tool you are considering.

One way to get better integration is to purchase a service management tool suite. As described earlier in this chapter, these tools feature integration without additional effort on your part. Integrated suites allow incidents and problems to be related to changes and allow changes to be related to configuration items. These are fundamental integrations, and it would be difficult to argue that you are aligned with ITIL best practices if your tools don't support them.

One of the issues with integrated suites, however, is that they seldom provide solid release management functionality. You need to either deploy a separate release management tool or customize the change management tool to accommodate release management as well. This poses integration problems, because the integrations native to change management aren't necessarily correct for release management. In addition, when bolting release management functions on to an integrated suite, you need to consider how to build integration between change and release management into your customizations.

If you've chosen to implement stand-alone tools, the integration issue becomes even more important. You need to look for tools that not only support integration at the data layer, but also support user interface integration to some extent. Being able to relate configuration items to a change record is important in the data model, but if you can't look up configuration items while working in the change management interface, the relationships may not be very strong. User interface integration allows you to call out to external programs from the main screens of the change and release management tools.

The most important integration standard today is Extensible Markup Language (XML). Ask your tool vendors if they support XML, or even web services protocols such as SOAP. Following these industry standards makes integration between tools from different vendors a relatively simple process. If you have to define integrations without these standards, you will spend much more time doing it.

Using a Trade Study to Choose Tools

You now have all the information you need to make a wise decision about change and release management tools. But having plenty of information and using it might be two separate things. This section presents a decision-making tool that can help you turn information into action. This tool doesn't apply strictly to change and release management, and it isn't even limited to choices about tools. A trade study is a generic decision-making tool that helps clarify several alternatives and helps guide you to the best one.

Defining Requirements

The first step of doing a trade study is to define a set of requirements. This might be a subset of the overall requirements you defined for change and release management, but it necessarily is more focused on just the decision at hand. For a tools decision, you need a set of requirements defined at sufficient depth to distinguish one tool from another.

For example, you may already have a requirement defined that your tool should support searching on change record numbers. But every tool in your short list can satisfy that requirement, so for the purpose of the trade study, you should add more details, such as support for partial numbers and searches on ranges of numbers.

Perhaps you have special needs for one or more data elements. I once worked with an organization that supported a forty-two-character chargeback code. In a general requirement it might be sufficient to indicate that the organization needs to support chargeback information. But in a trade study the organization would need to specify this unusually long code. Think carefully about potential friction points in implementing the tools, and turn those into requirements for your trade study.

Requirements for a trade study need not be as formal as those for your project. Project requirements lead others to specific actions and need to be tested. Trade study requirements only need to differentiate one tool from another. Rather than complete, unambiguous statements, trade study requirements can be just a listing of desired features, as long as the list is descriptive enough for everyone to agree whether a tool has the feature.

Establishing Weighting

As soon as your list of requirements is long enough to differentiate between the various tool options, it is time to move on to the numeric portion of the trade study. Start by assigning each requirement with a weighting factor indicating how important it is to your decision. Use something simple, such as 1 for the least important, 3 for the most important, and 2 for somewhat important. For the math to work out well, you will want to use greater numbers for greater importance and lesser numbers for lesser importance.

Try to avoid dramatic differences in importance among the requirements. If one requirement really is dramatically more important than others, you might consider trimming the list of options to just those that meet this requirement, because it is unlikely that you will pick an alternative that doesn't meet it. The trade study technique works best when all the requirements are relatively of the same importance.

Evaluating Alternatives

As soon as the requirements have been defined and assigned an importance factor, the actual evaluation of alternatives can begin. For this stage, determine a scoring system that you can use consistently to indicate how well each potential tool meets each requirement. One scale that works very well is to assign 0 for "does not meet," 1 for "meets with heavy customization," 2 for "meets with minimal customization," and 3 for "meets out of the box." Using a scale based on the effort of meeting each requirement will help you find the solution that meets your needs best within the shortest time frame.

Each tool you are considering should be scored against all the requirements. Many times the vendors themselves will help in your evaluation. You can give them your trade study requirements and ask them to demonstrate their software to show you how it meets your needs. While the demonstration is going on, you can use the requirements as a checklist to evaluate what the vendor is showing you. Allowing the vendor to show the strengths and weaknesses of its tool against your set of criteria can be a very effective way to highlight the differences between tools.

Scoring and Judging

After you have established a weighting and a score for each requirement and each tool, you can calculate a numeric value by multiplying the two. If you followed the earlier advice and are using scales with a lower value for less important requirements and less adherence to requirements, higher scores indicate more desirable tools. Figure 6.5 shows an example of a trade study scorecard.

| | | Tool A | | Tool B | |
Requirement	Weight	Raw	Weighted	Raw	Weighted
User Interface	2	2	4	1	2
Search Input	1	3	3	2	2
Configurable	3	3	6	3	6
Architecture Scrabble DB Support	2	1	2	3	6
• • •	3	3	6	3	4
Total Score			21		20

Figure 6.5 A trade study results in a scorecard comparing tools.

Although a trade study is a good decision-making tool, you should always remember that it is simply a tool. Other factors, such as price, vendor relationships, and user preferences, might make you choose a tool even though its trade study score is lower than other tools. Use the trade study mostly to eliminate poor choices, and then choose from among the good choices using other techniques.

Looking Ahead

Tools can be a very emotional topic. Throughout this chapter, you have learned about the different common categories of tools that are either directly or indirectly used for change and release management. You cannot quell all the emotions with this knowledge, but you can at least shed a little light in the midst of the heat.

Certainly not every organization is in a position to purchase an entirely new tools suite. By looking at the survey of tools and capabilities in this chapter, you should be able to understand the gaps in your current tools. You also should be able to prioritize which tools are most urgently in need of replacing or modifying. When you get to that point and are ready to make a tool decision, the section "Using a Trade Study to Choose Tools" will help.

If you do end up with new tools, you need to read the next chapter, "Migrating or Consolidating Data." It is one thing to install a great new tool, but quite another to realize that you need to move all your data from the legacy environment to load that new database. Chapter 7 helps you do that.

CHAPTER 7

Migrating or Consolidating Data

Projects are derailed not by major things, but by simple things. Project managers usually do not overlook requirements or processes or tools, but many projects have gone bad because nobody thought about how to get the old data into the new tools. Migrating data from an older tool into a new one, or consolidating data from multiple legacy tools into a single new tool, are simple tasks that can significantly delay your project if they aren't included early on.

Although migration and consolidation are simple, they are not necessarily easy. Dealing with thousands of old change records and hundreds of release records is tedious and time-consuming, but not complex. You can use a few simple techniques to scale the highest mountain of data. This chapter describes those techniques and how to use them to migrate or consolidate data.

Dealing with Legacy Systems

Unless your organization is new, you probably already have a change management system of some kind. If that system is meeting your needs well, and it has the flexibility to adapt to your new ITIL-aligned process, you may be able to continue using it. Thus, you will not have to migrate change management data. Of course, if your modifications to align with ITIL include adding fields or changing the data layout, you will still be forced to do some sort of data migration.

Release management is a different story, however. Very few organizations actually have a release management process. Even those that do seldom have a tool that automates the process well. Release management data is likely to be found in a series of project control books, software inventory systems, or source code control systems. This data needs to be consolidated to create a single release management repository.

Accessing Legacy Data

The first step in moving data from a legacy system to a new tool is to get access to the legacy data. This may be easy, or it may require significant effort, depending on the nature of the legacy system and how it structures and stores data.

Many organizations have adopted unstructured information storage as part of their change management system. Information such as backout plans, test plans, and sometimes even change records themselves are stored in tools such as Lotus Notes®, where the information isn't available as simple rows and columns in a relational database. If this is your situation, you will most likely need to create a custom parser that can read the unstructured data and pull out the pieces you want to include in your new change management tool. Figure 7.1 shows the function of this parser.

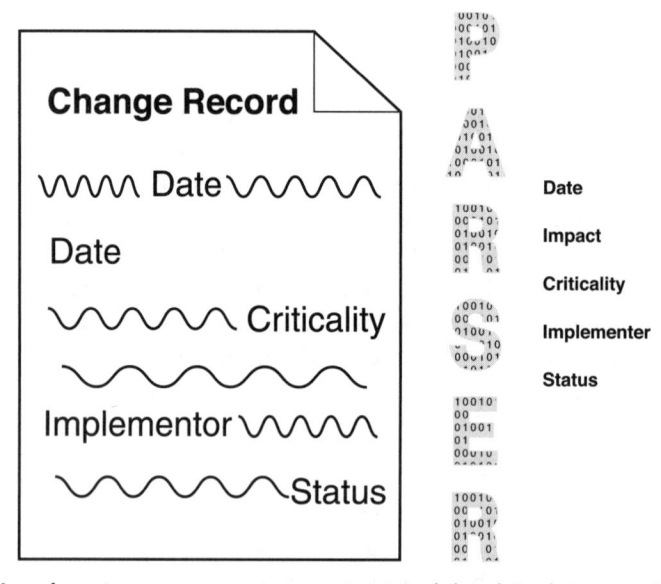

Figure 7.1 A custom parser can turn unstructured data into data records.

The unstructured data parser typically reads a document at a time, looking for keywords or other clues about where data is stored. For example, you might create a parser that will find all the strings formatted as times and then attempt to assign them to the date/time fields in your new tool. Unstructured information is particularly difficult to deal with, so be sure you really need to pull the data into your new tool before you go to the expense of building a migration routine.

Assuming that the data you need to migrate is structured as identifiable data fields, you simply need to create a program to pull that information. If your legacy tool uses a relational database, this could be as simple as creating some SQL statements to access the data you need. If the legacy tool uses some other format, you might need a more complex program that can read the database and pull out the data records.

Dealing with Legacy Systems

Determine how to access the legacy data, and then pull it into a format that can be easily manipulated. Many people find that comma-separated value (CSV) files are easy to deal with because they can be brought into a spreadsheet, which is the perfect tool for manipulating many rows of data quickly. Others find it convenient to simply emulate the old data structures in the new tool and port data directly. Then you can use any work flow, scripting, or programming capability of the new tool to populate the "native" tables with data from these "foreign" tables you have created.

Adding Values to New Fields

Missing data is a very common problem when migrating change and release management data. The legacy database probably does not contain all the data elements you want in the new tool. If it did, you probably wouldn't be moving to a new tool. In some cases, these missing data elements will actually be required fields in the new tool set, so you need to put some values in them. The challenge is in determining how to put values into those fields.

The first and easiest possibility is that you can populate the same value into each migrated data record. For example, imagine that your new tool requires a field for change requester, but the legacy data doesn't have this value. To create the new records, you can adopt a dummy value—say, "Legacy"—and simply put that into every field. This isn't very useful data, but at least it accommodates the need to have a value in the field in the new tool.

The next step in difficulty is a situation in which you can deduce a value from other fields in the legacy data. For example, suppose the legacy tool supports values for the complexity of a change and the organization that benefits from the change. You might use these two values by creating a formula that calculates the risk of a change by some combination of the complexity and the beneficiary. A complex change benefiting four or five parts of your organization would certainly have a higher risk than a simple change benefiting only one part of the organization.

Another possibility is to fill in the data values by cross-referencing each record with some external source. Going back to the example of the requester, if the legacy tool has information on the department charged for the change, you may be able to use your human resources system to look up the manager of that department and assign that manager as the requester of the change. You can leverage external data to fill in data values in many ways, but this often requires some programming, so be sure the value of the data is worth the cost of obtaining it.

As a last resort, it is always possible to manually create missing data values. After pulling the legacy data into a spreadsheet, you could break up the spreadsheet by sets of rows and ask a knowledgeable person to fill in the empty columns in each of the rows assigned to them. This is a slow and painstaking process that can result in data errors, but it is also guaranteed to produce meaningful data in a way that is impossible with formulas and cross-references.

Some vendors have developed reconciliation technology in their data import process. This allows you to prioritize sources of data to pick the "best" source first. For example, physical location might have a database source as the primary, and then a spreadsheet, and finally manual entry. An automated process would then look for data in that field. If there were data, the process would take the data first from the SQL source, and then from the spreadsheet, and finally would allow manual entry.

Converting Data Values

Another common issue with migrating data is that data in the legacy system may be formatted in a way that doesn't match the needs of the new system. This is an excellent time to use a spreadsheet and its ability to manipulate values. For example, imagine that the legacy data has the implementation date formatted as a simple text string, but your new tool needs it formatted as a date/time field. Simply put the text string in one column, and then put a formula in the neighboring column that uses the spreadsheet's text-parsing capabilities to create a date and time value. This same technique converts text to numbers and uppercase to lowercase, and performs a host of other useful conversions.

Sometimes, however, a simple function cannot perform the conversion, because more complex logic is required. For example, imagine that your legacy tool supports only three status values for each release—planning, development, and deployed. You want six values in your new tool based on the life cycle you've identified. The records that were identified as being in the planning phase in the old tool would have a status of "concept" if the requirements were not finalized yet, but "plan" if those requirements had been finalized and approved. To quickly deal with hundreds of rows, you might create a macro that read the current status, and when it was "Planning," looked at the date for requirements approval to find out whether to set the value to "Concept" or "Plan." This kind of complex calculation could be done with a compound formula or with a simple macro.

Converting data presents dozens of challenges. Always look for the simplest approach first, trying to define a formula or macro in a spreadsheet that will quickly convert all the rows of legacy data. In some cases, however, you need to address each row individually, which is slow but reliable. Be sure to allow plenty of time for this kind of data conversion.

Dealing with Unclosed Records

Of particular concern when migrating data is records that are in flight. These are records that are actively being worked on, such as changes that are still in the approval phase or release records that are still in the deployment phase. Closed records are simpler because they have no timing implications.

For unclosed records, you need to consider when to have people stop updates in the legacy tool and when to start making updates in the new tool. This decision must be made based on the "go live" schedule, the training schedule, and the schedule of activities around the record itself.

If possible, you should handle the problem of unclosed records by a slow migration. Implement the new system, and declare a date on which all new records will go into it. At the same time, keep the old system running, and allow unclosed records to be worked in the old system until they are closed. This requires two sets of reports and measurements for some transition period, but it prevents your having to move unclosed records in any way. This approach is particularly helpful for change records, which tend to have a shorter lifespan, but it may not be practical for release records, which can sometimes remain unclosed for many months.

If you can break your migration effort into closed records and then unclosed records, you will be more successful. This normally involves a concentrated effort the week before migration to close as many records as possible.

Data Retention Policies

One of the primary techniques for dealing with legacy data is to remove anything that is no longer needed. To safely do this, you need a strong organizational policy on data retention. This policy should describe what must be kept, what can be disposed of, and how long data must be kept. This section describes how to establish a data retention policy, and then how to deal with data as soon as that policy is in place.

Defining and Using Policies

In today's era of Sarbanes-Oxley and corporate responsibility, every organization should have a policy on data retention. Records destroyed prematurely and data retained past its useful life both represent significant exposures to corporate auditors. If you don't know your organization's policy on retaining data, you should find out what it is, and you should certainly push to get one created if it doesn't already exist.

Change records contain important data for regulatory compliance. In the U.S., IT changes to computers connected to laboratory equipment can impact FDA compliance for pharmaceutical companies. Application changes to financial applications in Europe can affect compliance with BASEL II and other EU regulations. Because change records have significant compliance implications, they should fall into your policy on data retention.

If your organization does not have a specific policy concerning retention of change records, the implementation of ITIL-aligned change management is a great opportunity to create one. Start with defining all IT change records as data that must follow the retention policy. It is theoretically possible that only certain categories of change really impact compliance, but with the plethora of new regulations affecting almost every industry, it is safest to simply assume that every change record will one day be affected by some regulation or other.

The difficult part of defining a policy is setting the retention times. Some regulations require that data be kept for three years, and others require that data older than 18 months be removed. This kind of conflict between government and industry regulations and corporate practice will most likely lead to a data retention policy with variable times based on change category. Three possible situations exist: Some records will require deletion before some set time has expired, other records will be required to be kept for some period of time, and others may require both retention for a minimum time and deletion after a maximum time. Understanding these times based on the regulations your organization must deal with is the key to setting up effective change management categories for data retention. For much more on managing compliance and data retention, see Chapter 14, "Auditing and Compliance Management."

Archiving Aged Data

Setting a data retention policy is quite important, but it is effective only if you enforce that policy. To enforce it, you need a mechanism to archive data that has aged. Archiving moves data from your permanent change or release management system to a long-term offline storage facility, normally using either tape or CD media. That data could be restored if it becomes necessary later, but usually it is simply stored until the data retention policy says it should be removed.

The first step in enforcing data retention is to create a process that selects data that has aged. Your policy should define some number of days past closure that records can be archived, so you need a query that quickly identifies these records so that you can archive them. The query should be executed at least weekly, and any rows identified should be extracted from the production database and sent to your secondary storage mechanism. This helps meet the data retention policy but also keeps the production database small enough to be effective.

As soon as you've extracted the data records that have aged, you have two options. If your policy calls for offline storage for some period of time, you need to put those records in secondary storage. Of course, if the data retention policy calls for permanent removal of records, you simply delete them from the production database, and there is no need to store them more permanently. Figure 7.2 shows the typical life cycle of data in a situation where data retention policies are enforced.

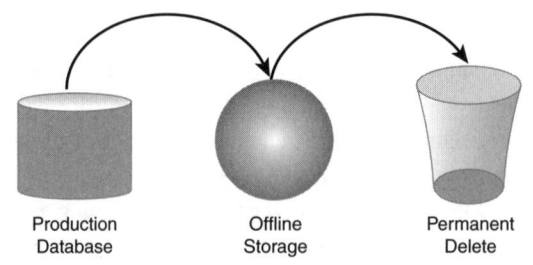

Figure 7.2 Data moves through three discrete locations when following data retention policies.

Your secondary storage mechanism should be tested occasionally. You should move some records, but not delete them from the production database. Then read the records from secondary storage to make sure that they match the production records. Any discrepancies indicate that there is a problem with how your archive is being created, and this could invalidate all the archived records. Any errors found with the archive should be taken seriously, because they might jeopardize your ability to respond to an audit.

Techniques for Consolidating Data

After all possible purging has been accomplished, you will still have data that needs to be merged into your change and release management tools. If that data resides in more than one system, you will be faced with a data consolidation challenge. Consolidation is more difficult than simple migration because you must deal with multiple source systems and determine how to combine the data. This section describes some important techniques for consolidating data from disparate sources. Figure 7.3 shows the general cycle for consolidating data.

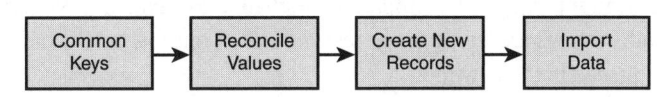

Common Keys → Reconcile Values → Create New Records → Import Data

Figure 7.3 Consolidating data from multiple sources requires four steps.

Identify Common Keys

When you work with multiple data sources, the first task is to find ways to relate those sources to one another through elements common to all of them. These common elements are called keys because they unlock the power to combine diverse data sources.

The best possible case is when keys are already unique within their own tools but are common across the tools you need to consolidate. Imagine that you need to combine data from three separate legacy change management systems. In each of the systems, the person who implemented the change is identified by his or her employee number from a common human resources system. This kind of common key makes it easy to find all the changes implemented by a single person, regardless of which system recorded those changes.

Unfortunately, it is rare to find a common key across all tools. More frequently you have to infer commonality by looking at different data values in multiple tools. Suppose, for example, that your source code control system maintains the name of the top-level executable module for each application, and your software inventory tool recognizes applications by an application ID generated specifically for that system. To combine data from these two systems, you may choose to use the last compiled date from the source code repository and compare it to the executable date/time in the software inventory system. By inferring that these date and time stamps should be the same, you can correlate applications between these diverse systems. When you have more than two sources, you may need to continue this technique. You would relate the source code control records to a software license management tool by an executable module name and then compare the license management record to your CMDB by configuration ID. The farther you build such a chain of related records, the more brittle it becomes, and the more likely you will fail to relate records to one another.

You might be able to find a common key only by including data from a system that wouldn't otherwise be in scope for your data consolidation effort. In many cases, you can find common keys from a human resources system, or perhaps a corporate locations database. Other enterprise databases probably contain lookup codes that are frequently used in IT systems. Any of these might become a good way to link data records between systems that you have been asked to combine.

Reconcile Similar Data Values

When combining data from multiple systems, you will often find data elements that have the same meaning but are formatted or expressed differently. For example, one legacy change management tool may express the impact of a change as "Low," "Medium," or "High," and a second legacy system might express the impact of a change as "None," "Moderate," "Significant," or "Severe." Both systems are trying to express the same concept, but the data needs to be reconciled before being placed in the new tool.

One technique for reconciling these data values is to build a mapping table. In essence this is a simple spreadsheet that takes all possible values from one system and maps them to a possible value in the other system and to the final value in the new system. Creating a mapping table normally is a manual activity, but after it is created, it can be used to both reconcile similar data values and translate to the value needed by the new tool. As long as the set of values is reasonably small, a mapping table can be stored in memory by the program responsible for combining the data records. Larger mapping tables can be stored in a working database and looked up by the combination program. Some vendors have or are creating ways to use the mapping table concept during data import to automate some of these features.

Mapping tables are useful when both systems support finite lists of defined values in their fields, but they are not helpful when the data elements to be combined are free-form. What happens, for instance, when two text fields need to be combined somehow? Imagine you are working to merge two legacy change management systems into one new tool, and each system supports a title for every change record. You have determined through common key values that a change record in system A defines the same event as a change record in system B, but the systems have different strings in the title field. In this case, you can either adopt the title directly from one system or concatenate the two strings into a single title. If you adopt a single title, you risk losing some important data, but concatenating two titles leaves you with titles that are not very readable.

Another challenge in reconciling data happens when two values are contradictory. Suppose, for example, that two different software inventory systems both describe the same application, but one of them says the application is on version 4.2 and the other says the most recent version is 4.3. Or imagine that you have determined that two change records identify the same event, but they have different implementation dates. These are cases in which at least one of the systems is in error. If you have good knowledge of the systems involved, you might be able to figure out which one is in error, but if you have never worked with these source systems before, you may have quite a lot of detective work to do. Work with the people who have entered the data (if they are available) to determine what the right data value should be, and then manually adjust the data to indicate the correct value.

In addition, it is important to "close the loop" with this incorrect data. After you have consolidated and reconciled all the data, determine if and how you should fix the data in the various legacy systems. This is important, because some groups in the enterprise may still be using those legacy systems, and they may be making (incorrect) business decisions based on the incorrect data.

Form New Data Records

After you have found common keys and correlated like records and data elements, it is time to build the consolidated data that will flow into the new change and release management tool. Building this data is a matter of putting together the pieces in a temporary storage location and then moving the constructed records into the permanent database of the new tool.

To start assembling a new record, you must first understand the needed structure. Fortunately this can be obtained from the documentation of your new tool, combined with whatever customizations you've made to that tool. If you've added some fields, they need to be part of the new records you are now creating. If you've hidden or even removed fields from the standard data model, you don't need to put data in those fields as you build the temporary record.

Your new tool set will support many different types of records, including release package records, release records, change records, approval records, and probably many more. The best way to assemble temporary records before importing into the new tool is to make a complete copy of the new database to use as temporary storage, but then to relax any constraints such as required fields, indices, and data triggers. By doing this, you will have the structure of the new database that you can populate in any order you want. Of course, this kind of testing is best done in the test environment before you make wholesale changes to production.

Your consolidation program can now populate data rows as they are assembled from the legacy tools. This might involve going to spreadsheets, mapping tables, external sources, and a whole variety of other tricks described earlier. As each row is assembled, it is placed in the temporary storage location.

When all data assembly is complete, you can run reports to determine the quality of the data in the temporary store. If you were able to automate most of the assembly, your data should be very clean, but if you did much of the work manually using spreadsheets or other tools, the data might still be unsuitable for import into your new tool set. If this is your situation, plan to spend significant time cleaning up the data before the final import.

Run the final import only after all the data is clean and you are satisfied that it is complete. Importing bad data into a new tool is a certain recipe for failure. You should guard the new tool and its pristine database to ensure the highest possible chance of success in your overall implementation project.

Merging Release and Change Data

As you define the change and release management processes, you undoubtedly will define many ways in which the processes should integrate with one another. Because of this process integration, it is important to be able to integrate data from the two processes. This is really a special case of consolidating data between systems in which the systems are a change tool and a release management tool. This section presents some ideas to help you merge change and release data into a single system.

Configuration Items as a Common Denominator

To bring together change and release, you must start with configuration management, or at least some notion of what could possibly be changed in your environment. This idea of "what might be changed" is known more formally as configuration items in ITIL. Configuration items are the units that make up the entire IT environment.

The reason that configuration items are important when relating change management and release management is because they provide the best possible way to be sure that a change really describes the release you want to relate it to. This works through a series of relationships, as shown in Figure 7.4.

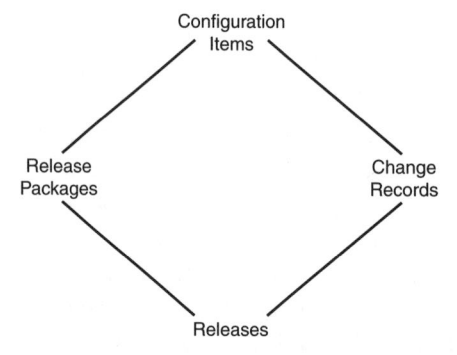

Figure 7.4 Change and release management are integrated through configuration items.

Each release package is made up of one or more configuration items. The release package is really nothing more than a subset of your IT environment, so it makes perfect sense that it can be described as a group of related configuration items. Using the CMDB, you should even be able to understand the relationships among the configuration items in any particular release package.

Each change record in the legacy system you are incorporating should also point to one or more configuration items. Because your legacy system is not necessarily ITIL-aligned, it may describe these as resources, components, or something else. Whichever word is used, most change management systems allow the requester to specify one or more things that are being changed in the environment. Now that you understand ITIL, you know that these are configuration items.

So the biggest issue is simply to associate the configuration items that are part of a release package with the configuration items that are described in a change record. Depending on how the legacy change records worked with configuration items, this might be very easy or extremely difficult. If the legacy system used something common like server names, application identifiers, or IP addresses to identify the resources that would be changed, you should be able to map these fairly easy to configuration items in your CMDB. On the other hand, if your legacy change system uses a free-form text identifier for resources, you will have no choice but to read every change record and make your best guess at the configuration items that were involved.

As soon as you can relate each change to a set of configuration items, you can determine which release package was modified by the change record. This leads you directly to which release belongs with this change record. The value of this information becomes clear when you begin planning the next release of the same package. You'll find that having a list of the changes that have been made allows you to quickly understand the work involved the next version. In addition, relating change records to a specific release also allows you to relate incidents to a specific release. This is a great way to track the quality of your testing efforts.

The cost of associating release data to change data can be very high. Because of this, you will want to carefully consider the value you will gain and determine whether relating legacy change and release data to each other is worth the cost. If not, you can always build a process and tool set that will relate the two going forward.

Looking Ahead

Data migration is the ugliest topic when you're implementing any new system. Everyone likes to think of the new system as a chance to start fresh and have great data management practices going forward. Unfortunately, reality normally dictates that you must move at least some data from the old system to the new, and that the data is unlikely to be pristine. In this chapter, you have learned a variety of techniques for dealing with old data and transforming it into new information for your change and release management processes. In the next chapter, you will learn how to implement the process to use that new information.

CHAPTER 8

Bringing the Process to Life

So far your fledgling implementation of ITIL change and release management has been done through small planning sessions, documentation, and some software. With this chapter, you will bring out your creation to face the rest of your organization. Nothing will make your effort more real than when people actually start executing the new process rather than the old. You might have the tools installed and the data migrated, but until the process actually changes, you haven't really implemented change and release management.

This chapter highlights several things that will help launch the process in your organization. From the inception of the process in a workshop format to measuring the success of the process in a concrete way, you will learn how to take all the plans and back-office work and bring it to life.

Running a Process Workshop

Chapter 3, "Defining Change and Release Management Processes," described how to define the change and release management processes. What that chapter ignored, however, is the social dimension of process design. No process worth writing down is executed by only one person. A typical change or release management process might require action from dozens of people, each of whom has thoughts about how the process should flow.

One way to gain consensus from all these people is to hold a process workshop. The workshop not only accelerates development of the process work, but it also helps socialize the ideas behind the process so that people will feel a greater measure of ownership. This section describes the mechanics of a process workshop and how it can help bring your change and release management processes to life.

Workshop Participation

The process workshop should include the key influencers from the community who will be affected by the process. Sometimes these people have titles like "team leader" or "manager." At other times, the influencers can be difficult to identify by title, but they are known as the most experienced member of the team or perhaps the person with the most ideas. You should gather these people from each organization that will be impacted by the newly defined processes.

Sometimes the people most eager to attend a process workshop do not make the most contributions. You should look for the critics and those who don't believe the process will be successful. Of course, you do not want a room full of people who complain, but you certainly want to get the key critics involved so that they will not have a chance to sabotage the project later.

As soon as you have identified the participants, it is important to get them all into a central location. Process workshops must be done face-to-face because they require the full engagement of the participants. If people are on the other end of a telephone or staring at their PDAs during the workshop, they won't be involved enough to really get the benefits of the workshop.

Agenda and Purpose

The purpose of a process workshop is more than simply defining the process documents. It is a way to get the IT team energized and ready to actually use the new processes while defining and assigning the action items to deploy the process. With that in mind, you should make a big deal of publicizing the workshop, including documenting a clear agenda before the meeting starts.

Normally a process workshop lasts three or four days. The workshop should start with an overview of the ITIL change and release management processes and end with a review of the work completed and tasks assigned. In between, you should follow the structure outlined in Chapter 3 by working from the top-level process to the policies and down to procedures. Table 8.1 shows a sample agenda for a three-day change and release management process workshop.

Table 8.1 A Sample Agenda for a Three-Day Process Workshop

Date/Time	Topic	Moderator
Nov. 14, 8:30 a.m.	Welcome and introductions	Project leader
9:00	Overview of ITIL change management	Process architect
10:30	Break	
10:45	Overview of "as-is" change management	Process owner
12:00	Lunch	
1:00	Overview of ITIL release management	Process architect
2:30	Break	
2:45	Overview of "as-is" release management	Process owner

Date/Time	Topic	Moderator
4:00	Agenda for the next two days	Project leader
5:00	End of day one	
Nov. 15, 8:30 a.m.	Change management high-level flow (group discussion)	Project leader
10:30	Break	
10:45	Document policies and procedures needed for change management	Project leader
11:00	Change management policies (group discussion)	Process architect
12:00	Lunch	
1:00	Continue change management policy discussion	Process architect
2:00	Change management procedures (break into groups)	Process architect
3:00	Break	
3:15	Continue change management procedures discussion	Process architect
5:00	End of day two	
Nov. 16, 8:30 a.m.	Release management high-level flow (group discussion)	Project leader
10:30	Break	
10:45	Document policies and procedures needed for release management	Process architect
11:00	Release management policies (group discussion)	Process architect
12:00	Lunch	
1:00	Continue release management policy discussion	Process architect
2:00	Release management procedures (break into groups)	Process architect
4:30	Summary of workshop and list of action items	Project leader
5:00	End of day three	

Use techniques such as brainstorming, whiteboard recording, and facilitated breakout groups to work through the process deliverables. A strong moderator is important for each of these techniques. The goal is not just to get to the end result, but to form a strong working relationship with the team along the way. Be sure not to let a single person dominate any discussion. When breaking into smaller groups, make each group as heterogeneous as possible. This will help people get to know one another and thus work better together when the process goes live.

Expected Workshop Outcomes

It is extremely unlikely that you will finish all process documents in a three- or four-day workshop, so set expectations accordingly. It is much more likely that you will be able to work out high-level flows based on the ITIL processes and then identify the policies and procedures your organization needs. As soon as the flows are worked out, base the list of other necessary documents on those flows.

In most cases, the workshop will complete the discussion of flows and have time left. Use this time to start working through some of the policies and procedures so that people have an idea of how to approach these process documents. The goal should be to create outlines rather than completed documents, because outlines will help you quickly get at the important ideas your workshop participants can contribute.

Be prepared to quickly publish the outcome of the workshop, ideally the day after the workshop ends. If you've done a good job of setting expectations up front, people shouldn't be disappointed when they see that the workshop didn't produce complete and polished documentation. Instead, people should be pleasantly surprised by how much ground was covered and how much thought went into the outlines and flows that the workshop produced. Use this momentum from the workshop to push the overall project forward.

One of the outcomes of the workshop should be a committed plan to turn the workshop outlines into full process documents. While everyone is still at the face-to-face meeting, you can get agreement on who will tackle which policy and procedure documents and get some idea of where work instructions might be required. Put all of this into the overall project plan, as described in Chapter 3.

Building the Right Organization

Although defining good processes is important, the key to the overall success of your implementation is building an outstanding change and release management team. Highly skilled people can make up for inadequacies in the process, but no amount of process documentation can make up for people who are unwilling or unable to do their jobs.

The right organization consists of both good people and good job descriptions or roles for those people to play. This section describes some of the roles needed in change and release management, and also gives you some tips for building a strong organization. These roles are shown in Figure 8.1.

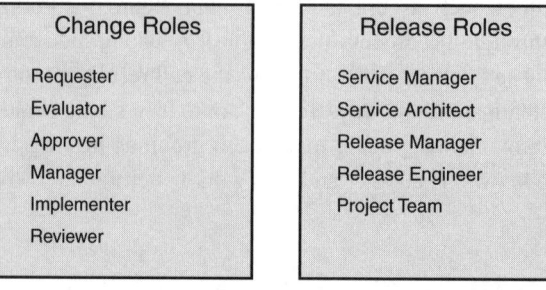

Change Roles	Release Roles
Requester	Service Manager
Evaluator	Service Architect
Approver	Release Manager
Manager	Release Engineer
Implementer	Project Team
Reviewer	

Figure 8.1   Many roles are associated with change and release management.

Change Management Roles

Change management roles are reasonably familiar to most organizations because they have been fairly static over the past thirty years. This section considers some of those roles and how they may be impacted as you align your change management practices with ITIL.

Change requesters come from many parts of the organization. They might be from IT or from the business community. Anyone who asks for an IT change can play the role of change requester. This role will not change dramatically with the advent of ITIL-aligned change management, but the kinds of information that a requester must have to initiate a request for change (RFC) might be different.

You may not currently have people assigned to evaluate changes separately from change approvers. The evaluation role is separate in ITIL to reflect the practice of understanding both the technical and the business impacts of a change. Typically changes are evaluated by technical peers of the person who will be making the change and by business peers of the person who requested the change. When aligning your process to ITIL, change evaluators may be a new role, or change evaluation might be a new set of responsibilities for your approvers.

Change approvers will continue to be important in an ITIL-aligned change management process. The logistics of approval may change with the implementation of the change advisory board (CAB), but the fundamental role is still to take responsibility for approving or rejecting requests for change.

The change manager is an administrative person responsible for process compliance and marshalling changes through the new process. The change manager sees that requests are complete, that the proper reviews take place before the CAB meeting, that approvals are recorded in the tools, that change records are in the correct status, and that reviews are completed when needed. The extent of the tasks for the change manager is largely determined by the measurement points you choose to put into your process.

The change implementer role continues to be important in change management but probably will not be significantly impacted by the alignment to ITIL best practices. The implementer may need to provide additional configuration information and details for the post-implementation review, but the core technical tasks of making changes in the environment are unaffected by the ITIL change management processes.

If your organization has not been conducting post-implementation reviews, the change reviewer role might be new. The key responsibility of this role is to review what happened during the implementation of a change and to gain lessons that can be applied to future activities. The post-implementation review is a best practice identified by ITIL, and it should be part of your new change management process.

Release Management Roles

Release management roles are less familiar to most organizations because very few organizations have a release management process before they align with ITIL. The role descriptions in this section equate release management roles with some roles you may already have. This should help as you seek to implement release management.

The service manager is a high-level role responsible for overall management of a release package. Theory dictates that a release package should provide some identifiable service to either the IT organization or the business. The service manager is responsible for defining and managing that service regardless of how many releases or versions of the service get produced. In that way, the service manager is very similar to a product manager for any product an organization might produce. Service management looks at the larger picture and makes long-term strategic decisions about the service.

A service architect is responsible for defining the technical solution for how the service will be delivered. This role also operates across all releases of any particular release package. The service architect takes the wants and needs of the service manager and builds solutions that satisfy those wants and needs. The service architect works to implement a technical strategy across all releases of a service.

A release manager is focused on a specific release rather than the big picture. Outside of release management, this role normally is called a project manager. If you view the release as a project, the release manager does all the normal things a project manager would do, including dealing with schedule, resources, budgets, and the overall quality of the release. Normally the release manager is the leader of a project team that is responsible for building, testing, and deploying a particular release.

The release engineer is a technical role that oversees the technical solution for a specific release. This role is equivalent to a project architect or system engineer for a traditional IT project. The release engineer takes specifications and general architectural direction from the service architect and creates a detailed architecture for the current release. As soon as the architecture has been defined, the release engineer is responsible for technical content throughout the project and verifies that the release meets its requirements.

Within release management are also all the normal project roles. As a new release is defined, designed, built, tested, released, and deployed, the project team needs all your normal project-related roles. This might include additional application designers, infrastructure architects, developers, test engineers, quality assurance support, documentation specialists, integration engineers, or a variety of other roles. All these roles will play a part in your release management cycle.

Staffing the Roles

Seeing all these roles defined might have you wondering how many people you will need to achieve change and release management. The number of people you need is unrelated to the number of roles. Some very large organizations might have dozens of people whose only job is to evaluate change requests, and dozens of others who are dedicated service architects. In a small organization, one person might play the roles of service manager, service architect, release manager, and release engineer. It is quite possible to have multiple people play one role or to have one person play multiple roles.

The real answer to how many people you need comes from your own experiences. If you have thousands of change records to process each month, you need more people than an organization that handles only one hundred change records per month and many more than an organization that handles only ten change records per month. The size of the change management staff is not dependent on the overall size of the organization, but it is dependent on the amount of change activity in the organization.

Aside from a count of how many people you need, you also need to know what kind of people to put into the roles for both change and release management. The different roles require a wide range of skills and experience. You should put the most effort and money into finding highly skilled people for the service manager and service architect roles in release management, and the change evaluator and change reviewer roles in change management. These roles will have the most impact on the overall success of your release and change management programs, and putting your best people in these roles will give you a greater chance of success.

Some roles, such as change approver and members of a project team, do not require a dedicated commitment. Other roles, such as change manager and release manager, should be the only task a person performs. This isn't a question of workload, but more an issue of focus and ability to go beyond the daily work to help improve the process in substantial ways. If your organization is simply too small to allow for a dedicated change manager, you should at least share a person with another ITIL process area such as incident manager or perhaps service-level administrator. It is also quite possible for a release manager to be dedicated to release management but to manage multiple releases of different services at the same time as long as the individual projects are not too big or complex for a single person to manage.

Training the Team

One of the most frequent causes of failure in implementing IT processes is a lack of training. Regardless of how good your people, how detailed your process documents, or how self-explanatory your tools, people still need training. This section describes how to prepare and deliver good training for your change and release management organization.

Preparing Training Materials

When building training materials, the first step is to consider the audience for the training. Will new people be hired from outside the organization? If so, you might need to include some information on the organization and its purposes in the training. Even if everyone receiving the initial training is a senior member of the current IT team, consider how often people change jobs or even come and go from the organization. You should try to build training materials that will last for as long as the process and tools are relatively stable.

Build your training materials as a series of small, reusable modules. By building the materials as a set of small blocks, you can build interesting and innovative training programs much more easily. You might consider creating complimentary sets of blocks. For example, one module could cover the organizational policy on when to approve a change and when to reject it, and the complimentary module could cover how to approve or reject a change in the tool. Then, if the tool changes, you can reuse all the process modules.

The audience also determines what format you use for training modules. If you are training a few people in a single geography, you might prepare some slides and plan to stand in front of them to teach the material. If you have to deal with people who are widely dispersed, you might want to consider something more elegant, like a training video that they can watch at their leisure. People who understand the process relatively well might need only a few quick work flows and a short description of what has changed. People who are new to the topic of change and release management need much more background on what ITIL is, why it is important, and how it drove the creation of the process.

Your goal in preparing training should be to meet the requirements and no more. Although a twelve-hour training class complete with lab exercises might seem like a complete training solution, it will not be very helpful to the person who just needs a high-level process overview that could be gained in two hours. If you need both extremes, however, be sure to create those small modules so that the two-hour version is nothing more than a very small subset of modules out of the twelve-hour version.

You should plan to create training programs for each role. This is another reason for small, reusable modules—the change evaluator and change approver will have many modules in common, and perhaps only two or three modules different. By creating the training in a modular way, you can quickly build additional training programs as needed.

Delivering Training

Preparing training materials is only half the battle. The training must also be delivered, which in larger organizations can be a major undertaking. Between scheduling, logistics, and making sure the training is effective, there is plenty to do.

Unless you have decided to make all the training self-directed, you need to decide how to schedule all the members of your change and release management teams without disrupting their normal jobs. Change requesters and change approvers are particularly difficult, because normally there are many of them, and change management is not always their top concern. Sometimes a conference call format works well, or a web conference, in which a presentation can be quickly shared with a large number of people.

Scheduling for the dedicated staff, such as change managers and service architects, also can be difficult, because they frequently have nobody to take over their tasks while they take training. If these roles are staffed by more than one person, you will most likely need to stagger the training. But if only one person handles these roles, you need to schedule training for a time when that person is the least busy. Either way, be sure the training focuses on the essentials and doesn't take more time than it needs to.

If the team you are training is large, you will inevitably run into people who cancel at the last minute. Therefore, you need a way to track who has been trained and who hasn't. This tracking should be used to schedule additional sessions, send reminders, and generally hound people until the entire team is properly trained. Experience shows that people generally view training as a low-priority activity until they need to actually execute the new process and realize they don't know how. To help avoid this syndrome, you should schedule training as close to your process start date as possible, but be sure to leave time to train those who legitimately cannot make the scheduled times.

Many people are skeptical about the value of tests administered at the end of training, but they can be very helpful when a significant work process is being changed. Tests help measure the effectiveness of the training and show whether people were paying attention. If you choose to use them, you will want to be sure they are not intimidating but still are difficult enough to see if the concepts came across clearly. If you do choose to use tests, be sure you look at the results between multiple sessions of the same training so that you can decide whether the training materials can be made more effective before the next session. Many times you will find that the tests point out problems with the materials more than problems with the people being trained.

First Steps Toward Success

When training is over, the big day finally arrives. The purpose of ITIL is to share best practices. In this spirit, this section describes some of the best practices in launching a new IT process. You'll find it helpful not just for your change and release management efforts, but also for almost any IT service that requires new behavior from the organization. Figure 8.2 reminds you of the main steps in implementing a process.

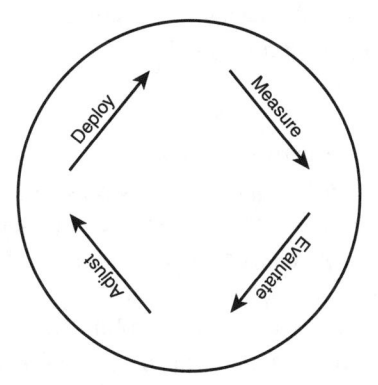

Figure 8.2 Deployment follows a proven cycle.

Certify Key Staff

It is difficult to overemphasize the importance of your people to the success of your implementation. If they are fully trained and completely understand the benefits you are seeking with the ITIL implementation, they will be able to make up for poor process definitions, poor tool selection, and even a poor project plan. On the other hand, if your team is unsure of the project or is not adequately trained in their new tasks, no other part of the project can overcome the deficit. Because people are the biggest dependency in the project, it makes sense to test their readiness. This is done through certification.

The IT industry has been using certification for a long time. At its core, certification involves validating someone's readiness to perform a job. For change and release management, this means making sure that your team is ready to follow the process and use the tools.

Certification can be as formal or as informal as you like, as long as it validates that people are ready for full operations of the new processes. A formal certification might include a role-based written test, an oral presentation demonstrating skills, or some combination of the two. An informal certification might be as simple as following someone around for a couple hours and watching to be sure they are performing the role as it is intended to be performed. Whether you choose formal or informal certification depends largely on the confidence you have in the training and the staff's skills.

You certainly do not need to certify every person associated with the change and release management processes. Roles played by multiple people, and especially roles that are part-time, do not need every person to be certified. You may want to check only a few of the change approvers or the release project team members to validate that people understand their role based on the training they received. Certifying every person playing these roles would be expensive and unnecessary. If you believe there is a problem in a certain area, you can always come back later and certify people in that particular role or area.

Best practice dictates that you certify all service managers, service architects, change evaluators, change managers, and change reviewers. These are the key roles that evaluate your process, and they largely determine success or failure.

Measure Frequently

Another step you should take in the early days of production is measurement. During the process definition, you probably defined some monthly measurements, but during the first days of production, you should implement some weekly or even daily measurements. People love feedback, and the more frequently you can give feedback to your stakeholders, the sooner they will gain confidence that the program is a success.

Because change management is all about controlling the environment, there are dozens of good measurements that can be produced. In the early days of production, you can measure how many changes are being requested, how many of the requested changes are being approved, how many approved changes are implemented successfully, and how many changes need to be backed out. In a larger organization with lots of change, these can be measured daily for the first few weeks. For a smaller organization, weekly measurements make more sense, but they are just as important for gaining precious momentum.

A really important measure for deploying change management is the number of unauthorized changes. This gives the change management organization a way to understand the penetration of the change management process and how much the organizational culture is changing.

It is more difficult to find short-term measurements in release management, because activity is less frequent. If your organization has chosen to implement retroactive projects such as getting every release package documented or putting all controlled software into a definitive media library, you can choose percentage complete as a good measure. If you are introducing release management more slowly, you may have to settle for less-frequent measures.

Your measurements should be featured in weekly status reporting. The project is not finished just because the process has gone into production, so you should still be meeting regularly with your stakeholders. Use this time to highlight the team's accomplishments, and use the measurements to demonstrate the value being gained.

Evaluate and Adjust

Measuring the process frequently gives you an opportunity to adjust as needed. No matter how well you've defined the process, issues will arise in the rollout. Perhaps people will have forgotten some of the training, or the process will be unclear in some area. Often you will find that the world in which the process must function is different from the one you envisioned while creating the process. These are all reasons to adjust your process during the rollout phase.

The primary basis for making process adjustments should be your measurements. If the measurements indicate that the process isn't as successful as you would like, you should adjust the process and then see if the measurement shows improvement. Do not make too many adjustments at once, because you will not be able to determine which ones helped and which ones did not. Adjust, evaluate, and then adjust again.

Although measurements are the most helpful, you should also consider anecdotal evidence in evaluating the process rollout. If key people are overstressed, there might be a better way to execute that can reduce their stress. If you are hearing that things are worse, even though the process measurements show improvement, you should investigate to see if you might be measuring the wrong things. Conversely, if one or two people seem to be succeeding much more than others, you might want to investigate what they are doing differently to see if you can incorporate that practice into the process for everyone else.

Do not be afraid to have a long settling-in period for the process. It is not uncommon to still be making modifications to the initial process six months after rollout begins. It is critical to get everyone comfortable and working at full capacity. If this takes fifteen modifications of the process, that is how many you should produce. Be sure not to change simply for the sake of change, but as long as legitimate improvements can be made, you should continue to make them.

Looking Ahead

The process rollout is in many ways synonymous with deployment. Using the process workshop technique, you can be sure that the entire team understands the process. Building a strong organization to support the processes will move you closer to deployment, and when training day actually arrives, people will know that vision is becoming reality. This chapter has given you some background on rolling out the process. In the next chapter, you will learn even more about the first steps toward production as you see how to implement a pilot program.

CHAPTER 9

Choosing and Running a Pilot

If change or release management is new to your organization, you should establish a pilot program to test the waters. If your organization has tried and failed at these ITIL disciplines, you should establish a pilot program to help regain lost confidence. As a matter of fact, the only time a pilot program doesn't make sense is if you've already been successful and currently have an effective change and release management service. Otherwise, choosing and running a good pilot program is a great way to find out how much your organization can benefit from implementing ITIL.

So what is a pilot program, and why is it so important? First, it is important to understand that by pilot I do not mean test. A pilot is a full production implementation of change and/or release management on a small scale. All the people executing the steps should be the people who will have those jobs for the long term. All the processes should be the ones you intend to use when you go to full scale. The tools should be fully installed and verified before you start the pilot. The only thing that differs between a pilot program and full-scale production is that you have a narrow focus and very close scrutiny.

The pilot program offers an opportunity to validate your execution capability in a short-term way. It should be treated as a separate project inside the larger project of implementing change and release management. As a separate project, it will have a planning phase, an execution, a measurements baseline, and an evaluation phase. These short phases are wrapped in all the normal disciplines of project management, as shown in Figure 9.1.

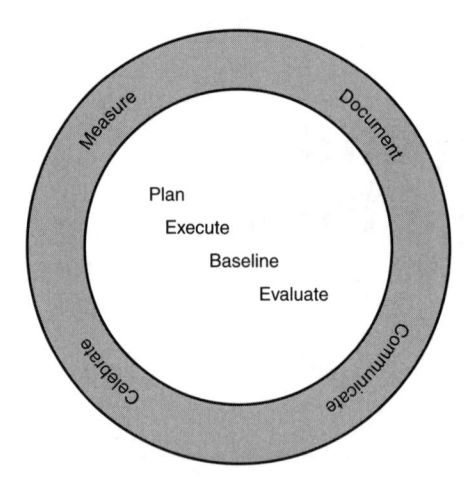

```
        Measure              Document
              Plan
            Execute
            Baseline
              Evaluate
        Celebrate          Communicate
```

Figure 9.1   The phases of a pilot are the same as those for a full project.

Reasons to Perform a Pilot

Performing a pilot for any kind of IT work has many benefits. Change and release management has very few risks that must be weighed against these benefits. Especially if release management is a new discipline to your organization, you should always plan to do a pilot. This section and Figure 9.2 describe why a pilot is almost always a good idea:

- Validating the processes work for your organization
- Exercising a new organization or new role assignments
- Practicing with the Key Process Indicators (KPIs)
- Building momentum for the long deployment ahead

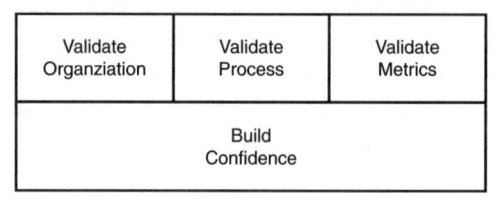

Validate Organziation	Validate Process	Validate Metrics
Build Confidence		

Figure 9.2   The phases of a pilot are the same as those for a full project.

One of the best reasons to perform a pilot is to make sure you have the correct processes defined. Tools are fairly easy to test. Many organizations have well-defined procedures for unit test, system test, integration test, and user acceptance test. There are organized ways to plan the tests, execute the tests, and record defects against tools that are found as a result of the tests.

Processes, on the other hand, pose a whole different set of issues. Most organizations are not very good at testing the process work they have done. Those that have tried tend to use their development methodologies and wonder why the testing of processes isn't very effective. Fully validating that the processes are working well requires several executions of the process in a setting that is as close to reality as possible. Fortunately, a pilot program offers this opportunity.

I said earlier that a pilot is not a place to conduct testing, and that is true. You aren't really testing the process during the pilot. Testing would involve consciously causing every possible process decision box to be executed and every branch of each procedure to be executed in sequential order. A pilot simply puts the processes into production, which inevitably leads to the most common branches and flows being executed multiple times. Some less common scenarios might never be encountered during the pilot phase, but that is acceptable as long as the processes work in the real world. So although a pilot isn't a test of the processes, it is a great way to overcome whatever weaknesses might have occurred during the test phase.

If processes are difficult to test, organization structures are even more so. Unfortunately, experience shows that most IT projects fail exactly because the organization can't execute the process effectively. Thorough testing of the organization would involve verifying that each responsibility is adequately assigned to a role, that everyone clearly understands the roles they've been asked to perform, and that everyone is fully qualified and trained to execute the roles they've been assigned. This kind of thorough testing is seldom completed, usually because of time pressures or because nobody really knows what all the roles and responsibilities will be until after the project has started.

So a second great reason to perform a pilot is to confirm that the organization is ready to meet the overall needs of your change and release management services. Like process validation, this is not a test as much as it is a way of overcoming the normal weakness of not having a prior test of the organization. If change or release management is new to your organization, and especially if you've created a new team or department that is responsible for the new process, it is important to emphasize that this is not an employment test. If the organization does not work, it isn't because the people are defective, but because the roles were insufficiently defined, the training was insufficient, or perhaps there were too many responsibilities for one role to handle.

Processes and organization are difficult to test before production, but measurements are impossible. Until you actually start executing the process against production data, you cannot really capture any of the metrics associated with configuration management. There are two classes of measurements:

- Those associated with the entire service
- Those used to track just the success or failure of the pilot

We'll talk about the second group a bit later in this chapter, but for now let's focus on measurements that report the day-to-day and month-to-month health of the change and release management services.

A critical part of the pilot effort should be making sure that all the measurements are in place and working from the beginning. How do you know if a measure is working? By comparing the data collected against the soft evidence of perceptions about that part of the service. For example, suppose you're counting the number of incidents that get resolved more quickly because of change management data. The reports after a week of the pilot show that only two incidents were marked as having been solved more quickly, but when you interview a server administrator, she can easily recall three or four times when going to the change management data helped her resolve an issue more quickly. Your only conclusion would be that the measure isn't working, because it is too difficult to record the data needed or because somewhere in the process the data is getting confused.

Chapter 16, "Reports and Service Levels," is devoted to helping you create and use good measurements. This is a very important topic, especially if you are implementing change and release management in a series of phases or releases, because getting future funding depends on showing the value of the service you're building. Use the pilot to really understand and refine the metrics you will gather.

At the end of it all, a pilot is really about increasing confidence. For yourself and the implementation team, the pilot helps you validate the planning you've put into the process, the organization, and the measurements. For your sponsors, the pilot is the first chance to see if their investment in the project will yield returns. For the skeptical people who are sitting on the sidelines wondering if this whole ITIL journey has any value, the pilot shows that the first steps are positive and the rest of the journey is possible.

The rest of this chapter talks about how to make your pilot successful so that you can build this kind of confidence. And just in case your best-laid plans don't work out, read the next-to-last section, "What Happens When Pilots Fail."

Choosing the Right Pilot

Now that you know all the reasons to perform a pilot, it is time to think about what shape that pilot will take. It sounds simple to start a pilot, but when you think about it more deeply, you'll find there are many ways to go about it. This section describes how to choose the right shape for your pilot program.

One easy way to select a pilot is by using geography. You might decide that the pilot will do change and release management within your headquarters building, within a specific site that your organization operates, or perhaps even within a designated country if you are part of a very large organization. The common factor is that it is relatively easy to identify the boundary for the pilot based on geographic borders.

A geographically based pilot is a great choice for many. For better or for worse, the pilot set will be selected as much for political reasons as it is for technology reasons. Perhaps your organization in South America is having difficulty passing audits, and you want to implement change control there first to see if you can resolve that issue. Or maybe the eastern European part of your company is driving phenomenal growth, and you want to implement release management there to capture all the activity going on. You'll certainly want to choose a pilot that gives you the highest possible chance of overall success, and that is not always the one that is technically easiest.

Of course, one issue that will quickly arise with a geographic pilot is what to do with changes and releases that span multiple geographies. For example, if you are changing the routing on a circuit between Australia and Singapore, you need to decide if this change is within the scope of a pilot whose scope is supposed to cover only Australia. Of course, this issue also needs to be decided for logical entities such as a business application used by people all over the company. Determining the scope of a pilot by geography requires detailed decisions about where to place the pilot's boundaries.

If your organization is managed very hierarchically, with strong distinctions between business units, divisions, or even departments, it might make sense to choose a pilot based on business organizations. You could do release management for just one division, or perhaps even a single department. This is slightly more complex to do than a geographic pilot. You need to make everyone aware that if a change or release affects the selected organization, the new processes are in play, whereas changes and releases outside this part of the organization will still follow the old path.

For example, suppose you've chosen to pilot release management with just the research division. You need to notify application developers, release managers, project teams, change management review boards, and anyone else who might come in contact with Research about the pilot choice. All those groups will need to behave differently if their work is on behalf of Research. That can be a complex communication and training challenge, but it might be worthwhile if the political advantage of working with Research is big enough.

As with a geographic pilot, seams or cracks in an organization pilot must be considered. These normally are in the form of shared infrastructure. Consider the payroll program, which supports not only Research, but also other parts of the organization. Odds are good that it is shared by many different organizations, so you need to decide whether it is in or out of scope for an organization-based pilot program.

A third dimension you can use to choose a pilot is technology. Perhaps you could do change management for only servers, only workstations, or even just the mainframe equipment as a pilot program. A technology-driven pilot is the easiest for IT people to understand and define, because we are used to categorizing things by networks, applications, servers, workstations, and so forth. Unfortunately, a technology-based pilot often shows the least value outside of IT, because the benefits might be scattered among several different parts of the business.

Of course, the three dimensions of geography, organization, and technology can be combined in interesting ways to identify the scope that is best for your organization. You might choose to control changes for the servers in the Dayton datacenter, or all equipment supporting marketing in Singapore. On the other hand, you could form a release management pilot of just the release packages used by manufacturing or containing SAP applications. Use your knowledge of the organization and your assumptions about difficulty to choose a pilot that provides the best combination of value and chance of success.

Be sure to carefully document the pilot scope. Nothing is worse than having mistaken expectations at the beginning of the pilot, because it is almost impossible to recover if you are planning to build one thing and others expect you to build something else. The scope document should be concrete and should give examples of both what will be included and what will be excluded. This document should be carefully reviewed and widely published after it is approved by your sponsor.

Measuring the Pilot Project

As soon as a suitable scope is chosen, you should begin thinking about the definition of success for your pilot. Because your goal is to build confidence, you will want to be able to demonstrate success in the most quantitative terms possible. Although good feelings and happy IT people definitely help, solid, uncontestable numbers will really convince your team and your sponsors that your change and release management effort has gotten off to a good start with the pilot.

Note that the pilot does not need the same set of measurements as the overall change and release management service. The pilot has a shorter term and therefore must be measured in weeks rather than months. Release duration, for example, is a long-term measure that normally takes months to establish. Usually measures that require months to determine are unsuitable for a pilot.

Focus instead on the benefits your organization hopes to get from change and release management. If you hope to see fewer failed changes, create a measurement related to how better review techniques affect your success rate. If the goal is to improve your compliance posture, choose your pilot accordingly, and create a measure around how change control helps improve compliance. The measurements you choose should be able to be measured at least a couple of times during your pilot, and they should demonstrate conclusively that your pilot is trending toward the promised benefits. You shouldn't expect that the pilot will completely overcome the startup costs of an immature organization, but you should at least run the pilot program long enough to see a trend toward improvement.

Don't get overly ambitious with measurements. Three or four solid numbers can be enough to demonstrate the success of a pilot, whereas thirty or forty different measurements will only confuse everyone about what the real goals are. And although strong numbers will prove your case, don't forget to gather the "soft" benefits as well. Specifically, solicit comments from people who have benefited from the pilot, and use those "sound bites" to decorate your measurements presentation. Although they aren't as powerful as the numbers, if the comments you get are positive, they will build confidence more quickly.

Ultimately your measurements should be used as acceptance criteria for the pilot. Suppose you establish a measurement for reduced release defects based on having better release data. You could say that pilot is successfully concluded when you see a 10 percent decline in defects. These kinds of very specific and measurable criteria are what will take all the controversy out of the pilot's success (or failure).

Although you probably won't be publishing all the measures for the full change and release management program during the pilot, this is a good time to at least establish baselines for the critical measures going into the future. Going back to duration, just because you can't measure it several times and see a trend during the pilot doesn't mean you shouldn't at least start to establish a baseline for the future. This is a part of validating the overall measurements—a key reason that you are performing the pilot in the first place.

Running an Effective Pilot

A key thing to remember while executing your pilot is that you will be under a microscope. Every success and failure not only reflects on the pilot, but also indicates to your sponsors and the wider organization what they can expect from the entire change and release management service. If this seems like a lot of pressure to put on a single project, you've got the right impression. Success of the pilot is a critical component for going forward and can lay the foundation for the entire future effort.

To manage this level of visibility, you should start your pilot project slowly and publicly. Celebrate small victories such as capturing your first change record, defining your first release package, or getting past the first execution of any of your processes. These small successes will communicate to everyone that the effort is valuable and that you will achieve the pilot's larger goals.

While the pilot is executing, be sure to actively look for ways to improve. A quick adjustment to a process or a fast change to the data schema when done in pilot might save thousands of dollars or hundreds of hours in the future. Although you shouldn't change just for the sake of making changes, the pilot is a time for some degree of experimentation and adaptation. Take advantage of the lessons you're learning while you're learning them.

To make a change during the pilot, you should have an abbreviated control mechanism. This change control should include a communication mechanism to ensure that everyone knows about the change, some evaluation criteria to allow rapid assessment of the change, and a tracking mechanism so that you can measure the results of the change. You don't need fancy tools to track changes in this informal way. E-mail for communication and a spreadsheet for tracking are suitable.

During the pilot, just like during the full production change management service, you should constantly look for ways to validate controls. If there is any hint that changes might be done without change records, or if records are not following the process, be aggressive in getting it corrected or completed. If the process controls are perceived as less than completely useful, your sponsors will get the impression that this is just another failed IT project that had good intentions but ultimately will not deliver on its promises. Nothing will kill the spirit and momentum you're trying to build in the pilot phase faster than unauthorized changes that are not caught.

But how do you avoid these issues? During the pilot, you should have the luxury of double-checking nearly everything. Because the set of changes you're managing is intentionally small, you should be able to add extra steps to validate your controls frequently. Make that extra effort to ensure the pilot's success and a solid foundation for your change management service.

Finally, during the pilot phase, you need a strong issue tracking and resolution process. Keeping track of all issues, regardless of how trivial they might seem, is the best way to increase the satisfaction of your stakeholders. You should announce how issues can be reported and work with anyone reporting an issue to assign the correct severity to it. Work on the highest-severity issues first, but be sure to give each issue a status. Be attentive to details, because, again, the smallest change in the pilot might save you money and time in the longer term.

Some issues might be too big to correct during the original pilot time frame. If the issue is very critical or describes something that simply can't go on in further production, you will have no choice but to extend your pilot or even postpone it until the issue is resolved. If the issue is small enough, however, don't be afraid to let its resolution wait until after the completion of the pilot.

Evaluating the Pilot

After the pilot has completed, take stock before rushing on to production. You should evaluate the pilot not just for success or failure, but for lessons that can be learned and improvements that should be made. The evaluation step should not just help improve your change and release management service, but also help other IT projects in their pilot efforts in the future. Figure 9.3 shows the components of a complete assessment; they are discussed in the following paragraphs.

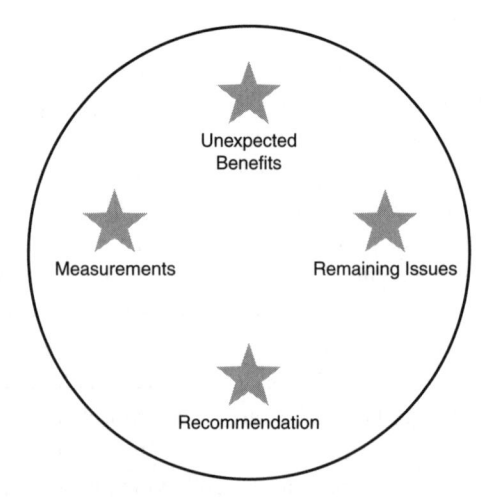

Figure 9.3 The pilot should be evaluated based on several criteria.

The evaluation begins with an analysis of the measurements you decided to track. The measurements should show what is working well and what is not working as well as expected. Use all measurements taken during the entire pilot to compile an overall assessment, including strengths and weaknesses, action plans, and recommendations to proceed or wait. This assessment should be reviewed by the team first, and then provided to your sponsors as a summary of the pilot project.

Your assessment should also contain some comments on unexpected benefits from the pilot program. In most projects, you can find benefits that weren't expected, but that are real nonetheless.

You might discover during the pilot, for example, that you've actually improved the quality of configuration management data. Although you didn't plan to improve the configuration management process, this can certainly be claimed as a benefit of the change and release management pilot work. Thus, you would expect all other configuration data to be more accurate after you've completely rolled out your change and release management service. Spend some time in your evaluation thinking about benefits to the other operational processes that have occurred because of implementing change and release management.

Of course, your assessment should also document any issues that remain out of the pilot program. Document the issue clearly, and indicate any steps being taken to resolve the issue. At the end of the pilot program, you should close out your issue management by either resolving all remaining issues or documenting in your assessment how they will be handled after the pilot.

In its summary and recommendations, your assessment should provide concrete information about how your project achieved its acceptance criteria. Each criterion you defined before the pilot started should be revisited to assess whether the pilot missed the mark, partially met the goal, or completely satisfied the standard. The recommendation you make should be based on this objective assessment of the acceptance criteria. If it is, there should be no doubt about whether your recommendation will be accepted.

What Happens When Pilots Fail

Hopefully you will never have to read this section. Maybe your pilot will meet and exceed its goals, and you can sail smoothly in your implementation. Just in case that doesn't happen, however, this section describes how to understand and recover from a failed pilot. Figure 9.4 shows the full recovery cycle.

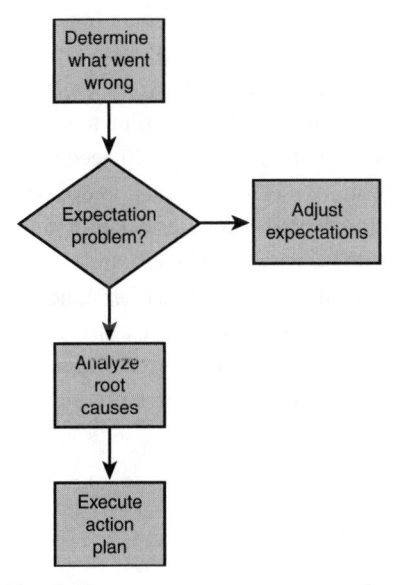

Figure 9.4 If you follow the right process, you can recover from a failed pilot.

Of course, the first thing you need to do with a failed pilot is find out what happened. Was this a real failure of the change and release management service, or a case of failing to meet undocumented expectations? In many cases, you'll find that the pilot is declared a failure because you failed to do something you never intended to do. Someone read your scope document or perhaps your acceptance criteria and thought you meant something different than you intended. This can be a difficult situation to get out of, because it is hard to have a retrospective discussion of motives. In many cases, this kind of dispute needs to be worked through the issue management process. If the dispute is significant enough, a new pilot may need to be run with a different scope or acceptance set defined.

If the cause of the pilot failure is not found to be mistaken expectations, you should do a root cause analysis. Dig beneath the symptoms of failure to find the underlying causes. You might find processes that were inadequately or incorrectly defined, team members who didn't receive enough of the right kind of training, tools that failed to provide needed functions, or even requirements that were poorly specified. Whatever you find should be documented and worked until you are fairly satisfied that the root cause is well understood.

The integrity of the root cause process can often be enhanced by inviting people outside the project team to participate. If your organization has an independent IT quality group, they would be ideal members of the root cause team. If no such group is available, ask a peer manager or one of your stakeholders from outside the project team to help you understand the causes of the failure without prejudices associated with having been on the team.

As soon as the root causes have been clearly stated, you can formulate action plans to address them. Document the actions, including the person taking the action and definite completion dates. Track this mini project plan to completion to get your effort back on track. If the actions will take a long time to complete, you may need to address some other things before coming back to change and release management. For example, your pilot might have failed because of lack of process discipline among those who deploy software. Releases went out on time, but the documentation was shoddy or didn't exist. You would create an action plan that helped people understand the need for documentation and find the time to do it.

If you are faced with long-term action items, you need to announce to the organization that although ITIL process implementation is a great thing to do, your organization is not yet mature enough to accomplish it. Then work on the long-term action items, and come back to change and release management as soon as those issues are taken care of.

When your action items are all complete, whether in the short term or after some time, you should run another pilot. It is important to have a successful pilot before moving on to a wider-scale rollout of the service. This is especially true after you've had a failed pilot, because the confidence *in* the team and *of* the team will both need to be bolstered.

Looking Ahead

Choosing and running a pilot program provides a short-term way to either achieve success in your deployment or understand what needs to be improved. In this chapter, you've learned how to select a good pilot scope, how to effectively execute and measure a pilot program, and how to recover when a pilot goes off course. Using these techniques, you can run a successful pilot program that creates the cornerstone for your complete enterprise deployment.

The next chapter expands on the work begun in the pilot by describing how to move beyond pilot to full production.

CHAPTER 10

Moving from Pilot to Production

As soon as your team finishes celebrating the success of the pilot, you should begin thinking about the long, slow march to full production status. Between the limited number of changes and releases in pilot and the much larger number in production lie a lot of effort and probably many unforeseen obstacles. This chapter helps you plan your route and navigate the course from pilot to production.

Determining the Implementation Axis

Your first concern should be how you will approach the production rollout. Unless your organization is very small, you cannot implement change or release management all at once, like turning on a switch. Instead, you should implement one piece at a time, but of course this demands a solid definition of what a "piece" is.

The implementation axis may well have been determined by your pilot. If you did a geographic pilot, the logical next step would be to expand to an additional geography. Similarly, if your pilot covered a specific part of the organization, you might want to implement change and release management in a complementary part of the organization next. On the other hand, no rule says you must use the same method to roll into full production that you used to select a pilot. It is quite possible to choose an entirely new approach.

Organizational Implementation

Rolling out change and release management one organization at a time will definitely make your training burden easier. You can simply train each organization as you reach it, giving each group the overall schedule so that they know when other groups will come on board with the new processes. This organizational approach to deployment also makes the scope and schedule for the deployment project clearer, because the organizational units within the enterprise should already be well known.

Deployment by organization is especially helpful if your IT group is closely aligned with the business. For example, suppose you already understand which set of applications aligns to each business process, and you know which business unit implements that business process. You can quickly determine which applications will need release management and change control when you move to each new business unit. This strong alignment between IT and the business also reduces the number of changes that cross multiple organizational units.

An organizational implementation is more difficult if you have gone through a significant data center consolidation or if you frequently use shared infrastructure in deploying your applications. If you had applications from accounting, finance, research, and manufacturing all hosted on a single shared database server, it would be difficult to manage changes for that server while in the midst of an organizational deployment. Changes made to finance applications might be well managed, but if the manufacturing organization wasn't yet under change control, it might be difficult to coordinate the needed outage windows. Sharing IT infrastructure has significant financial benefits, but unless your change and release processes are mature, shared infrastructure can be much more difficult to manage.

As an example of an organizational deployment, imagine a simple company with three divisions—manufacturing, sales, and corporate. The pilot managed all changes within one of the three manufacturing sites and did release management for one manufacturing application. You decide to continue the organizational deployment by reaching out to the other two manufacturing sites first and including all manufacturing applications in release management. As part of the pilot, you trained some of the IT staff that deals with manufacturing applications, so now you train the rest. Note that like IT components, IT staff might also be shared, so you may need to train your database analysts even though they work with databases for both manufacturing and sales applications.

After the staff is trained, you determine a start date for the wider use of change and release management. On that day, release managers begin defining the release packages that make up the manufacturing applications, change requesters start using the new change management process, and the change advisory board (CAB) that started in the pilot begins to consider changes across all of manufacturing. Of course, you need to make a clear statement about applications, servers, and networks that are shared by manufacturing and other business groups so that everyone understands whether they are in or out of scope.

After the manufacturing group has been running for a while, and the measurements show that the new processes are taking hold, you determine that the corporate division will be the next target. Following the same plan, you train the staff, document the scope, and start to implement the new processes for corporate. Every shared resource, including staff, that was pulled into scope in manufacturing stays in scope for corporate and represents some bit of work that has already been accomplished. Run with just corporate and manufacturing using the new processes for a few weeks, and then repeat the process for sales. With sales, you reach the full scope for both processes, and your deployment is complete.

Geographic Implementation

Deploying processes geographically makes sense for many organizations. Often the people who will execute the processes are distributed geographically and are accustomed to working together, so training is easier. Hardware and software are located in some geography, so fewer questions about scope occur when you deploy geographically.

Deploying processes by geography is a technique that works for any size of organization. If your organization is very small, you might want to deploy by the floors within a building. On the other hand, global corporations might deploy by continent and then by the countries within that continent. The size of any piece you choose to deploy as a unit will be based on the overall size of your organization, the number and skill of the people on your deployment team, the organization's tolerance for change, and the risk you are willing to accept. In general, larger chunks introduce more risk and faster change but get you to the end of the rollout more quickly. Smaller pieces tend to cause fragmentation in the overall scope and make the period of change last longer, but they reduce the risk that a single piece failing will significantly impact the overall project.

As an example of a geographic rollout, imagine a medium-sized enterprise with a corporate office in Paris and four smaller branch locations in France and Germany. One possibility is to introduce the change and release management processes one location at a time. The pilot could be done in one of the German branches, simply exercising change and release management on the few pieces of IT that exist solely in the branch office. For full-scale deployment, you might want to first deploy to the rest of Germany, and then move to the remote offices in France, and finally tackle the corporate office. Because headquarters probably contains the bulk of the IT environment, it might make sense to deploy there immediately after the pilot, which will make the remainder of the rollout very easy.

Rolling out geographically is almost the only option for large global enterprises, in which the deployment normally is done by continent, and then perhaps by business unit or technology within the continent.

Technology Implementation

The third potential axis for implementation is by technology area. Technology areas are easy for the IT community to understand, because most IT people naturally think in technical terms. It may seem most logical to the IT team to implement change and release management for business applications, and then for servers, networks, workstations, and so forth. The scope of a technology-based rollout is very easy to define, and surprisingly very little confusion or combination occurs between the various technology layers.

Deployment by technology alone works very well in medium- or small-sized enterprises, but for a large enterprise that has hundreds of servers and hundreds of business applications, it can become unwieldy to tackle an entire technology group at once. In these cases, it always makes sense to mix the implementation types. For example, if an organization has data centers in Europe and North America, it might make more sense to deploy release management for applications running from the European data center, and then change management in the European data center, and then release management in North America, and then change management in North America. This four-part rollout combines both geography and technology, and it stages the processes instead of trying to accomplish them both at once.

The trouble with a purely technological deployment is that it often makes little sense to the business. One of the goals of ITIL is to align IT more closely with the aims and goals of the organization, but implementing ITIL by technology area often defeats this goal. It is difficult for people who don't focus on IT to distinguish between a change that affects a business application and a change that affects the server that the business application runs on. From a business perspective, both changes represent some period of time in which the business doesn't have the service it normally gets from IT. The subtlety behind why the service is unavailable is unimportant from a business perspective, so indicating that some of these reasons need to be in change control and others do not will make little sense to people who are simply trying to get their job done. Figure 10.1 shows the three possible axes for implementation.

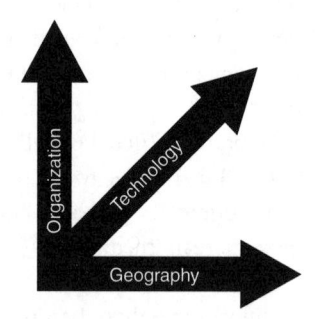

Figure 10.1 The phases of a pilot are the same as those for a full project.

Measuring to Show Benefits

In case you have not gotten the message yet, measurement is the only reliable way to determine whether the processes are showing the promised business benefits. As you move from pilot to production, the measurements focus softens a bit, but the measurements are no less important. This section describes some of the more common measurement points in production change and release management processes. This is not a complete catalog of all possible measurements, but it can serve as a springboard to help you develop a complete set of metrics for your own organization.

Change Management Measurements

Change management is concerned primarily with control of the IT environment, and, like most control mechanisms, it is full of measurement opportunities. This section focuses on measurements that help reduce change management errors and those that integrate multiple processes. Tracking errors is a somewhat subjective exercise. All measurements of errors in any process require people to acknowledge that errors have been made, and sometimes people are hesitant to admit mistakes. If you want to measure errors, it is important to let everyone know what the measurement will be used for, and that it not be used for punishment of any kind. Metrics involving errors found and removed can be extremely helpful, because over time they provide a clear indication of improvement.

The most positive error measurement is a count of errors found during change review. Each error found during the review phase of a change is one less possibility that the change will result in a failed implementation, so the more errors found in review, the better. Typically this measurement is determined by change reviewers. For the sake of a change review, an error is defined as any discrepancy that is significant enough to cause the change to be implemented incorrectly. Some examples of errors that might be found during a change review include changes with the wrong configuration item, changes assigned to the wrong reviewer, incomplete or incorrect implementation or backout instructions, or changes that have an incorrect estimate of the time required to complete the change. Again, some of these are subjective, but each is a potentially serious problem with a change being reviewed.

Most likely you will find that your change reviewers are reluctant to point out errors when you first implement the process. Because change reviewers are likely to be less familiar with the environment than the change requesters, they often assume that the requester cannot be mistaken, and thus they don't catch the errors. As your process and people mature, however, people will get more accustomed to the kinds of errors to look for, and you should see more errors found in review. This is a very positive trend, because it should accompany a decrease in the next measurement, errors found during implementation.

Errors found while implementing a change come in two varieties. Some errors are found and corrected by the implementer while the change is going in. These are somewhat innocuous, but they still cause confusion and perhaps some delay in the change. Other errors are not found until the change is being verified, and they may cause the changed system to not work as expected. These errors often are found when verifying the change after it has been made, and they result in rework. You could measure these two types of changes together, or create separate measurements for each.

Errors found during implementation are more serious than those found in review. When you first start working with change management, most errors will most likely be found during implementation, but over time you should strive to find more of these errors during review so that implementations become easier and less risky. Errors found early in the process cost dramatically less to repair than those found late in the process.

Of course, the worst possible place to find errors is post-implementation review. Errors found when reviewing the implementation will most likely need to be corrected through the incident or change management processes, often by implementing a second change to repair the damage caused by the first change. This is extremely expensive for your IT organization, and it should be seen as a significant failure of the change management process. An immature organization might find one error for every ten implementations, but over time you should seek to push this number to less than one post-implementation error for every hundred changes implemented. An ideal balance of errors for every hundred changes would be ten or more errors found during review, three found during implementation, and, at most, one found after implementation. Figure 10.2 shows a healthy ratio between these three sources of errors.

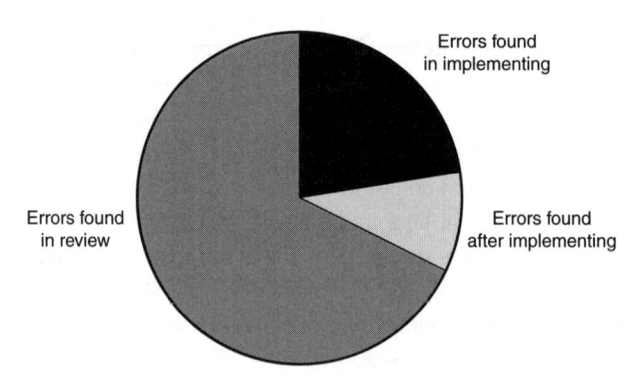

Figure 10.2 You should strive to discover more errors in change review and fewer after implementation.

Another excellent type of measurement to use in assessing your change management process is the relationships with other ITIL processes. Because ITIL provides a rich set of interconnections between process areas, the value of change and release management to your organization can be measured by how well the processes are integrating.

One measurement of process integration is the proportion of problems that are closed by change records. In a mature ITIL environment, the problem management process should proactively identify trends that might lead to outages. After they are identified, these problem areas have one or more root causes identified, and for each root cause, some number of action items are defined to permanently repair that root cause. If your processes are integrated in a healthy way, those action items will result in changes to the IT environment. Measuring the number of such changes shows how well your organization is moving toward best practices in both change and problem management.

To measure problems closed by change records, you need to allow each change record to be associated with one or more problem records or action items. When this association is possible, you can train your teams to indicate which change records are happening as a direct result of action items based on problem records. Over time, you should expect to see an increasing number of changes that occur as a result of action items. This is a great indication that you are moving from reactive management to proactive management, and that the problem management process is well integrated with the change management process.

Another good way to understand the integration between ITIL processes is to measure the number of changes that resolve incident records. In ITIL terms, an incident is a degradation of the services that IT provides, whether that is an outage of a key resource or a slowdown of some business application. In an immature organization, technicians simply fix these incidents by doing whatever needs to be done. As you mature, the fixing of incidents should be controlled by change records that are carefully planned and executed. Unfortunately, you will never get away from emergency fixes when significant outages occur, but even these should be governed by emergency change records so that the entire organization can understand what was done to resolve the incident.

Like problems, incidents should be able to be associated with a change record. In fact, two types of associations are possible between an incident and a change—either the incident is resolved by the change, or the change caused the incident. Both types should be measured, and you should try to increase the number of changes that resolve incidents while you shrink the number of changes that cause incidents. Everyone knows that IT components will fail, but a mature organization will control its response to those failures and take calculated actions rather than flailing away at a solution.

Finally, a great way to measure the maturity of your change management process is to understand the relationship between changes and configuration items. Configuration management is the discipline of documenting the entire IT environment in the configuration management database (CMDB). Before implementing ITIL change management, most organizations have a very loose relationship at best between the assets providing IT service and the changes to those assets. A key policy of an ITIL aligned change management process is that each change should point to the assets (also called configuration items) that are being changed.

You should specifically measure the number of changes that have no configuration items associated to them, and also the total number of configuration items that are being changed each month. The first measurement tells you how well the organization is adhering to the stated policy, and the second gives you a gross estimate of the pace of change in your organization. Changes without configuration items should be avoided. You can control the pace of change by scheduling changes more or less frequently as desired.

An organization that understands its environment well enough to associate each change to one or more configuration items adheres to best practices in both change and configuration management. On the other hand, an organization that cannot link changes to configuration items probably struggles with configuration management, change management, or both.

Release Management Measurements

Release management measurements can also help you move from pilot to production. Because release management is a bilevel process, two sets of measurements are important. The first set measures at a release package level and aims to understand how well you are planning for the long term. The second set of measurements is obtained at the release or project level and helps you understand how well you execute against specific plans. This section describes both of these sets in more detail.

One important measure of your ability to plan for the long term is the number of release packages your organization has identified. The number of packages shows how much of release management you have successfully implemented, and it is also a gauge of how complex your IT environment is. Most organizations find that they begin by defining too many packages, so initially the number of packages grows quite dramatically. With some maturity, however, the number of individual components within a release package increases and the total number of packages decreases. Closely associated with the number of release packages is the percentage of configuration items in your CMDB that are not part of any release package. This measurement shows how well your organization is adopting release management as a discipline. Most mature organizations find that they have one release package for each of their business applications and an additional 10 percent for infrastructure-related releases.

Another measurement that can be useful in assessing your strategic planning is the number of releases that are planned per package. In general, you should plan three to four releases in advance. You will not necessarily know the exact dates or contents of those releases, but your policy should dictate at least which quarter of the year each release will fall into and a rough outline of contents. If you are planning fewer releases ahead of time, you may need to define better release policies. On the other hand, if you are planning five or six releases into the future, you might want to think about larger releases or perhaps even combining the release package with additional components to facilitate larger releases. Like any good rule, however, there will be exceptions where it is perfectly normal to plan six or more releases into the future.

A very telling measurement is the number of releases that are actually started according to your plan. It makes no sense to plan three or four releases in advance if you never hit the quarter or contents you had planned. If you find that your plans are not coming to fruition, this problem likely has one of two causes. Either your execution on the previous release is poor, so you aren't finished with release one before release two should start, or your planning does not match your organizational funding, so you need to be more realistic in your planning. As the entire organization becomes more familiar with the release planning and management process, you should be able to avoid poor execution by scheduling more lag time between releases. You can avoid funding obstacles by scheduling fewer overall releases into any given time period.

Timing and Productivity Measurements

A third category is productivity measurements. These measurements normally are based on the time between two control points. They are called productivity measures because they point out whether people are expeditiously moving the process along or are taking additional time and introducing waiting time for others.

In the change management process, a change record traverses a series of well-defined states. These states present ideal measurement points, and each interval can help you assess something about the overall process. Looking at the interval between the recording of a request for change and the completed review can indicate whether the reviewers are taking too long or perhaps not long enough. Reviews that span several days to a week might indicate that the review process is getting bogged down due to inattention or overworked reviewers. If you find that reviewers are not acting quickly on the reviews, you can probe a bit deeper to see if their workload is too heavy.

On the other hand, properly conducted reviews take time. If the review time seems too short, reviewers may not be taking the time to deeply consider each change. Normally very short review times coincide with a lack of errors found during the review process. As discussed previously, errors found early in the cycle are much less expensive to fix. If you see a trend toward very short reviews in your measurements, you should consider repeating the training for change reviewers and perhaps adding some review checks to be sure the reviews are thorough.

Other interesting intervals in the change cycle include the time from review completion to final approval of a change record, and the time from implementation to completion of the post-implementation review. These two intervals often get longer as the workload gets heavier and the people involved with the change management process get pulled in too many directions. If you see this happening, you can refocus your organization's energy by asking your sponsors to reiterate the key values of the process. If your sponsors are part of the problem because they are asking people to work on other things besides change management, you may have to use the metrics to again sell the benefits of change management.

Release management productivity measurements are easy to define at the project level but difficult at the release package level. The productivity of individual releases can be measured in any traditional way, such as function points, actual versus estimated task durations, or the number of resources needed to accomplish similar tasks. All these measures are well documented and in use by project managers today.

It makes much less sense to talk about productivity measures for complete release packages. You could certainly work with the average length of time to complete a release within the package. But because the contents of releases could be significantly different from one another, even within a single release package, this metric is not likely to yield useful data. Perhaps the best way to measure productivity in the strategic planning aspect of release management is to measure the rework necessary between first formulating the plan and then later implementing it. This is very similar to the metrics mentioned earlier.

Measurement Summary

We've looked at only a few potential measures that will help you assess progress as you roll out the change and release management processes. Many more measures could be defined, and not all the measures documented here will apply to every deployment. The unifying theme of your measurements should be pragmatism. It takes some amount of effort and therefore money to formulate a measurement and then produce the needed data month by month or project by project. Before spending that effort, be sure that the measurement will tell you something worth knowing and that your organization will be willing to act on what it finds.

You should be aware that your ability to measure the processes will mature along with your ability to execute the processes. Measurements that work well in the early stages of deployment or operations might lose value later. Entirely new measurements might become possible as you make incremental process or tool improvements. Never be afraid to try new measurements for a few months, and never become stuck on a measurement simply because it was once useful. A dynamic and vibrant measurement set will become a key part of the continuous-service improvement, which is a cornerstone of ITIL.

Corrections for Common Implementation Problems

Regardless of how well you have planned and how successful your pilot effort was, your implementation will run into some problems. This is simply the nature of complex work such as deploying the ITIL processes. Rather than being dismayed by these problems, you should be prepared to deal with them as obstacles that might slow you down but will not stop you. In this section, you will learn about several common implementation problems and how you can overcome them.

Lack of Resources

More than any other cause, IT projects fail for lack of resources. People either leave a project or get pulled off to pursue other work. Budgets get cut because of unexpected business priorities or downturns. If your organization is very small, you might not find time to work on projects because of the crush of day-to-day operational responsibilities. If your organization is very large, the time needed for deployment might simply be too long for people to be dedicated to a project. When you run out of resources, this can be a difficult blow for a project to overcome.

So what can you do to prepare for a lack of resources? The first strategy is to implement your project in small, contained segments. Rather than an eight-month effort to deploy release management to a large, global corporation, implement a two-month project in North America, a two-month project in Asia, a two-month project in Europe, and a two-month project in Latin America. You'll find it easier to obtain and keep resource commitments for these small projects. And if your resources are taken away between projects, you can keep the knowledge and plans gained from the first projects until the resources can return to finish the later phases.

A second technique that helps level resources is to intentionally schedule people at less than full capacity. If you know that a person has operational responsibilities, simply schedule her participation in the project at 25 percent rather than 100 percent. If you suspect a person will be able to work on the process deployment for six weeks and then get pulled for three weeks, schedule his work to happen in the first six weeks, and then resume when he can get back. Be realistic about the amount of time people can give to your project, and you will avoid having to reschedule later when those people cannot dedicate all their time.

The techniques just described consider human resources, but the same techniques can work with monetary resources. By breaking the project into smaller phases, you can deal with budget cuts by eliminating the later phases. As soon as your initial deployments show significant value, you will be in a better position to build a business case to get the last phases funded. Similarly, you can sometimes build a project schedule that spends money in the quarter in which it is available and delays some spending to a time when a further budget can be allocated.

Overwhelming Data

Another common issue with process implementations is data overload. Especially in large or complex organizations, you might have so many change records or so many release packages that the implementation of the process gets bogged down. As an example, consider a large multinational organization that decides to implement ITIL change management. It builds a CAB structure such that a single board considers all changes that will have a significant business impact. This might seem like a good idea during the pilot, and even during the initial implementation. As the process gets rolled out to a wider portion of the company, however, the global CAB meetings get longer and longer. Eventually everyone realizes that the number of changes has overwhelmed the process deployment and that different policies or board structures need to be created before the deployment can continue.

One form of data overload happens when a particular person or group serves as a choke point in the process. For example, you may have a policy that every change must be approved by the CAB. If you have more than three hundred changes a week, however, that CAB might become a bottleneck simply because of the volume of data they are trying to handle. Review your processes, and redesign any points at which a single individual or group may become a bottleneck.

Changing the process or realigning some part of the organization is usually the right approach to dealing with overwhelming data. If people have too much work and too few hours, you might need to either supplement the staff or perhaps find a process improvement that automates some of the tasks or eliminates the need for them. The world's largest corporations are successfully implementing ITIL, so there is no reason why you cannot deploy change and release management in even the most complex environments.

Looking Ahead

Congratulations! At this point, you have implemented change and release management for your organization. You have determined and followed your implementation axis, implemented measurements to understand how well things are going, and overcome some of the common implementation issues.

The rest of this book focuses on what happens after implementation. Starting in the next chapter, we will examine some of the operational issues you are likely to face with your developing change and release management services.

Part III

Operational Issues

Deploying the change and release management processes is only the first step in a very long journey. After deployment, many different operational issues will arise. In this part, you will learn about some of the issues that make change and release management both interesting and rewarding. Successfully working through these issues will make your ITIL deployment produce more value for your organization.

CHAPTER 11

The Forward Schedule of Change

Among change management professionals, no operational topic seems to be as hotly debated as the forward schedule of change (FSC) that is called out as an ITIL best practice. The intent of the FSC is to create a single place to see what changes will affect the organization in the future, although it also often contains changes that have recently been completed. This complete picture of change activity is powerful, but it can be difficult to produce. This chapter explains the power and helps you avoid some of the difficulty.

The Basic Contents of the FSC

Many organizations read about the forward schedule of change and think it sounds like a great idea, but they have no idea what it should look like. Ultimately the FSC is a list of changes, with some details about each change. This section will help you make informed decisions about which changes to include in your FSC, along with how many details. Figure 11.1 summarizes the guidance you will find in this section on the contents of the forward schedule of change.

Which Changes to Include

Because the FSC is simply a list of changes, you must decide which changes to put on the list. This decision is driven largely by what you want to use the list for. Most organizations find that the forward schedule of change makes a great tool for the change advisory board (CAB) meeting. After all, the CAB exists to review changes, and they need a list to review, so why not use the forward schedule of change as that list?

	Schedule		Impact	
	When	Duration	IT	Business
Past Changes				
This Week's Changes				
This Month's Changes				
Future Changes				

Figure 11.1 The forward schedule of change consists of groups of changes, with schedule and impact information for each change.

Many organizations also use the FSC as a way to plan operations over weekends or evenings. When blended with normal operations duties such as running scheduled jobs and monitoring the health of the IT environment, the forward schedule of change provides a way to tell operations what additional duties can be expected during any particular time period.

The forward schedule of change can also be used as a planning tool for people looking to introduce new changes. If you can see when existing changes are scheduled, you can select times when new changes can be introduced without the risk of conflicting with the already planned work.

Keeping in mind these uses for the FSC makes it easier to decide which changes to incorporate into the schedule. If you want the CAB to be able to discuss changes, you need to include changes that are in the future. But in many cases, the CAB will also want to discuss changes that have been recently implemented, especially if those changes resulted in an incident or a failed implementation. Thus, the forward schedule might also contain some changes whose implementation is in the past. If you are using the FSC to warn operations about extra tasks, you probably want to go at least as far into the future as operations plans their schedule. Using the FSC to allow others to plan change dictates that you go even further into the future to support planning as far ahead as possible.

The best practice for most organizations will be to put changes on the forward schedule of change if their implementation date ranges from one week in the past to six weeks in the future. This span should allow for discussion and should focus on recently implemented changes while allowing plenty of opportunities to look ahead to changes coming in the future. Many times changes are grouped on the FSC by the week in which they are scheduled to be implemented. This allows people to ignore past changes or changes that are further into the future than they care to know about.

For organizations that deal with high rates of change, a seven-week time span may create a report with too many changes. When that is the case, you can further segregate the changes on the FSC by their status. Changes that are simply proposed or requested might be removed so that the report can focus on those that have been reviewed or even just those that have been approved. If your CAB is an approval body, you might need to focus on just those changes awaiting approval. On the other hand, if you are primarily using the FSC for operations and planning, you might want to reflect only those changes that are approved to eliminate planning uncertainties.

As with the time frame, you can use status to group the records on the forward schedule of change. Grouping completed records allows people to either pay attention to what was recently finished or ignore it. Likewise, grouping all records that have been reviewed helps approvers see what they need to approve. Grouping records that have just been created helps operations ignore them and focus instead on what really needs to be accomplished.

What Information to Include for Each Change

After deciding which changes to include in the forward schedule of change, you still need to decide how much information to include about each change. The most popular change management systems have between eighty and one hundred twenty fields for every change record. Putting all those fields on a single report means that each change record would require almost a full page, and even a report with very few changes would quickly become unusable. On the other hand, if you are expecting CAB members to use the report to view changes or operations to use the FSC to arrange their schedule, the report must contain enough information for you to accomplish these tasks.

The balance between too much information and too little information is a common theme in reporting. Striking the right balance is especially important for a report that will be used as often as the forward schedule of change. Again, the decision about what to include should be based on how the report will be used.

One important use of the FSC is to find out when changes will happen. The CAB needs schedule information to understand the risks involved in the change. Operations teams certainly need schedule information to weave the tasks required by the change into their overall schedule. People planning other changes are interested primarily in schedule information to see when they can schedule their own changes. For all these purposes, you should include in the FSC information about the scheduling of each change. Although most change management tools store dates for estimated and actual implementation, estimated and actual duration, and several other schedule-related bits of information, experience shows that the FSC needs to reflect only the date, time, and duration of the implementation. For changes that are already implemented, these can be the actual values, and for other changes, these can be estimated values.

The other critical piece of information about a change is its impact. Assessing the impact of a change is a complex subject and receives its own treatment in Chapter 15, "Business Impact Analysis." For now, it is enough to assume that the impact will be documented in two separate areas—IT impact and business impact. The IT impact of a change is a simple list of components or configuration items that will be affected by the change. For example, if a server must be rebooted during the change, that server and all applications that run on it are affected. The business impact is a more complex assessment of what part of the organization will be unable to function because of a temporary loss of IT service.

These impacts might be simplified values such as "High," "Medium," and "Low," or they may be short comments such as "Payroll down." Whatever form impact information takes in your change management practice, that impact information should be displayed in the forward schedule of change. Impact information is especially important for changes that failed during implementation and for changes that are seeking approval. Impact forms the basis of analyzing the risk of a change.

Ultimately, then, a forward schedule of change contains four groups of change records:

- Those implemented recently
- Those to be implemented within one week
- Those to be implemented within one month
- Those to be implemented more than one month from now

For each change record, four pieces of information should be included in the FSC:

- The date and time the change was or will be implemented
- The amount of time required to implement the change
- IT components impacted by the change
- Business functions impacted by the change

FSC Timing Issues

One significant issue with the forward schedule of change is that it can represent only a single point in time, whereas the change management process is continual. Because the FSC is only a snapshot, you must decide when to take that snapshot. The timing of the FSC not only determines its usefulness, but probably also dictates behavior in your organization. This section describes some of the issues of timing and how to know the best time to create the forward schedule of change. One of the timing issues concerns using the forward schedule of change as an agenda for the CAB meeting. Ideally an agenda should be sent out before the meeting so that participants have an opportunity to prepare by familiarizing themselves with the changes that could be discussed. Of course, by capturing the agenda and distributing it, you eliminate from consideration any changes that happen between the time the FSC is distributed and the time of the meeting. Figure 11.2 shows an example. Suppose that the CAB meets on Tuesdays at 9 a.m. To give everyone time to prepare, the forward schedule of change is documented on Monday at 8 a.m. and distributed. This effectively means that to be considered, a change must be recorded in the tool by end of day Friday. This may seem like a reasonable amount of time to some organizations, but it could be far too slow for more nimble organizations.

Assembling a Useful FSC

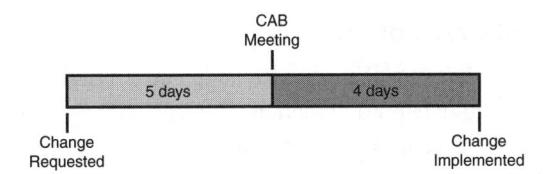

Figure 11.2 This example shows a lead time of nine days for a change.

This time challenge is exacerbated by the fact that most organizations enforce a policy that a certain number of days must elapse between the approval and implementation of a change. Normally this "cooling-off period" allows time to notify everyone of potential outages, put the change on the schedule, and arrange resources to implement the change. Unfortunately, this time is added to the overall time between requesting a change and being able to implement that change. Continuing the preceding example, assume that the organization has a policy of four days between change approval and implementation. Now a change requested on Friday must wait at least until the following Saturday to be implemented.

If your organization has a policy that says that CAB approval or review is required before implementing a change, a change requested at 10:01 a.m. Tuesday (right after the CAB meeting ends) will need to wait a full week for approval, and then an additional four days before implementation. Eleven days could elapse between the request for change and the implementation. For well-planned activities, this should be no problem, but for changes that must be implemented to resolve an ongoing incident, eleven days probably is unacceptable.

The solution to this timing dilemma is the urgent change process. Changes that must be implemented more quickly than standard policies and meeting schedules allow could be approved by an electronic vote. An e-mail is distributed to members of the CAB, and when each has responded that the change is acceptable, the change can be implemented immediately. For truly urgent changes, phone calls might replace e-mail. You should strive to define policies that make change lead times practical for your organization and reduce the number of urgent changes that are needed. However, you should always make allowances for truly critical changes to be made outside the standard policies.

Assembling a Useful FSC

Now that you understand what a forward schedule looks like and when to create one, it is time to uncover the details of how to create the FSC for your organization. Although documenting changes is a straightforward process, some techniques can make creating the FSC easier. You also must consider additional details if you are in a very large organization that has decided to implement multiple CABs that handle different parts of the organization. This section is a step-by-step guide to building the forward schedule of change.

Automating the FSC Creation Process

Because the forward schedule of change will be created regularly with the same set of parameters, it is an ideal candidate for automation. There are two approaches to creating an automated FSC. You can build a standard report, or you can provide an online query that allows anyone to pull up the FSC whenever they want to.

If your organization has a standardized way to generate reports from your service management tooling, you can leverage that function to create the FSC as one of those reports. Use the information you learned earlier in this chapter to build a report using tools offered by your platform, and then schedule the FSC to be created on the desired schedule.

A more interesting possibility is for your IT service management tools to let you extend the online interface. This might be through integration with a web service, or perhaps directly by customizing entirely new screens. If you have this capability, it might make sense to create an online application that can generate the forward schedule of change whenever the user wants it.

Such an online tool would allow the user to specify parameters for how far back in the past and how far forward in the future she wants to see changes. In addition, you could allow a user to specify whether she wants to include approved changes, exclude completed changes, or see all the changes in the date range. You could allow the user to determine which information would be displayed for each change. This flexibility allows the FSC to be used by a wider audience than a simple, fixed report. Figure 11.3 shows a screen mockup of an online forward schedule of change.

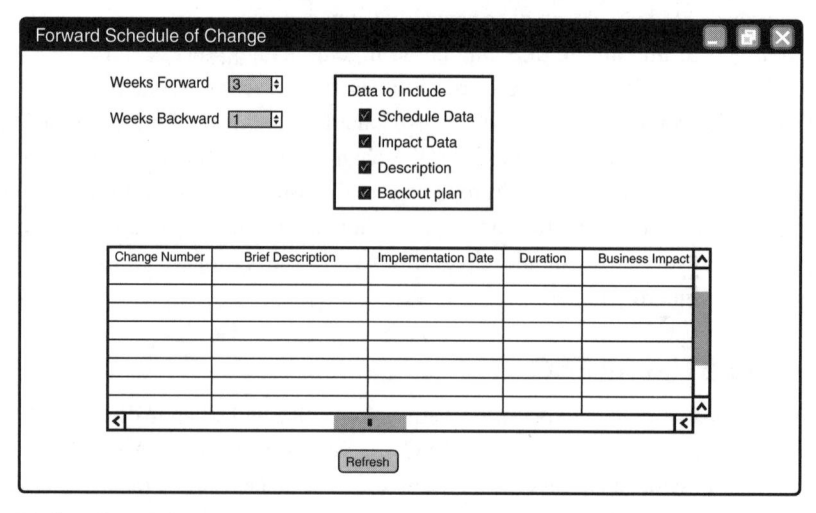

Figure 11.3 A real-time query is a great way to display the forward schedule of change.

Multilevel FSC for Multilevel CABs

If your organization is very large or complex, you will probably need to set up more than one change advisory board. You might need to establish a different CAB for each business unit, separate

CABs for each country or site, or perhaps even some combination of business unit and geographic CABs. The best practice is to organize these multiple boards hierarchically, with the chair of each individual board representing that entire group to the next-highest level. You also should implement a single CAB as the top-level authority on change control matters.

If this kind of implementation is necessary for your organization, using the forward schedule of change as a CAB agenda becomes more difficult. You need to be able to generate an FSC for each different CAB. Normally this means that you will want to define the domain of each CAB using some accessible field in the change record itself. For example, imagine that your organization operates in forty-two different countries around the world. You have decided, based on the volume of ongoing change activity, to form a country CAB for each country reporting into regional CABs for North and South America, Europe and Africa, and Asia and Australia. These three regional CABs then feed into a single global CAB. This complex structure requires the ability to generate forty-six separate views of your forward schedule, one for each CAB.

To generate these views, you need to create a country field in each change record that records the "owning" country for the change, even if that change is actually implemented in more than one place. In addition, you need to create a lookup table that matches each country to the desired region so that you can generate the regional CAB agendas by picking changes that belong to countries in that region.

The best way to deal with complexity of this kind is to create policies that filter what needs to be seen by each separate CAB. Higher-level CABs should consider only changes that have a high level of risk or a significant business impact. Lower-level CABs normally consider all changes in their scope. These policy decisions can be encoded in your CAB generation software, or you can simply create an owning CAB field in each change and have people set this value as part of your normal process. Either way, you will have the data you need to automatically create a different agenda for each CAB.

Of course, the best way to deal with this complexity is to create an online forward schedule of change application. You can add a field to the query asking which board or boards the user would like an agenda for, and the application can show the user the agenda as it will be seen by any specific CAB. In addition, you can allow the user to blend agendas by asking, for example, for a single list of all changes being considered by any CAB in the Europe and Africa region. This kind of powerful online query utility will allow even the most complex organization to really control the flow of changes through the review and approval stages.

Integrating Change and Release Management Schedules

The forward schedule of change normally is registered in weeks and deals with your everyday operations. Release management schedules can deal in years and are the primary domain of the application development and project management teams. But there is value in taking both a macro view and a micro view to really understand both the pace of change in your organization and the longer-term direction in which your changes are taking you. This section considers some ways to blend the long-term view of release planning with the short-term view of change control.

Changes Implement Releases

It may seem obvious, but every release that goes into production does so through one or more change records. As release managers prepare project schedules and think about the deployment phase of their projects, they should be scheduling the actual dates when those changes will happen. In other words, release managers will most likely be the first to know the date of many changes that will eventually end up on your forward schedule of change.

Of course, when the release is still being formed, requirements, resources, and schedules are still in flux. The release manager initially does not have enough information to create a change record, even though a tentative date may be on the calendar. What is important in these early stages is that the release manager adds a task to the project plan to formally request the changes that must be made to implement the release. This task normally is assigned to the project architect, who understands the technical details needed to fully document the change request.

As the release progresses through the definition and build phases, the details of the desired change become clearer. As soon as possible, the architect should open the change request, which moves the release from plan to reality. After the change is recorded with a proposed implementation date and time, it begins showing up on the forward schedule of change like every other change record.

The FSC Versus the Release Road Map

Many ITIL novices confuse the forward schedule of change with a release management road map. They think that if seeing changes scheduled for the next six weeks is good, seeing tentative dates for the next year must be even better. The problem with this line of thinking is that it blends two different purposes. The release road map is prepared by either the service manager or the service architect and documents a strategic plan for each release package. Some organizations then combine the release road maps from their most important release packages into a single document that can be used for strategic planning and portfolio management.

The forward schedule of change, as you have learned, is designed to provide decision makers and change implementers with a close-up view of the work at hand. It helps plan for the next couple of weekends, but certainly not next year. Your FSC should stretch out to whatever your organization normally uses as an operational planning horizon. If that is six weeks or even a month, let your FSC reflect that time period. Stretching beyond your normal operational view will only dilute the power of your forward schedule of change and confuse the very people it was intended to enlighten.

Looking Ahead

The forward schedule of change causes confusion in many organizations that are new to ITIL. This chapter has shown that it is simply a list of changes that can be generated in a number of ways. As you have seen, determining what to include on the list and when to generate the schedule can help you integrate your problem and release management processes.

The next chapter continues this survey of operational issues by looking at another topic that confuses newcomers—the Definitive Media Library.

CHAPTER 12

Building the Definitive Media Library

Even a medium-sized organization can have thousands of different software packages that are installed somewhere in the IT environment. Using the CMDB, you can track what you have. But what happens when a technician needs to reinstall one of the more obscure packages? The CMDB cannot help find the right CD or point to the correct website where you can download the executable code. You might ask the technicians to keep copies of software as they install them, but if you have more than two or three people installing software for your organization, you'll quickly find that it is difficult to keep track of the different forms of media they use. If you have several international versions of each package to accommodate your global organization, the task of tracking the right copy of the software becomes almost impossible for technicians.

The ITIL answer to this dilemma is the Definitive Media Library (DML). The DML is a single place where any technician can go to get a copy of any piece of software that must be installed or reinstalled in your organization. You can think of it as a vault where software is stored until it is needed, much like a bricks-and-mortar library is a location where books are stored until someone needs them. This chapter describes why and how you should build a DML.

Overview of the DML

Before ITIL version 3 was published, there was much confusion about whether the DML (or the Definitive Software Library, as it was called in the v2 books) should be a physical entity such as a room or a logical entity such as a database. Version 3 cleared up that debate by declaring that the DML is both physical and logical. It must contain physical objects such as CDs, tapes, and disk drives, but it also should allow for storage of bits and bytes that aren't in any particular physical form. The goal of the DML, whether it is physical or digital, remains the same—it allows people to quickly and easily access supported versions of your software assets. In this section, you'll learn what the DML looks like and how you can implement a DML for even a global organization.

Physical Aspects of the DML

The first rule of the DML is that it must occupy some space. The library is a physical place somewhere in one of your facilities. This could be as simple as an unused closet or as complex as an environmentally controlled room, but some space must be allocated to keeping a DML.

Because the library should be controlled, your space should provide some type of physical security to keep the contents from wandering away. If you're using a closet, install a simple lock on the door, and control who has access to the key. If your organization uses electronic security badges, put a badge reader outside the DML space, and control access to which badges can get into the library. Whether you use a key or an electronic badge, you should implement some sort of logging to keep track of who is going into and out of the library.

Why must the library be physical? Because you need to store some concrete, physical objects there. Although you could certainly keep software in electronic format only, copying files from disks and tapes into a repository, it is often easier to keep them physically. In addition to the software, your DML should store the documents showing what licenses you have purchased and describing how those licenses entitle your organization to use the software. This documentation usually comes in paper format, although you may want to scan it into electronic format for faster retrieval. The library should definitely be a physical location that can hold all the physical forms of media for your organization.

Logical Aspects of the DML

Although the DML is a physical storage depot, it can certainly contain software in nonphysical ways as well. Although commercial software normally is distributed on CDs or tapes, applications that your IT organization has developed do not need to be distributed this way. The DML allows these custom-built software applications to be stored in electronic format.

To create a software library, you simply need a file storage system. This could be as simple as a file system on a Windows® or UNIX® server, or as complex as a dedicated document management system such as Documentum. The key capability that you need to make a software library is simply any technology that can store files and that has an access control mechanism to track who accesses those files.

Many organizations use the logical aspect of the DML to support their software distribution process. To support automated distribution of software, you need to build a repository of all packages that can be installed in your environment. By definition, this is the logical part of the DML. You can use this repository to automatically push out software to hundreds or even thousands of devices at a time, or you can set up the logical software repository to allow users to browse its content and download software as it is needed. Either way, the repository is a storage area for authorized versions of software, and that makes it part of your DML.

Building a Distributed DML

Although the DML must have a physical location, it is not restricted to a single location. It is quite possible to build a distributed library to support an organization that operates in multiple geographic locations. Such a distributed DML requires even more stringent controls than a library in a single location, but often the convenience of having more immediate access to the resources in the library offsets the added costs. Figure 12.1 shows an example of such a distributed library.

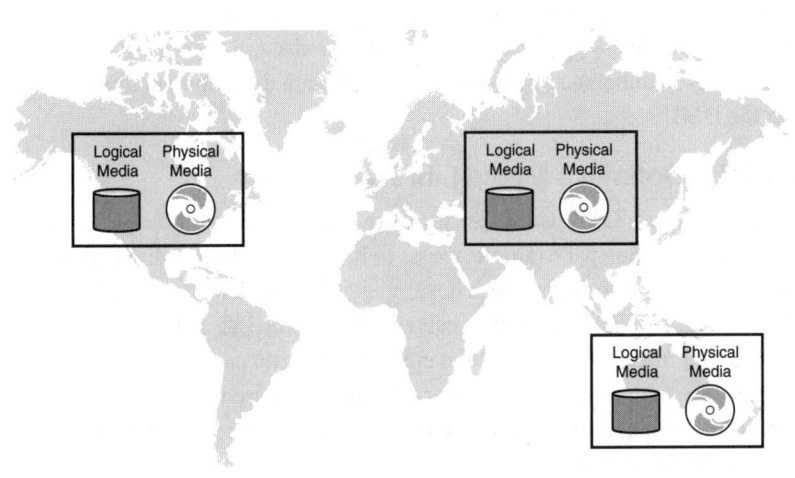

Figure 12.1   Your Definitive Media Library might be distributed to multiple locations.

The first requirement of a distributed DML is a strong centralized indexing system. Your configuration management system can provide the naming convention and can assign names to the specific media being managed. But you need a separate indexing system to indicate which distributed library holds which pieces of media, because the CMDB is not designed for that task. The indexing scheme should be flexible enough to support multiple copies of the same medium, because it is often convenient to make copies for several locations. In addition, there should be a means in the indexing system to allow for transfer of media from one location to another and for indicating media that are temporarily outside of any library location because they are out on loan.

One strong reason to set up multiple physical library locations is that software sometimes has different versions based on locality. Operating systems, for example, come in different versions in different countries to accommodate the differences in keyboards, language, currency, and date display. If your organization supports computers in multiple countries and languages, you are probably painfully aware of these differences. Having a separate DML in each country, or at least each geographic region, lets you track these region-specific instances of software. Of course, you could have all versions within a single location, but having the software closer to where it is likely to be used generally is a better idea. A distributed DML also allows continuous operations even if one physical DML site is affected by a disaster.

If you decide to distribute your DML, you need to create additional procedures and policies to handle transfer of media between locations and other media inventory tasks that are not required with a single library location.

How the DML Differs from Other Software-Tracking Tools

If your organization develops software either for your own use or to distribute, you most likely already have several tools that store information about software. Source code control systems, software configuration management systems, and others keep source code, scripts, data files, and other pieces of your business applications safe and organized. But you still need to build a DML. This section helps you understand why traditional software development tools are insufficient for the needs of the DML.

Purpose of the Definitive Media Library

The difference between a DML and other software tools begins with the purpose of each tool. A source code control system, for example, exists to help track all the individual components of an application. Using source code control, a developer can select the single piece of code that needs to be modified and make all necessary changes. Then he or she can put that one piece of code back into place with full confidence that the entire application can still be compiled. The purpose of a software license management tool is to track what software is installed and running in the IT environment. It is compared to the software that is entitled to be running based on license agreements with a variety of software vendors.

In contrast, the purpose of the DML is to assist IT operations. In any event that requires the software environment of either a single server or an entire data center to be restored, the DML helps by having the correct version of every piece of software needed. There is no need to compile anything, nor is there concern about what is licensed or entitled. The DML is strictly an inventory keeper that allows the inventory to be accessed readily when needed.

Contents of the Definitive Media Library

Another difference between the DML and other software management tools is the content that is stored by other products. A source code control system stores the software but doesn't keep it in an accessible format. Instead, the code is kept as a series of modules that programmers can use. A software configuration management system stores many details about each piece of software, including the number and size of each executable module, the location of each installation and administration document, and information about where the software should be deployed. Software configuration management does not store the software itself, however. A software configuration management system (and other solutions) can and should have links to the DML based on a user's access and the user's ability to self-provision software. The DML stores electronic versions of the software and any instructions for how to install it quickly. It maintains the software in a form that is immediately installable and kept accessible for the operations team. Another key difference in content is that no other software tracking tool deals with physical media, which is a key component of a DML.

Uses of the Definitive Media Library

Finally, one of the biggest differences between the DML and other tools that track software is how each tool is used. License management systems are used to ensure that your organization complies with all license agreements. Source code control is designed to keep track of development activities as bits of code are changed and built into applications. Software configuration management tools help you understand the application software environment and help you organize software releases. Each of these tools has a place in the overall environment, especially if your IT organization includes multiple software developers who are working on more than one project at a time.

The DML serves as a focal point for operations. It is intended to be a storehouse for the software tools that operations technicians might need in the course of their duties. Deskside support technicians use the DML to get the latest copies of applications they can restore to a user workstation. Server administrators use the DML to keep all active releases of any software they may need to put on a new server as it is being provisioned. Database analysts and others who support various kinds of middleware use the DML to keep the authoritative copies of the software they have installed in the course of their work. The DML is used by anyone implementing a change if that change involves software.

Table 12.1 summarizes the differences between the DML and other kinds of software management tools.

Table 12.1 Differences Between the Definitive Media Library and Other Software Tracking Tools

Definitive Media Library	Source Code Control	License Management	Software Configuration
Used by operations	Used by developers	Used by asset managers	Used by developers
Stores actual software, both physical and electronic	Stores source code usage information	Stores contract and about software	Stores information
Provides software inventory	Provides development tracking	Maintains license compliance	Documents the application environment
Links to release management	Links to software development	Links to asset management	Links to release management

Tracking Versions in the DML

You will quickly discover that the DML is complicated by the variety of software versions that must be maintained. You need policies for acquiring new versions, archiving old versions, replacing lost media, and allowing people to borrow media from the library. In this section, you will learn about some of the procedures necessary to successfully operate your DML.

Acquiring New Software

The first procedure you should work on is how to integrate the DML into the software acquisition process. This integration will most likely involve both your organizational procurement process and software development process.

During procurement, you will acquire software licenses and sometimes get media with those licenses. At other times, you might simply purchase licenses that permit you to download software. In either case, your purchase process should include steps to ensure that both the media and the software license documents are included in the DML. Most organizations prefer to enforce a policy that all software licenses and media are put directly into the DML after they are tested and then are borrowed from there as needed to install in the environment. Letting software license documents and media go directly to technicians for installation before they enter the DML is likely to result in a discrepancy between what you purchase and what actually ends up in the library.

Your organization uses the DML as an operations center. New or untested software should not be in the primary DML library. It is important to keep this software out of your primary DML library, because you don't want to distribute software before it has been fully tested in your environment. You may want to section off your DML into production and prerelease software areas. This division will allow you to control who has access to prerelease software and will significantly decrease (and hopefully eliminate) unauthorized deployment of software prior to final testing and approval.

If your IT organization includes software developers, you need to define an interface between the development process and your DML. There is no need for untested software to be in the library, because operations is not interested in untested software, so the most common time to put software into the library is immediately after testing has been completed in a test lab and pilot deployment group. As part of your final checklist before bringing software into production, the development team should be responsible for moving the code into the DML.

Retiring Software Packages

Removing items from the DML is at least as important as adding items. If your IT group is like most IT groups, you are very good at putting new projects into place and very bad at retiring software or hardware from your environment. This is an area where the DML can really help. By keeping better track of all versions of every piece of software, you will be able to see very quickly when old versions should be retired. Create a project with all the discipline you use to implement new solutions, except that the goal of the project is to remove a legacy IT solution.

Part of the project should be to remove software licenses and media from the DML through the change management process. If the licenses do not have an expiration date on them, check to see if your license terms allow them to be upgraded to newer versions. This may save you money over buying new licenses. Even if the licenses are still good, if you are certain they will no longer be used in your operational environment, schedule a change to remove them from the DML. The library is not an asset management repository, but an operational inventory system, so you should not keep software simply because you own the rights to it. You should keep only software that has ongoing operational use.

Lending Software from the Library

You will want to spend some time defining procedures for borrowing software from the DML. Your loaning procedures should include a way to make a copy of the software so that the original is still inside the library at all times. These copies might include physical media such as copying from one CD or tape to another, or simply a way to download logical files from a file share. In any event, the copy should be considered as outside the library, while the original stays inside the library.

Your library procedures will need to interface with asset management, so you can be sure that every copy of software you provide has a valid license somewhere. Nobody should assume that because software is in the DML, it is free or that unlimited licenses are available. The library should be another tool to help you stay in compliance with license terms and conditions, but it can quickly become a significant risk if your practices around making copies of software are too lax.

The interface to asset management should also allow people to turn software back in to the library so that you can investigate the possibility of reuse across your organization. When a project or a user is finished with a particular kind of software, he or she should be able to report that to the asset management team, and that team should then be able to send others to the DML to get an authorized copy of the software, thus reusing the licenses that were returned. In a medium-to-large organization, this policy alone might save enough money to pay for the DML and all the processes around it.

Replacing Lost Media

You may need to create some procedures for replacing media in the DML. There may be times when media is lost, either by careless housekeeping or by a failure of the storage on which you have housed logical software. At other times, you might want to refresh media due to technology changes. You certainly do not want 5.25-inch floppy disks or reel-to-reel tapes in your library when you can move files to CDs or tape cartridges. In the future, these modes of storage may seem antiquated, and you may want to move software to other types. This probably isn't a high priority for most organizations, but it will not hurt to have at least thought about how to keep the media in your DML current.

Using the DML to Optimize Change Management

Now that you have learned everything about building a DML, it is time to look at the value gained from your efforts. The DML is more than a check box on your ITIL list of things to do. You can significantly improve the change management process by maintaining a strong DML. This section describes how the DML can make your change management process more effective. Figure 12.2 summarizes these benefits.

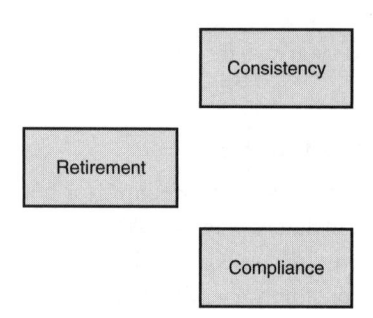

[Figure: three boxes labeled Consistency, Retirement, Compliance]

Figure 12.2 Building and maintaining the DML benefits your organization.

Consistency of Deployment

The primary benefit of the library is that software can be deployed consistently. Without a DML, it is often up to a server administrator or deskside technician to keep the right versions of software on hand. When the time comes to build a new server or restore software to a user's workstation, the technician uses what is on hand rather than worrying about corporate standards. Often the technical team downloads and installs the latest patches on a newly deployed system without considering whether those patches have actually been tested in your environment. When a critical patch does come out, you are dependent on whatever notes the technician made, or even on his or her memory, to determine which servers or workstations need that patch. Without a single source to get authoritative versions of software, you are left with an inconsistent and poorly documented environment.

With the DML, however, the technician is relieved of the burden of having to keep copies of software with him. He no longer needs to carry a large CD case holding his own treasured copies of each program. Instead, the technician can retrieve whatever software he might need from the DML. He knows that he always has the standard version with every patch that has been tested in your environment. The technician can quickly deploy the needed software and doesn't need to keep notes or remember what he deployed, because he knows it follows your organizational standards. You will end up with a consistent environment that is easier to support and less prone to strange differences between systems that are supposedly the same.

Helping the Sunset Problem

Another significant benefit of the DML is that it allows you to retire software from the environment as part of your release management process. When an organization first implements release management, it uses release management to carefully control the introduction of new hardware and software and immediately realize benefits. As your practice matures, however, you will realize that to truly manage a release package, you need to plan for the time when each release will give way to the next and when the entire package becomes obsolete and should be retired. You can start building retirement plans for your release packages.

To ensure that a piece of software really gets retired, you can simply remove it from the DML. If your organization has the discipline to use the library for every software deployment, removing software from the library will immediately stop deployments of that particular package. Along with a project to remove existing deployments, this ensures that the software is removed from your environment. At that point, you can stop paying maintenance costs for the software and know that you are still complying with all license terms.

This policy will have compounding benefits within your organization in areas such as incident management, problem management, and other ITIL disciplines. These areas will benefit because only supported software will be deployed, and you will not need to support legacy software.

Improving Audit Posture

A third benefit of the DML is compliance management. This is really an offshoot of the other benefits. By consistently deploying software at the same release and patch levels, you reduce this risk of security exposures, thus improving your ability to pass an IT security audit. By removing software in a timely manner when it should no longer be deployed in your environment, you reduce the risk of having unlicensed software, and thus failing a license management audit.

The DML also helps you identify and track software releases more accurately, which helps you achieve and maintain ISO 20000 certification. Although the definitive media library is not just a check box on your ITIL to-do list, it certainly counts as credit if you're trying to build an ITIL-compliant environment.

Looking Ahead

ITIL declares that a DML is a necessity for good reasons. You've learned in this chapter that the DML stores the authorized versions of all media. It also significantly benefits the deployment part of release management by ensuring that only tested and approved versions of software get deployed to your environment. You will need to define some important procedures for using the DML, but after you have implemented these, you will begin to see a significant return on your DML investment.

The next chapter looks at another significant operational issue—how to design and specify release packages.

CHAPTER 13

Defining Release Packages

Managing even a simple release package can turn into a complex project. The most basic business application can have a database management system from vendor A, server operating systems from vendor B, a web server from vendor C, and custom scripts and integration code from your own in-house development team. Each of these vendors and teams operates on an independent schedule, so planning when to create a new release of your business application is a matter of juggling these four schedules to create the right timing.

This challenge gets greater when you introduce hardware releases and the need to schedule before vendors' new products are even announced. This chapter investigates the operational issues of defining and managing release packages when you don't control the schedules of every piece needed to build the release.

Understanding the Software Stack

Defining release packages is the domain of an IT architect, so this chapter begins with a brief refresher on application architecture. If you are already a practicing architect or application designer, you can safely ignore this section, because you already understand how applications are pieced together in a series of layers. For everyone else, this section provides a brief introduction and establishes a common vocabulary for the rest of this chapter and for your future conversations with the service architects in your organization. Figure 13.1 illustrates the software stack as it is described in this section.

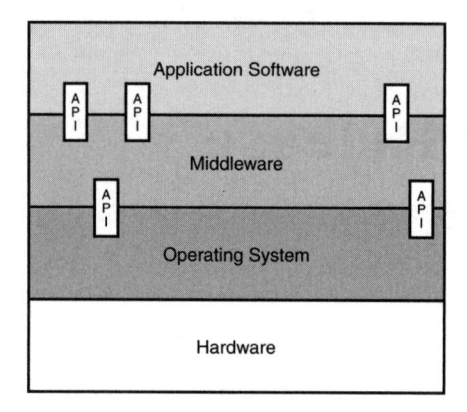

Figure 13.1 Understanding the software stack helps in defining release packages.

Application Software

Architects love to arrange things in neat layers and therefore find the metaphor of a stack of things very convenient. To describe business applications and the many things they depend on, architects use the notion of a "software stack." At the top of the software stack is application software. The placement is not an accident. Application software is placed at the top because it is the layer that is most visible. The application is used directly by the people in your organization to accomplish their business tasks. All other layers support the application software, and if there were no application software, those other layers would not need to exist. Conversely, if all layers of the stack are operating normally, only IT people should care about layers beneath the top.

When building release packages, the normal and correct instinct is to build packages around application software. This makes great sense, because the application is what delivers value to your organization directly. A new application release is likely to have features that will make your business processes operate with higher quality, lower cost, or possibly both. Those features can get both your IT organization and your business users excited about a release and can provide business justification for putting forward a new release. All these reasons make an application software package a good basic unit for building a release package.

In some cases, however, it makes more sense to bundle application software packages to form a single release package. In doing this, you are essentially going above the software stack into the business process stack. Here application software is at the bottom of the stack, and a product or service that your organization delivers to your customers is at the top. Using this enterprise architecture model, you may discover that a specific business process uses two or more business applications to automate the entire process. You can then define one release package to contain all the applications required for the entire business process.

The benefit of these larger release packages is that a single release offers your organization significant benefits by improving a business process in more than one way. You can accomplish quite a bit in a single release. The disadvantage of this approach is that each release carries more complexity and thus has a higher risk of failure. Use business-process-oriented release packages only if your project disciplines and release management skills are mature enough to be able to successfully manage this higher level of risk.

When you consider how to define release packages, it is important to understand that not all application software is the same. Broadly speaking, two classes of applications have an impact on release management planning. The first class is applications where you purchase the basic code and use defined interfaces to customize the application without programming. Large Enterprise Resource Planning and human resources systems, such as those from SAP, JD Edwards, and PeopleSoft, follow this basic model. Although you can build a release by choosing different customizations for the same base code, normally a release of one of these packages would be based on waiting for a new base code version from the software publisher.

The other class of application software involves writing the code yourself, either from scratch or using a development toolkit approach. If you have a group of application developers who define, design, and build applications, you are likely to have software of this type in your organization. Building a new release of these packages generally involves defining a desired business benefit and then refining that into a set of requirements that can be developed into a new custom application release. Instead of being dependent on a software publisher, you depend on your development organization to tell you how soon new releases can be ready.

Middleware

Directly supporting the application software is a set of middleware tools. These have names such as database management systems, web application servers, portal servers, access servers, and message brokers. These tools exist to provide a set of services to your applications so that you or the software publishers you choose don't have to build those services into every application. Normally you find middleware tools in the list of prerequisite software for an application system.

You typically have some choices to make in the middleware space. If you are developing software in house, your developers choose which database management system and web application server with which their code will work. If you are purchasing application software, the vendor tells you which middleware products will work; typically it offers a choice of several of each type. Choice in middleware is a very good thing, because it allows your organization to adopt standards for each product category so that you can focus on developing skills and procedures for supporting that kind of middleware.

Middleware is a secondary consideration in planning release packages. Most organizations don't plan to update all their web application servers or message brokers as a separate release. There simply isn't enough business benefit to justify rolling out a new access management server without at least some application software demanding it.

Being a secondary consideration does not mean that middleware has no part in a release package, however. Frequently a new release of an application requires that you upgrade one or more of the middleware packages supporting that application. Even if the application release does not demand that middleware be upgraded, it often supports a newer version of the middleware, allowing you to upgrade if you choose to do so. Your normal practice should be to combine into a single release package all the necessary middleware components with the application software they support. This doesn't imply that you must change every component of the release package with every release, but it does mean that each release of the application gives you an opportunity to update the middleware if you choose to do so.

One exception you might encounter is when middleware is deployed in shared pools. Many organizations find, for example, that it makes the most sense to deploy a cluster of very large servers backed by a storage area network to support the database needs of many different business applications. Such a database "farm" normally requires that all servers be on the same version of the database management system. This makes it impractical to have different servers bundled into different release packages.

If your organization has chosen to implement database farms, web application server farms, or any other middleware farms that support many different applications, you will most likely create a release package specific to that middleware so that the entire farm can be upgraded at once. Of course, then you need to test all the applications being supported by the farm at the new middleware level. This might occur only by coordinating release plans among all those applications so that each has been tested on the new release when the farm is upgraded.

Middleware generally comes from software publishers, which dictate the schedule for both deploying new versions and supporting older versions. In your release planning, you should be aware of dates when new versions of middleware will become available and when older versions are no longer supported. Those dates should be clearly communicated to all service architects and release architects so that your release plans can be aligned to avoid depending on a release that is not yet available or one that is no longer supported.

Operating Systems

Below middleware are the operating systems that support both middleware and applications. Operating systems are essential. Although it is possible to develop an application that does not require middleware, it is impossible to create an application that doesn't depend on an operating system.

Because of the marriage between operating systems and the hardware they run on, often a big fuss is made about operating system upgrades. Operating system developers spend millions advertising that their latest operating system is better than every else's. More people locked in to their particular operating system means more sales of their server hardware.

Despite all the noise around operating systems, they really don't provide much value to your business community. Even the operating systems that run on desktop and laptop computers seldom provide significant business value. They focus on the latest media players and graphical interface without significant new capabilities that help people get their jobs done more effectively. The operating systems on servers are even less visible, because all they do is support the middleware and applications.

When release packages are formed, operating systems are in a neutral zone. Modern server operating systems are not bound very tightly to application software, and seldom do you see a real business application that requires a certain version of an operating system. On the other hand, a release of an operating system by itself violates the rule that a release should add significant business value. Many IT organizations have tried in vain to produce a sound business justification for an operating system upgrade. The business people just do not understand the need for newer plumbing when the old seems to be working.

Occasionally a major new release of a business application or middleware package requires an operating system upgrade. Because this happens so seldom, the dependency is often missed. The problem is compounded because the IT group that supports the operating system doesn't communicate well with the group supporting the business application, so the dependency lies dormant until late in release planning or early in release testing. If you find this scenario happening in your release management effort, it might make sense to bundle operating systems with business application release packages.

It is generally best to bundle operating systems in the same release package as the hardware they support. A piece of a hardware refresh project should be upgrading the operating system to the latest version supported by that hardware. In many cases, the purchase of new server hardware includes an operating system license, further supporting the notion that the hardware and operating system form a unit that should be released together.

Release packages consisting of hardware and operating systems suffer from the same problem as release packages containing only middleware. Each time a new release is made available, you need to confirm that all your middleware and applications work with that new operating system release. Fortunately, most software publishers today already provide high-quality testing of their operating system with the most common middleware products. Some vendors have even created certification processes by which middleware and application vendors can certify that their software works flawlessly with the operating system. If you have unusual middleware products or have developed your own applications that link directly to the operating system without the help of middleware, you need to conduct this kind of testing yourself.

Like other software you purchase, operating systems have their own schedules. As with middleware, you should keep your IT planners aware of the introduction and retirement of key operating system products that are likely to be used in your environment. Although you cannot necessarily depend on software publishers to release their operating systems on time, you should certainly plan to retire an operating system before the publisher stops supporting it.

Hardware

The final layer of the software stack is not really software, but the hardware that runs under everything else. Although hardware vendors work hard to create distinctions between their products (and certainly a variety of server, storage, network, and workstation devices fit into the category of hardware), for the sake of release management, all hardware can be lumped into one bucket.

Projects to replace hardware normally are handled as part of asset management and are called hardware refresh. ITIL suggests that these projects should be treated as releases, and that different categories of hardware that share the same refresh cycle should be grouped as a release package. As described, you probably want to include the operating system with any release package that includes servers. It makes the most sense to update operating systems with new hardware rather than as a separate release.

In many ways, hardware has become a commodity, even at the server level. Manufacturers frequently introduce new products. But ultimately it is the hardware specifications rather than any particular model or version that dictate when it is time to create a new release. Most mature organizations have three- or four-year hardware refresh cycles for servers, which allows either a third or a quarter of the servers to be changed out each year.

Because of the standardization and commoditization of hardware, little functional testing needs to be done specifically for hardware. The operating system will have been well tested before you acquire new hardware, and other layers of the software stack simply don't interact with the hardware enough to cause issues.

Guiding Principles for Release Package Design

With this common understanding of application architecture in hand, it is time to consider how to define the release packages that will be the backbone of your release management process. Rather than describe every possible scenario and combination, this section describes some general rules that should help you build sensible policies for your organization.

Design Packages from the Top Down

You have already learned that a release package should be designed to ensure that each release will provide some significant, measurable business value. The best way to ensure that value is to design packages from the top of the stack downward.

The most common release packages in your organization should be designed around your business applications or business processes. If you are discovering a tendency to design more release packages around infrastructure items such as hardware refresh or middleware upgrades, you will not get business benefits from release management. You might be able to sell infrastructure releases if your organization puts a high-enough value on standards and keeping current, but in the toughest economic times, those releases won't be funded over releases that save money or increase revenue.

Starting at the top does not imply that the application software should be the only component of a release package. In most cases, you will want to craft an entire release package based on what other components that application software interacts with. Typically this includes multiple middleware packages; it could even include operating systems or dedicated hardware devices.

As an example of designing a release package, consider a fairly sophisticated implementation of software from SAP. Your release package would start by including the SAP software itself, with all the modules your organization is using. You will require a database management system and a web application server to run SAP, so those should be included in your release package. Perhaps you also want to include the operating systems and the hardware that run the dedicated SAP application servers. All these components get included in the release package documentation.

If you have an operational configuration management database, you will find it easiest to use the configuration item identifier for each component to precisely specify the contents of the release package.

In defining a release package, you should always document the dependencies. In our example, often a dependency exists between SAP and a specific version of the database software. Occasionally a dependency exists between a database version and an operating system. These cascading dependencies are critical to the team producing the release, and they should be documented clearly in the release package.

Keep Packages as Simple as Possible, But No Simpler

The concept of simplicity can be overdone in IT. Everyone knows to keep things simple, but be sure you don't oversimplify your release packages. The point of doing a release rather than lots of independent work is to leverage the overhead effort involved in preparing a team, building a project plan, designing a solution, creating and running tests, and deploying to the field. Each of these activities has a balancing point between managing too much and managing too little.

The goal of release package design is to create a package that optimizes these release management activities. To understand the kinds of releases you want to manage, look back over recent projects that your organization has completed. Do you succeed more frequently if projects last a month or less? Do you always fail if more than ten people are assigned to a project team? Do software development projects succeed more frequently than implementations of commercial software? The answers to these questions will help you develop release packages that will result in projects that your organization is likely to succeed in deploying.

You also need to understand the goals of the releases you will produce. If the release package contains an application that drives the control rods in a nuclear reactor, each release will be about safety. If the release package contains a funds transfer application, each release will be about accuracy. You will want to optimize the release package around the purpose of the releases that will result.

Using the earlier example, suppose you look at projects your organization has attempted in the past year. You find that integration projects tend to miss their schedule because so many issues are uncovered in testing that they cannot be fixed in the time initially allocated by the project schedule. Use this knowledge to create one release package including SAP and its associated components, and a second release package for updating the interfaces between SAP and your other business applications. By designing the packages this way, you increase the likelihood of success with each deployment release and allow more management focus on the interface releases.

Test Each Release from the Bottom Up

Packages are designed from the top down, but the releases that get deployed are tested from the bottom up. Why is this important for package design? The test strategy that you will deploy for each release is based largely on the contents of the release package. If your package includes hardware and operating systems, each release that updates those components will have a longer testing cycle than a release that simply updates applications and middleware. On the other hand, packages that include only middleware might require complex testing, because they interface with many different applications.

Each release package should document the general strategy to be adopted when testing releases built from that package. The test strategy does not need to be specific, but it should include some policies for each component. These might include what to test if the component is being updated in the release, and what needs to be tested even if the component is not scheduled for update in a particular release. This documentation alone can save significant time for each subsequent release project, because a testing strategy won't have to be created from scratch for each release.

The testing strategy for the sample package is reasonably straightforward. If a release includes refresh of the application servers and the operating systems on them, the first tests verify that your standard systems management tools and server operations utilities work with the new operating system. If you are not upgrading your operating system, you skip these tests. Next, if the release is planning to upgrade the database management system, a quick certification of the DBMS is done against the new operating systems. If the web application server is being refreshed, you conduct a similar test against the new operating system and then test that the web server and database work well together. After all other testing is complete and any issues have been resolved, the application software and any new customizations are tested.

It may seem overly complex to develop this kind of test strategy for each release package, but experience shows that logically developing a test strategy up front greatly improves the quality of testing that actually happens during release deployment. During project scheduling or execution, people tend to gloss over the need to test in a misguided attempt to reduce the deployment schedule.

Never Count on Vendor Release Schedules

This principle is so obvious it almost does not need to be stated. Unfortunately, many IT projects still fail because release packages and release schedules are built on software publishers' schedules. This is particularly true of middleware and operating system products. These products are incredibly complex and often miss their originally published schedules by three to six months. Also, if you are up against a vendor's schedule, the odds that your final applications have really been tested against it are low. You'd rather have someone else find the first couple of big issues with a major release.

When defining a release package, be aware of how often the components are likely to change and how reliable the vendors will be in predicting the schedule for those changes. Normally you cannot avoid being dependent on a software supplier, but sometimes you can align package boundaries in a way that minimizes the disruption when a supplier misses the schedule.

When actually planning releases based on a package that includes vendor software, always make the safe assumption, and use the currently available release, no matter how tempting the new features look.

Using the Release Packages

To summarize the release package design rules, consider what will become of the SAP release package described earlier. As soon as the package has been defined, the service architect and the release manager begin planning releases. They consider how often SAP releases new versions because they designed the package from the top of the software stack. If the vendor supplies new functions in the first and third quarter of each year, the release manager may decide to schedule releases in the first and third quarter, with each release using the software that was available six months earlier. This provides a cushion against the vendor missing its schedules.

When considering the contents of each release, the service architect checks the schedules from the database management and web application server suppliers. The architect does this to determine whether current software is going out of support or new software might be available. Because the organization normally succeeds with medium-to-small-sized projects but struggles to adopt too many technical changes at once, the architect may decide to alternate releases in which the database or web application server is updated.

Finally, the architect realizes that the application servers with their operating systems should be refreshed every three years, so every sixth release will include this extra effort to both upgrade and test the operating systems as the hardware is replaced. A complete road map going out for three years is compiled based on thoughtful creation of the release package and preliminary planning from release management. Figure 13.2 shows a sample road map. Imagine how useful this kind of road map could be if you had one for each of your top twenty business applications.

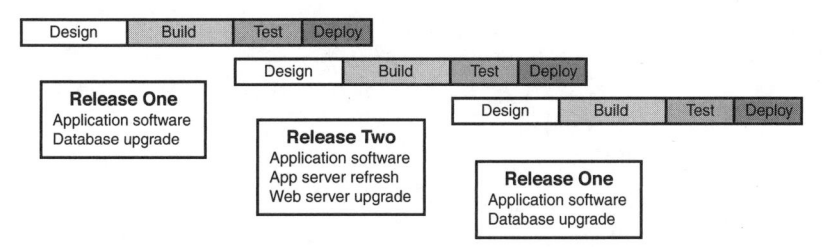

Figure 13.2 A high-level road map helps determine the priorities for each release package.

Looking Ahead

Defining the units that will form your releases is an important job. In this chapter, you've learned about the architectural concept of a software stack, and you learned to use that concept to develop your own release packages. With this information, you can define your release packages to facilitate stronger releases.

The next operational issue is compliance with regulations and policies. The next chapter describes how compliance can be managed through change and release management.

CHAPTER 14

Auditing and Compliance Management

You have many good reasons to have firm control over the changes in your IT environment. Perhaps the most important of these reasons to IT management and the executives of your organization is that controlling changes helps you stay compliant with the many regulations your organization faces.

Almost every industry today is heavily regulated. If you are in the finance or insurance markets, your organization has been working with national and even international regulations for years. Regardless of where it does business, every pharmaceutical company needs to deal with the U.S. Food and Drug Administration or an equivalent in another region. Manufacturing organizations frequently need to deal with the regulations imposed by import and export of the goods they produce. Nonprofit organizations have a completely different set of regulations than businesses that try to earn money, but they are no less regulated. In addition to external regulations such as the U.S. Sarbanes-Oxley Act, each organization has internal policies and checkpoints that it chooses to govern with.

Your requirements for change and release management should include compliance requirements. Many times audit and compliance items are not brought forward or recognized early enough. And when they surface later, they impact a project's scope, cost, and schedule.

At times, the weight of all the regulations, policies, laws, and interpretations can make an IT manager think it would be better to allow no changes. However, that isn't realistic. Even if it were, sometimes the regulations themselves change, and IT must adjust to stay in compliance. This chapter examines the operational issues of compliance management and auditing and recommends ways to build compliance into your change management process.

Control Points

To have control, you have to establish some handles that your organization can hold on to. These handles are called control points, and establishing them is the beginning of compliance management. Although the notion of a handle is useful and intuitive, it is not very specific. This section describes control points and provides some guidance on how to define and create them for your organization.

Defining Control Points

A control point is specifically designed and created to allow control in a process or data set. In a process, a control point is a specific step or action that allows a person to make a decision and thus exercise control over the process. In a data set, a control point is a specific field or data element that allows measurements to be created. In either case, the control point has been specifically and consciously created to allow better management of the process or data set.

Every organization has hundreds of examples of control points. An expense reimbursement process might include a manager's review of the expense before it is paid. That review is a control point for the process. An inventory database might contain a field for the last time an inventory item was updated. This field can be used to validate the quality of data, because inventory updated more recently can be assumed to be more accurate than items updated much earlier.

Control points often have other names. They might be called approval, authorization, visual inspections, checkpoints, or any other name that implies stopping to make sure that the organization is really doing what it wants to do. Often the names help explain the purpose of the control point. When you find that a database stores "data validation criteria," you have no doubt that this is a data control point.

Process control points are relatively simple to define. They consist of a role and a responsibility. Typical roles are inspector, approver, reviewer, or the more generic title of manager. This role is the person who is exercising control in the process. After the role is defined, normally it is sufficient to insert one or more simple steps into the process to be controlled. This can be adding an approval or inspection step, for example. Almost any process can be more closely controlled with this kind of simple addition of a new role and a new responsibility. Figure 14.1 shows a generic example of defining a control point.

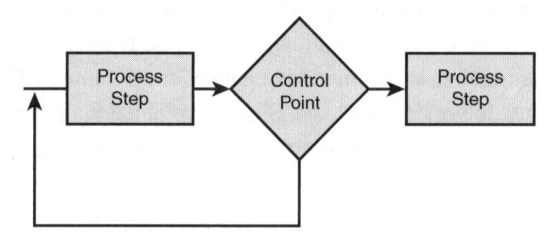

Figure 14.1 Control points can be inserted into almost any process.

Data control points are equally easy to implement. Here you simply add controlling data and a procedure for using it. The most common example of a data control point is a password.

You simply add a password to whatever data you want to control, and implement a procedure for people to get and use the password. You have instant data control. As another simple example of a data control point, imagine a typical payroll application. You want to make sure people are not being paid too frequently, so you insert a data element called "last payday." You implement a procedure that says that each time a paycheck is to be cut, the application will continue only if the "last payday" date is more than six days ago.

Implementing Control Points

By this point, you should be getting the idea that you could literally spend hundreds of hours and implement thousands of control points throughout not only your IT shop, but your entire organization. Although that may or may not be a worthwhile project, it won't help you implement change and release management.

If we focus on change management, you can now understand that it is probably a good idea to implement specific control points in your change management process. This is exactly the point of the techniques advocated throughout this book, such as change authorization and post-implementation reviews. These control points will ensure that you have a firm grip on the change activity in your organization.

Beyond the change management process, you should document the control points that already exist to help you maintain compliance with internal policies and external regulations. As soon as you have a catalog of control points, you should determine whether these control points are sufficient to maintain compliance. If not, define and implement enough new control points to make sure you stay in compliance or at least understand when you are drifting out of compliance.

Control Point Guidelines

Several guidelines will help as you define and implement control points for your organization. Like all guidelines, these are suggestions rather than fixed rules. Use them to help set up your control points, but don't become a slave to these rules.

The first general guideline is that you should not be overly controlling. Just because control points are easy to establish does not mean you should insert too many of them. Each control point adds a bit of time and expense to your processes and creates the perception of bureaucracy. People are creative by nature. If you add too many control points to any process, people will create ways to avoid dealing with the controls, or, worse yet, they will create ways to avoid the process.

The easiest way to know when you have introduced too many control points is through continuous-process improvement. As you're seeking ways to improve your process, you may notice that you can significantly increase productivity or streamline a process by removing some of the steps. If removing those steps doesn't jeopardize the integrity of the process, you probably have too many control points.

The second general principle for control points counterbalances the first. You do not want to be too lax in your control points. If a process or data set does not have enough control points, it may drift out of compliance. The general tendency of most organizations is to introduce too few control points when a process is first defined. This is probably OK with an immature process that does not affect your compliance posture. However, if the process is intended to fill a compliance gap or bring more control to an area that was found lacking, be sure to add extra control points to it.

You generally know when too few control points are associated with a process or data set by conducting an audit, as described later in this chapter. The key way to remediate issues found in an audit is to add control points to the process or data.

The final and overriding rule of control point design is to always maximize value. The best way to find the right balance between too many control points and too few is to control what has the most value to your organization. If you are part of a manufacturing organization trying to build a reputation for great quality, you should put lots of control points into processes that directly affect manufacturing. If your organization counts on bringing innovative products to market before your competitors, you should have strong controls around intellectual capital and marketing information. A health services organization should put strong controls around patient care processes and data to ensure that the highest possible standards are maintained. Whatever is of the most value to your organization should be the best controlled, which means focusing there when creating control points.

Controlling Changes Across Control Points

After the control points have been identified and put into place for any business or IT process, you can manage your compliance by keeping records of what happens at those control points. Fortunately, ITIL has just the right process for tracking and keeping records—change management. To stay in compliance, you should modify your change management process to pay special attention to what happens at the various control points you have defined.

To understand the interplay of change management and control points, let's revisit the simple example of a control point in expense reimbursement (see Figure 14.2). The control point says that each expense report must be reviewed and approved by a manager before it can be paid. This is a very simple example of a control point that almost every organization should implement.

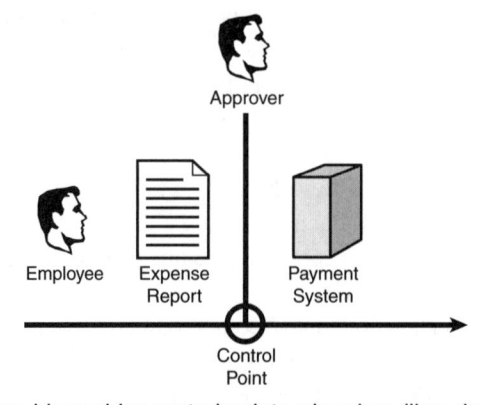

Figure 14.2 You should consider control points when handling change requests.

Now imagine that the expense reporting process is automated by a tool that allows employees to submit an expense report online. The tool then notifies the appropriate manager that a report has been submitted and allows the manager to review the expenses online and either approve or reject the report. This tool is an example of a simple business application.

Like any application, new versions of the expense reporting tool will be created from time to time. Each version will be defined, built, tested, and deployed by release and deployment management, under the governance of change control. This is exactly where your change control process should include the appropriate policies and procedures to govern not only the overall change, but also the control points that are affected by the change.

Say, for example, that the new release of the expense reimbursement tool will allow for managers being out of the office. If the expense report is not either approved or rejected within three days, the tool automatically assigns a different manager to be the approver and notifies both the new approver and the original approver. Clearly this is a direct change to the control point and how it was originally intended to work.

For each change that could potentially impact a control point like this, the change reviewer should take special note of the degree of impact. The assessment of the change should include special consideration of whether the organization really wants to modify the control point. Let's return to the example of the expense reimbursement application. The change reviewer would need to determine whether it is acceptable to have an alternate manager responsible for reviewing the expenses of an employee he or she might not know as well.

In most cases, changes affecting control points need special documentation that will serve as proof of compliance. The change reviewer can collect this documentation and either attach it directly to the request-for-change record or at least place a pointer in the record to the documentation for that change. As a governing process, change management is responsible for obtaining and maintaining whatever level of documentation is required by the regulations and policies that your organization must deal with.

Some examples of documentation that might be appropriate include test plans and test results, system logs of who performed each activity, records of any changes to access control so that you can understand who might change the system, or control points and specific history of transactions across a control point. The number and type of documents that must be maintained is directly related to the number and type of regulations and internal policies you must comply with. The more complex your regulatory environment, the more documentation you will end up keeping. In response to the complex demands of the FDA, many pharmaceutical companies maintain both logical and physical data vaults much like the Definitive Media Library described in Chapter 12, "Building the Definitive Media Library."

Generating compliance documentation from your change management system, or at least linking your change records to the appropriate compliance documentation, can be a large and expensive project. Although many change management tools today can attach external documents, most of them do not have the complete document management capabilities needed to keep documents that can serve as proof to external auditors. These capabilities might include access controls on attached documents that are different from the controls on the change record itself, the ability to automatically remove and destroy attached documents when their retention period expires, and the ability to apply an electronic signature to a document. Although many organizations choose to extend their change management tool in these ways, others decide to implement a separate compliance management tool that integrates with the change records but handles the compliance-specific documentation.

Compliance record keeping is a complex subject unto itself. From the standpoint of change management, the important point is that everyone who reviews, approves, or executes changes should be aware of the control points in your organization and should know what documentation must be maintained and how to maintain it.

Regulations and Release Management

Unfortunately, control points are not static in the environment. When new projects take place, they introduce new control points, alter existing ones, or perhaps remove some control points. Because new projects are the domain of release management, it is important to understand how your release plans and deployments will impact the control points in your organization.

To operate effectively in a regulated environment, each of your release road maps should consider the possibility that new or modified regulations will be required. Determine in advance which releases will contain functionality to automate those control points, and be sure to include extra testing and documentation time in those release plans.

Fortunately, most regulations are announced well before they take effect. This gives your organization time to understand how the regulation will impact your IT function, so it can plan to modify the appropriate applications and infrastructure. These changes should be planned into a specific release and put on your road map. Looking ahead in this way can make it seem less like you are always reacting to some external legislation or regulation and more like you are in control of your own IT shop.

When you reach one of those unusual situations in which you have insufficient lead time to implement a requirement, you should document the issue you have with compliance. This documentation must include your action plan to get to compliance, complete with dates. This kind of exception document saves the auditors time and effort because you already know that you cannot comply with the regulation by the date requested.

When a release includes regulatory content, the release architect and release project manager can do several things to make that release more successful. First, the architect should review all current control points and understand what will happen to each. Will the role or procedure around a control point change? Will new control points be added? Each of these should be noted and understood in the context of the entire release.

The release project manager should add extra tasks into the project plan to accommodate the necessary regulations. These include the control point planning (just mentioned), additional policy documentation, time to define new procedures, tasks for training affected employees, and plenty of time for extra testing. Figure 14.3 shows the additional points that regulatory compliance adds to the typical release deployment cycle.

Define → **Build** → **Test** → **Deploy**

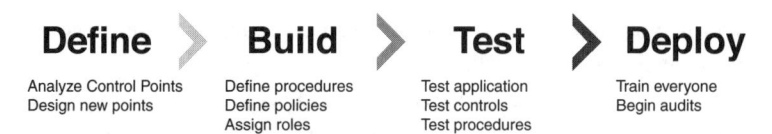

Analyze Control Points / Design new points | Define procedures / Define policies / Assign roles | Test application / Test controls / Test procedures | Train everyone / Begin audits

Figure 14.3   Regulations affect every part of the release management cycle.

Data Auditing and Process Auditing

In theory, keeping track of control points and recording activities occurring at those control points should keep your organization compliant with all the regulations you know about. Then again, theories hardly ever work out perfectly in the real world. Rather than base your compliance solely on change control, you should conduct periodic audits to find defects and repair them. In this section, you will learn about the different types of audits and how an audit program helps you maintain compliance.

Process Audits

Ultimately an audit compares the real world to some ideal baseline. A process audit, for example, compares the actual way your organization operates to the ideal process that is documented. This comparison is designed to show weaknesses where the actual practice could be better aligned with your intended practice. Process audits normally focus on the control points defined within the process, but they also can note discrepancies in other parts of the process.

Of course, such a comparison assumes that your documented process is better than actual practice. A continuous-improvement practice makes sure that as people find better ways to accomplish the process, these methods are incorporated into the process documentation rather than simply being adopted and leaving the process documents out of date.

Process audits require both interviews of the people executing the process and examinations of the documents involved in the process. An audit of the patient admission process in a hospital, for example, might include an interview with someone who normally admits patients. This interview is designed to find out if the person is really following the process or is simply doing the job the best he or she can.

In addition to interviews, an audit of the admission process would most likely include examination of some patient records, possibly with any identifying information removed. This examination would show whether all the data is being captured according to the process. Other records might also be examined if they are used as part of the overall patient admission process.

The net result of a process audit is a series of discrepancies between the documented process and the actual practice. Each of these discrepancies represents an opportunity for improvement. You can respond to an issue found in a process audit by either changing the behavior to line up with the process or changing the process to line up with the current behavior. Behavior is changed by retraining people and motivating them to use the process to accomplish their work better than they currently do. The process can be changed using process reengineering, which often results in retraining as well.

This general discussion about process audits applies to any situation where you want to strengthen a process or improve the degree to which your organization adheres to the process. For processes that comply with regulations in particular, however, you often will not have an opportunity to modify the process. In most cases, you need to improve your compliance by helping people follow the process more closely.

Data Audits

A data audit pays more attention to your data than to the processes that produce it. With a data audit, you compare two pieces of data that should match to see if a discrepancy exists. For a data audit to be successful, you almost always need two pieces of data to compare with one another, or at least a guesstimate of what the data should be to compare against what the data actually shows.

Data audits are performed through random samples. The auditor determines how much data is needed and then pores through that data, making comparisons. Sometimes audit tools make the comparisons more quickly, but often a data audit involves manual comparisons.

Just like a process audit, a data audit results in some discrepancies between the audited data and the expected data. If the audit compares two different values, two possibilities exist. Either one of the values is considered the baseline, and any value that differs is suspect, or neither of the values is known to be accurate, and both become suspect when a discrepancy is found.

An example will help illustrate possible outcomes of a data audit. Imagine that a retail organization is auditing register sales. A comparison is made between the actual cash in each drawer and the point-of-sale computer record. For every drawer where the amounts differ, the auditor can assume that the computer record is an accurate baseline and that the amount in the drawer is wrong due to employee error or misbehavior. This is an example of using one value (the computer record) as a baseline.

This discussion of data audits in general can help you understand audits dealing with compliance. Many financial regulations can be examined by regular data audits. In fact, the whole concept of double-entry accounting is predicated on having two different data values to compare when an audit is conducted.

Discrepancies in data audits usually are repaired by a corrective entry somewhere. A general ledger update, an administrative inventory entry, and a correction of an account balance are all examples of changing data in response to an audit discrepancy. To maintain compliance, it is important that you correct the data and address any underlying procedure issues that caused the discrepancy. In most cases, you will find that issues in data can be traced directly to people not following the correct process to keep the data accurate.

Internal and External Audits

Audits are a great tool for your organization to use to measure your compliance with the many policies and regulations you must follow. When someone within your organization performs an audit, it is called an internal audit. Although it is always uncomfortable to be examined, an internal audit generally is relaxed, and the consequences of discrepancies are minimal.

Many times, however, regulations require that your organization be audited by a third party. These external audits can become confrontational, because the results of a discrepancy can be severe. If you fail an external Sarbanes-Oxley audit in the U.S., for example, your corporate officers may be subject to legal investigations leading to indictment. A pharmaceutical organization that fails a regulatory audit may find itself unable to market one or more of its products for an extended time.

Because the consequences of an external audit can be so severe, you should spend a great deal of time and energy to ensure that only minor discrepancies are found. Some ways to prepare for an external audit include additional process training, increased internal data audits, and practice interviews with people who are likely to be selected.

Building an Audit Program

Audits are an important tool in building and maintaining an environment that is compliant with a variety of regulations. Anyone who needs to operate according to externally enforced regulations should create an audit program to accompany their change and release management disciplines. An audit program coordinates audit activity and regulates it to balance the need to ensure compliance with the expense of preparing for, conducting, and reacting to audits.

A good audit program takes a complete look at your organization and schedules internal audits to validate every control point at least once per year. For the more important control points, your audit program may want to schedule validation two or more times per year. The overall program should coordinate activities to ensure that no single business process or function is being impacted too frequently and that no control point is being left to chance.

In addition to scheduling and conducting audits, your overall audit program should track discrepancies and make sure that they get resolved appropriately. Keeping careful track of discrepancies found and the fixes that are implemented for them will help the organization get the most benefit from every audit you conduct.

Compliance management is an important topic and is growing more important each year. New regulations are being enacted while unscrupulous corporations are facing ever stiffer penalties for avoiding the rules. Even very small organizations are finding themselves subject to increasing scrutiny, and large corporations realize they need to make significant investments in compliance programs to keep their reputations spotless.

Your change management process should be designed to help create and maintain a compliant environment. Your release management process should consider each release and what it means for your compliance posture. Conducting a full-scale audit program serves as a backstop to catch compliance issues that might slip by these two processes. With good process discipline and a minimal investment in auditing, your organization can be assured that you comply with all necessary regulations and policies.

Looking Ahead

Now that you understand some of the key operational issues that might arise in change and release management, it is time to consider the benefits you can reasonably expect from all your hard work. Those benefits are the basis of Part IV of this book.

Part IV

Reaping the Benefits

So you have implemented change and release management. The long deployment is over, and you have overcome several operational issues. It is time to reflect a bit and then look forward to all the benefits promised in the first chapter. In this final part, you will learn about several of the benefits of a fully functioning and rapidly maturing change and release management process. Those benefits include business impact analysis, increased reporting capabilities, and better linkage across many of your existing and future IT processes.

CHAPTER 15

Business Impact Analysis

One of the most immediate benefits of change and release management is a better understanding of your IT environment. Eventually, however, this understanding will move beyond IT to the rest of your organization. As your change management discipline matures and your release management plans grow, you will be able to assess the impact of any particular change or release on the wider business environment.

This analysis of impacts to the business is beyond traditional user impacts calculated today. Today most organizations can perform an analysis that says "The accounting application will be down for two hours, so the accounting department will be unable to work." With mature change and release management processes, you can perform a deeper analysis. You will understand that a two-hour outage in accounting will impact next week's quarterly earnings statement and that if you delay a change by a week, you can negate that impact.

The power of business impact analysis is that it brings your IT group closer to the rest of the organization and helps you demonstrate the value of the change and release management disciplines.

Technical Impacts and Business Impacts

To reach business impact analysis, you need to distinguish between technical impacts and business impacts. Many organizations fail at exactly this point because they perform technical impact analysis and think they are generating business data. This section will help you distinguish between technical and business impacts.

Technical Impacts

The best practice in change management dictates that one or more IT components be associated with each change. After all, everyone should know what is being changed! In ITIL, this association is done by connecting a configuration item (CI) from the configuration management database (CMDB) to each change.

Using this simple association as a starting point allows you to better understand what each change will do to the technical environment. From a single server, you can predict an impact on the applications on the server and possibly the network segment the server is connected to. From one router, you can determine the impacts on both local-area and wide-area networks. Knowledge of one component and how it is related to all the other components comes from your CMDB. It helps you understand which technical pieces will be impacted by a change to any other piece. This is the basis of technical impact assessment.

As soon as your organization begins performing technical impact assessments, you will find them an indispensable tool. When an incident causes an outage to one of your key services, you no longer need to find just the right person to explain how a single broken disk drive can take down all of marketing. Your technical impact assessment will show exactly how and why this is possible.

A mature organization uses technical impact assessments as part of its forward planning. You can perform a technical impact assessment on several components to understand how running out of capacity on any of them will impact the overall system. This information forms the basis of a proactive capacity plan. Similarly, you can model different scenarios using technical impact assessment to understand the consequences of potential failures and build an availability plan to avoid any of those failures. This is an example of a classic "single point of failure" analysis using a technical impact assessment.

Business Impacts

Although technical impact is quite powerful, it provides only secondary benefits to your organization beyond IT. The IT team can use technical impact assessments to resolve issues more quickly, avoid problems before they occur, and make forward-looking plans. Certainly all of these benefit the business to some extent. With business impact assessment, however, the wider organization enjoys more direct benefits.

Business impact couches IT events in strictly business terms. Instead of learning that a network component or application is down, or even that some business people will lose IT functions, business impact talks about disruption to business events. If a server goes down, it is an IT event, but if that server causes a manufacturing line to go down, it becomes a business event.

Understanding business impact requires that IT understand the overall business. It may seem strange, but many people spend their entire career in IT without thinking that they support a company that sells insurance, makes soup, or distributes books. You learned about the application software stack in Chapter 13, "Defining Release Packages." Above that stack is a completely different stack for the business. In the business stack, shown in Figure 15.1, application software is the "plumbing" that is required but that mostly gets ignored. The business stack consists of business processes, which lead to business activities, which support business functions, which create the products or services that your organization exists to produce.

```
┌─────────────────────────────────────┐
│      Products and Services          │
├─────────────────────────────────────┤
│   Business Activities / Functions   │
├─────────────────────────────────────┤
│         Business Processes          │
├─────────────────────────────────────┤
│        Application Software         │
└─────────────────────────────────────┘
```

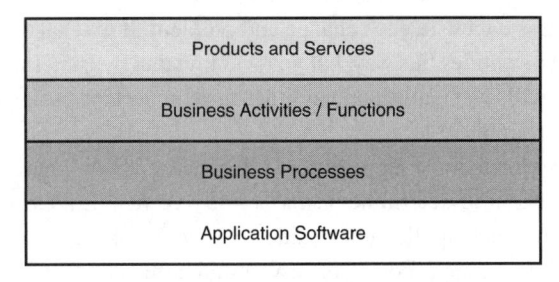

Figure 15.1 The business stack helps define business impacts.

Just as a CMDB helps you understand the relationships of networks to servers and servers to applications, so a true enterprise architecture can help you understand the relationships between layers in the business stack. When the IT people begin to see that the business has an architecture, they can begin to couch IT events in a way that business people can truly understand the impacts. This is the essence of business impact analysis.

How to Determine Business Impact

Achieving business impact assessment isn't easy, but with tightly controlled change management and carefully planned release management, it is possible. You can leverage your change and release management processes, along with extending your configuration management process, to link business activities to your IT activities and thus enable business decisions to be made from IT data. This section describes how to successfully implement business impact analysis.

Start by focusing on the post-implementation review of your changes. Invite one or two people who were affected by the change to discuss what that affect was. These should specifically be people outside of IT and people who can speak in business terms rather than simply saying that IT components were unavailable. You will not have time, nor will you find the right people, to do this with every change, but you should pursue additional business information for the changes that had the most significant impact on the business. Changes that had unintended or unforeseen consequences are particularly useful for this approach.

The information you gather in these post-implementation review sessions can initially be gathered in the change documentation, but it should eventually be used to extend your CMDB. Listen for business processes and business activities, and understand how they relate to one another and to other elements within the business stack shown in Figure 15.1. Capture those entities and relationships in your CMDB, extending the schema to handle business objects in addition to IT objects if necessary.

Most organizations do not have the skills or the funding to engage a full-time enterprise architect to define and populate all the configuration items and relationships in the business stack, but you can achieve most of the work without a dedicated project team. By using post-implementation reviews as well as the root cause analysis portion of your problem management process, you can capture valuable business data with each change and problem. It may take a very long time for the population of all business entities this way, but you will find that by gathering data from your operational processes, you will eventually populate the most important business entities without the expense of an enterprise architect.

As your CMDB grows into a repository of information about your entire organization, you will find that you can use it to determine business impacts. Just as a CMDB containing only IT components shows you which applications reside on a server, so the business-oriented portion of the CMDB can show you which products or services are affected when a business process is out of service. For example, if your CMDB has already captured the product design application and all the IT components it depends on, you can easily extend it to capture the product design business process. An additional extension could link product design, product development, and product marketing into the new product rollout business activity. Now, if a simple component failed, you could understand the threat to rolling out new products.

You need to exercise some caution in the early days of working with business impact analysis. Concepts such as redundancy, failover, and single points of failure are well understood in the IT space, but they probably are not as well understood in the business space. For example, perhaps your CMDB has captured a relationship between one of your applications and the warehouse receiving business process. Through some careful interviews with business people, you've learned that the receiving process links to both the inventory maintenance and vendor payment business activities. That inventory maintenance directly links to several of the key products your organization sells. This simple slice of a business CMDB is shown in Figure 15.2.

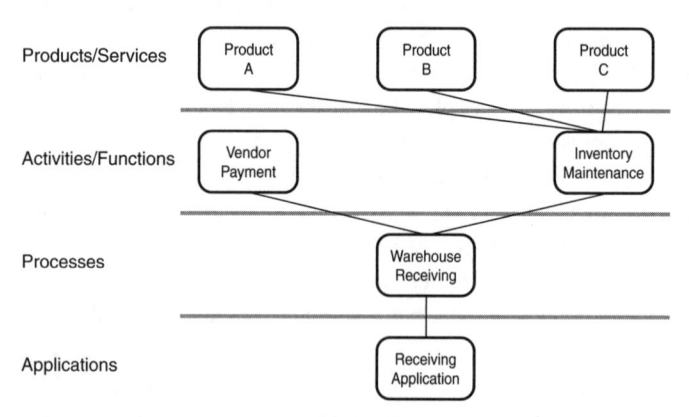

Figure 15.2 Products are dependent on the receiving application according to this simple CMDB excerpt.

Given this configuration data, an IT person might assume that an IT incident that causes the receiving application to fail might delay shipments of products A, B, and C. But a business person would look at this same information and assume that the inventory management activity keeps enough stock on hand to survive at least twenty-four hours of not being able to receive into the warehouses. Redundancy here comes in the form of redundant supplies to the products rather than in multiple technical widgets keeping the application alive, but the net result is the same. A failure lower in the stack can be safely ignored because of redundancy higher in the stack.

Capturing this notion of redundancy and the true impact on the business is very complex. You will be able to capture this information only after you start using requirements for your business entities and capture nonfunctional requirements for things such as business functions and processes. Determining the basic components of your business environment through change management reviews and problem management analysis is a great beginning. To go deeper, however, you should focus on one business environment at a time.

In defining a release package, you begin at the top of the software stack. To define and understand a business environment, you begin at the top of the business stack. Begin with a specific product or service that you want to optimize, and define all the activities or functions that support that top-level entity. This will most likely require significant interviews with people who understand that part of the business. If you have an executive who acts as a product manager or leader for that product or service, interview that person.

In defining a business environment, you need to understand not only the simple dependencies, but also the more complex relationships that might be invoked only when the primary function or process is disrupted. Gathering and understanding these complex relationships helps you define the redundancy and failover paths through the business, which in turn makes your business impact analysis much more powerful.

When you have gotten to this deeper level of understanding for one business environment, assess the value you will gain from the effort. If the value can prove itself for your organization, tackle the next business environment. If the value is limited or does not exceed the effort and expense needed to document an environment, you should certainly not extend any additional effort. This normally is not the case, but if it does happen, you should focus on increasing the value of the data you already have rather than documenting new environments. One organization used an analysis technique like this to realize that it could cancel the order for a redundant network line because the business process tolerated an outage of up to forty-eight hours without any significant impact. That was a real value that could be directly linked to the organization's analysis of a business environment.

Recording Business Impact in a Change Record

Assessing the technical and business impact of a change is important. But if you don't save this information and make use of it for the next change in the same environment, you run the risk of losing some hard-won intelligence. So it is important to record your analysis, but what form should that documentation take? This section looks at how you might want to record impact assessments and describes the benefits and drawbacks of each one.

Impact Assessments as Text

The obvious way to record an impact assessment is using text. Using a text box, you can capture the full analysis, describing the chain of events from a change or incident to directly impacted components right up the stack to the product or service that might be impacted. If the text is already documented by the person who did the analysis, it can be pasted directly into the change record as a long text field. For very long or detailed assessments, an external document might be attached to the change record but left in its original file format. Whether stored internally to the change tool or as an external attachment, text is a natural vehicle for conveying business and technical impact assessments.

The outstanding benefit of text is its flexibility. You can capture ideas in any format, you can insert drawings or other graphics into the text, and you can arrange the information in any way you want. There is no restriction on what can be conveyed, but this means that the skill of the person doing the recording influences the quality of assessment data captured. Not everyone can convey what they know in clearly illustrated prose.

Text is also simple. People understand how to work with the written word, and there is no frustration with trying to get the correct value in each field, as there is with data. It is intuitive to write words and have them flow onto the screen to convey the assessment information.

The most serious drawback of recording impact assessments as text only is that text is unstructured. It does not lend itself well to searching, correlating, sorting, or summarizing. With text-only impact assessments, it is very difficult to find all the assessments dealing with a specific business product or to count the number of times that a specific business function is impacted. If you choose to extend textual descriptions to external files, these problems are exacerbated because very few tools allow you to deal with text across multiple attachments. This unstructured nature of text makes any structured tasks more difficult.

Impact Assessments as Data Fields

If the unstructured nature of text is just too difficult to deal with, you could choose to store impact assessments as a series of data fields. You can create a field for the affected component, a drop-down list for the degree of impact, a time field for the duration of impact, and so on. These data fields can then be used to store the impact assessment data in a table of a database, which makes the data much more accessible than it would be as text fields.

Storing business and technical impact analyses as data fields has several key benefits. Because the thought behind formatting happens only once, when you create the data fields, the consistency of the data is much higher. You can use all the database tricks, such as default field values, required fields, and field validations, to further enhance the consistency of the impact data.

Of course, the structure in the data is a big advantage. You can search all impact assessments for using common database query tools. You can organize and sort the data into a format that best suits any required presentation. You can create meaningful statistics by counting impact analyses that meet certain criteria, or you can categorize these analyses by any value. The structured nature of impact analysis data stored as separate fields opens the door to data mining and other business intelligence techniques that can make the data more useful for a longer term.

The disadvantage of structured data is that it takes away the creativity of your analysts. If people are assigned to fill in a set of fields, their natural tendency is to look for the "answers" to the blanks rather than to do a thorough and detailed analysis. Data that is structured creates the perception that there are right and wrong answers and that looking any further or digging any deeper will not be beneficial. The analysis seems finished when all the fields are filled in rather than when the analyst's curiosity is satisfied. This might be helpful, because it puts a boundary around the amount of time an analysis might take, but it can also stop people from reaching some of the most creative and useful conclusions.

Impact Assessments and Relationships

Perhaps the most useful impact assessment data combines text and structured fields. This more complex data model requires some extra thought and effort, but the results overcome the objections to both text alone and structured data fields alone. Rather than store data in a single table, this model supports multiple relational tables that together hold impact assessments.

In the relational model for impact analysis data, the master table might be called "impacts" and might contain a single row for each impact analysis performed. This table can hold information about the overall impact itself, such as the date and duration of the impact or a reference to the change or incident record that causes the impact. It could even hold a long text field or an attachment with any form of analysis.

Related to the "impacts" table would be a table for affected components. Each row in this table would describe the impact on one component—either a technical component for a technical impact analysis or a business component for a business impact analysis. This table might include fields for the configuration item, the probability of impact on that component, and the severity of impact on that component. By creating a separate table, you allow any number of components to be impacted and each impacted component to be recorded. You could either assign technical components and business components to separate tables or create a flag column to indicate whether each row is a business component or a technical component. Figure 15.3 shows a simple view of this proposed layout for impact assessment data.

The disadvantage of keeping impact information in this structure is that it doesn't already exist in any service management tool. You would need to create the data model and then modify your tool set to support this advanced level of impact assessment. In addition, you would need to train your staff to understand the discipline of impact analysis well enough to use a more sophisticated model. Although recording this level of impact analysis is certainly not defined as part of the ITIL best practices, you should determine whether it could provide significant value for your organization.

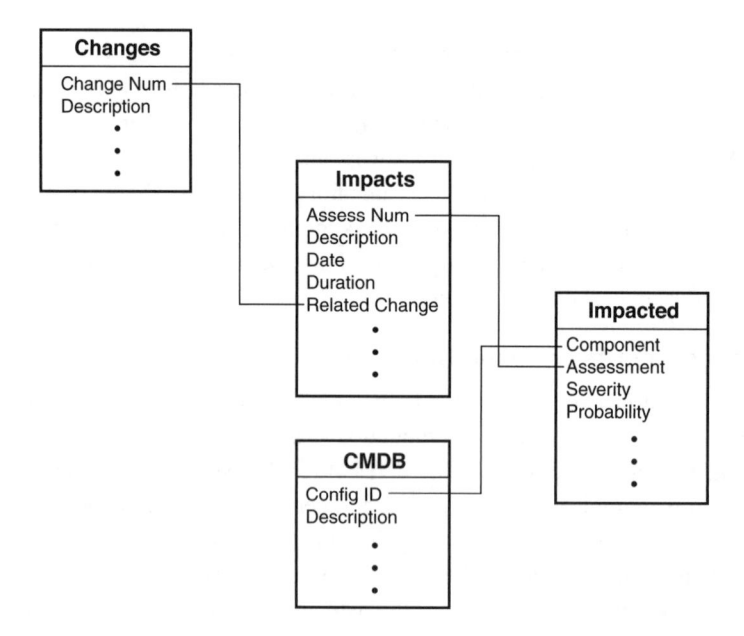

Figure 15.3 Business and technical impact can be tracked using related tables.

Using Business Impact Analysis in the Change Advisory Board

After the assessments are made and properly recorded, you have useful business intelligence at your disposal. The next important step is deciding who can use that data and how they should act on it. This is where a mature change advisory board (CAB) can dramatically help your organization. They use data from both the technical and business impact assessments to control changes in your environment. This section describes the ways in which impact assessment data is used to make decisions.

Scheduling Decisions

One frequent use of impact analyses is in making scheduling decisions. The CAB is in a unique position to look across the IT operational schedule and determine the best time for IT to execute a given change. With the addition of business impact analysis data, the CAB can look across the rest of the organization and schedule changes so that they suit the complete organization instead of the convenience of IT.

Imagine that the CAB is considering a change to a storage area network. Looking at the servers and applications using the storage, the CAB sees that the coming weekend is an acceptable schedule. With business impact data, however, the CAB can see that a major fund-raiser is scheduled for Sunday evening, and the donor data needed to coordinate the fund-raiser is on the storage that needs to be taken out of service. From this business data, the CAB can see that the change should wait until after the weekend.

In a large or complex organization, it may be very difficult to get timely information such as a fund-raiser happening next weekend. One of the side benefits of acquiring and using business impact assessment data is that closer relationships are forged between IT and the business it serves, so this kind of communication becomes more commonplace. When your organization, led by the CAB, considers change activity in light of the business rather than having a parochial focus, you will be amazed at how willing the wider organization is to share information with IT.

Authorization Decisions

Another use of impact assessments is in making authorization decisions about changes. Depending on your implementation of the change management process, a change may be authorized before it goes to the CAB, or the CAB may authorize changes. In either case, the CAB has the most complete information about all change activity in the environment. With the addition of business impact analysis, the CAB has the most complete information about the effect of any proposed change on the overall business.

Sometimes a change seems reasonable or even desirable to the IT community, but looking at the potential impact of that change to your whole organization makes it clear that it shouldn't be done. For example, what seems like a simple convenience in the employee benefits application might impact the organization's ability to comply with data privacy laws in Europe. Although IT sees a very sensible change, the business impact could be catastrophic.

The CAB should be able to override authorization decisions made by others. This allows maximum use of both technical and business impact analysis to make good decisions for all concerned.

Project Decisions

Finally, consider the funding decisions that every IT organization needs to make. What passes as a business case is often only a justification that IT uses to convince itself that what it wants to do doesn't cost too much. Using business impact information about a proposed project can help IT really understand the impact of each proposed project on the financial status of the whole organization. There are too many examples of projects that save IT a few pennies only to cost the overall organization thousands of dollars.

When solid business entities and relationships are part of your IT consciousness, your decision-making horizon can grow. The reputation of IT within the organization can grow, and you can make your CIO a true partner in the executive suite rather than just the person who spends all the money.

Looking Ahead

Business impact analysis is neither easy nor inexpensive. It is, however, powerful and valuable. Linking IT to the overall business allows stronger decisions and helps build a solid working relationship between the business community and the IT community. As with any other IT endeavor, you should determine the value proposition for business impact analysis in your organization. Most people who have looked deeply find that the value is far greater than the cost.

In the next chapter, you will learn about reports and measurements that are enabled after change and release management has been successfully implemented.

CHAPTER 16

Reports and Service Levels

You implement or revise an IT process to get the benefit of better information flow. This is especially true with change and release management. A wide variety of reports are possible when you have aligned these processes with best practices.

Many detractors will see additional reports as a negative feature of the new process. Indeed, the goal is not to generate more data in an overcrowded space. Instead, you should focus on improved reporting that really measures the capability of your IT services. Rather than putting the most data possible into each report, you should focus on making each report as useful as possible. The key reason to use these reports is to get the right information at the right level of depth in front of business and IT management so that they can make informed decisions that improve the quality of your services.

This chapter describes some of the reports you can use to measure and evaluate the change and release management processes. It is not an exhaustive list, but it is a good sampling of what various organizations have found useful to report on. Along with a description of each report, you will find some comments on how the report might be used and what it says about the maturity of your change and release management services. Figure 16.1 shows the four categories of reports, which include operational reports and process health reports for change and release management. As mentioned in Chapter 14, "Auditing and Compliance Management," reports play a key role in auditing and compliance management as well.

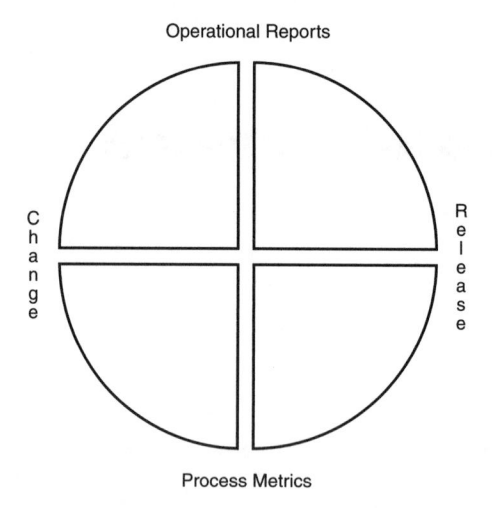

[Figure 16.1: Circle divided into four quadrants, with "Operational Reports" labeled at top, "Process Metrics" at bottom, "Change" on the left, and "Release" on the right.]

Figure 16.1 The four categories of change and release management reports.

Reports About Changes

The first group of reports deals directly with change records. These reports show information about the work that goes on and who benefits from it. They tend to be very operational in nature and can be affected only indirectly. These reports are fairly easy to produce. Any change management tool should provide some version of these reports without much customization.

Figure 16.2 summarizes the operational change reports.

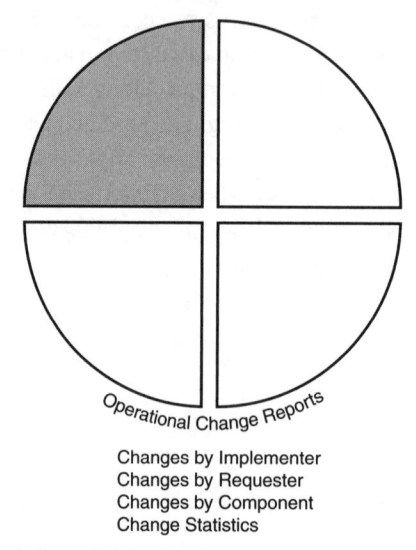

[Figure 16.2: Circle divided into four quadrants with the upper-left quadrant shaded, labeled "Operational Change Reports" below.]

Changes by Implementer
Changes by Requester
Changes by Component
Change Statistics

Figure 16.2 Operational change reports show what work is happening and for whom.

Changes by Implementer

One common report shows a summary of who is implementing changes. The report can provide details for every change record grouped by the implementer of the change. Alternatively, it can simply have a single row for each person and show summarized numbers for the changes implemented by that person.

Useful information on this report would include whether the person implemented the change alone or as part of a team, how long the implementation was scheduled to take, how long it actually took, and perhaps some estimate of time expended before and after the actual implementation. If you choose a summary-style report, you might want to see the number of changes each person implemented, the total time spent on implementing changes, the percentage of changes implemented within the allocated time, and the number of changes where the actual implementation duration exceeded the scheduled implementation duration.

Listing changes by who implemented them is a good way to understand workload balance in your organization. If one or two people always seem to implement the changes, you will most likely want to free them up as much as possible from incident management duties, because trying to do both could cause more changes to be implemented late. Conversely, if the workload is fairly even, except that one or two people have not implemented any changes, you might want to understand where their time is being spent instead. This type of report can also be used to assess the risk of a change based on the implementer. Implementers with a poor track record of failed or backed-out changes can have a higher risk value placed on their changes.

Changes by Requester

Changes by requester are another way to look at the changes in your environment. This report also can be formatted either as a detailed report with a single change in every row or as a summary with a single requester on each row. The choice between detail and summary may even be left up to the person viewing the report.

In a report by requester, you most likely will want to see each person's organization, whether each change was authorized, the time spent working on each change, the risk factors of each change, and the lead time provided for the change. For a summary report, you might just report the average of the time spent and the lead time, and a percentage of changes that have a high risk.

Reviewing the changes by requester allows you to see which groups are taking up most of your IT resources. If, like many organizations, you find that the requesters are almost always people within IT, you need to question whether all the activity is warranted. Is your IT group creating its own demand and then filling it? On the other hand, if most of the changes are coming from business units and people outside IT, you might want to see if IT changes are being properly recorded.

A healthy balance would be somewhere around one third of the changes coming from the business units and two thirds from within IT. This is fairly normal, because many changes are behind-the-scenes things that need to be done for maintenance or proactively to head off problems, and these should come from the IT group. The changes from outside of IT tend to deal with application changes and generally take much more time and effort to implement.

Changes by Component

Another interesting way to look at changes in your environment is by the component being changed. The fact that each change is associated with one or more configuration items allows you to produce an interesting report showing the amount of your IT environment that is changing regularly.

The report should list each configuration item (CI) that participates in a change, showing the number of changes to that component, how long the component was out of service for change activity, and the effort expended in changing that component. If you have it available from the CMDB, you should show the age of the component.

Looking at how many of your CIs are changing as a percentage of all components in the database can be very enlightening. If you see more than 5 percent of your environment changing in a given month, chances are that you have a stressed IT team. Most organizations find a change rate of 3 percent or less per month to be more comfortable and much less risky.

Your rate of change will depend somewhat on how you choose to define CIs and relate them to changes. For example, if you upgrade memory on a server and patch the operating system at the same time, that may count as three components changing (memory, operating system, and server), or it could be counted as only the server changing. For the sake of the 3 percent rule of thumb, assume that each server, router, application, network component, and so forth counts as a single component and that any subcomponents of these, such as a disk drive or memory module, do not.

Another common use of the changes by CI report is to look for equipment that should be replaced. If a specific component is being changed frequently, it might be too difficult to maintain, and thus more expensive than you want. By combining both changes and incidents by CI, you will see even more clearly that some equipment should be replaced before the standard refresh cycle would otherwise replace it.

One very key piece of data is to capture whether these changes are manual or automated. Automation involving standard changes to the environment (such as sending out patches to servers) has a tremendous return on investment because of a much higher success rate of changes, significantly fewer labor costs, and much faster and wider deployment of the changes.

It is truly faster, cheaper, *and* better to automate changes and releases. This is especially true in larger and more geographically dispersed organizations. Typically you see a full return on investment within six to twelve months of deploying the automation process and technology.

Change Statistics

The change statistics report is used to understand the kinds of changes made in your environment. Most change management tools support the idea of categorizing changes, and many organizations use categories such as data center changes, network changes, documentation changes, process changes, and so on. The change statistics report simply shows the changes summarized by these categories.

The information shown on a change statistics report is similar to that shown on the other change management reports. You will want to see the number of changes in each category, the amount of time being spent on them, the percentage that are implemented successfully, and the number of changes that failed for each category.

You can use the change statistics report to better understand your team's strengths and weaknesses. By seeing which changes fail most often by category, and understanding which changes take the bulk of your change implementation time, you can better understand where additional training or perhaps some additional resources may help.

You can also use a listing of changes by category to investigate whether people are using change management consistently. If you don't find very many documentation changes, for example, you can try to determine whether people know and follow your policy that documentation changes should be recorded. Likewise, if one category has too many changes, you can see if the policy should be modified to loosen control in that area.

Reports About the Change Management Process

The next set of reports focuses on the change management process more than on individual changes or even groups of changes. These reports help you understand the level of service that change management is providing. They are different in intent from the reports about changes just described, but they are not significantly different in content.

Figure 16.3 summarizes the change metric reports.

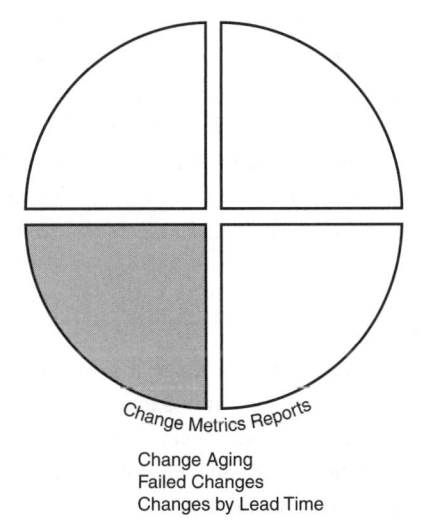

Change Metrics Reports
Change Aging
Failed Changes
Changes by Lead Time

Figure 16.3 Change metrics help you understand the maturity of the change management process.

Change Aging Report

The best overall view of the health of your change management process comes from the change aging report. This report displays the average time required for each step of your process. The categories found on the report may be somewhat different, depending on how you have chosen to customize the report. Essentially, anytime a record changes status, it should be seen as a milestone for the sake of the change aging report.

For example, if your change process dictates that a record start as submitted, and then go to awaiting approval, and then approved, implemented, and finally closed, your report would have four columns.

The first would show the average time from submitted to awaiting approval, which would indicate how long it is taking to do preapproval reviews.

The second column would show the average time from awaiting approval to approved, indicating how long people take to deliberate about approvals. This might reflect your CAB lead times.

The next column would show the average time from approval to implementation, which may be significant, depending on your process. If your change management process and your forward schedule of change are set up to approve changes right before they are implemented, this measure will be fairly consistent. On the other hand, if your process encourages early submission of change records by approving things when they are submitted rather than when they are about to be implemented, this time would show the degree to which your changes are planned in advance.

The final column, showing the average time between implementation and post-implementation review, is a good indicator of how hard your organization is trying to improve by quickly learning lessons from implemented changes.

By timing each phase of your change management process independently, you get a great picture of how well the process is working. You can get even more details if you further break down the change aging report by categories such as those used in the change statistics report. This allows you to see which types of changes breeze through the process and which ones tend to slow down. This probably reflects how your change management process is optimized. This also allows you to understand which area should be targeted for continuous-process improvement initiatives.

Failed Change Report

Another critical report for understanding the change management process is the failed change report. This report, which shows what changes failed in that period, should be run at least weekly. The report should include any change that was never successfully implemented, as well as those that were implemented outside of their scheduled windows. Both cases are examples of when the change management process did not work correctly.

For changes that could not be implemented, you would want to know what the issues were, whether the backout plan was successful, and whether the backout was completed within the allotted change schedule. Any change that failed and that did not have the backout plan successfully completed should be resolved through incident management, and that incident number should be present in the failed change report.

For changes that were eventually implemented, the report should show much of the same data. You will certainly want a summary of the issues, to understand whether anyone attempted to back out the change, and whether that backout was successful. In addition, you would want to understand if someone on your management team authorized the continued work on the change outside the originally scheduled window.

Failed changes should be treated exactly like problems—you should determine the root cause of the failure and define a set of actions to prevent that root cause from recurring. Failed changes should stay on the failed change report until the root cause has been found and the organization is satisfied that appropriate actions will be taken. Tracking the actions to remediate failed changes is properly the domain of problem management, so it does not need to be done as part of the failed change report.

In general, the percentage of failed changes should trend downward. As you pursue root causes and implement corrective actions, you are educating the IT community in how to avoid failed changes in the future. If the failed change report does not show a downward trend, you may need to introduce additional rigor and controls in your problem-management process.

Changes by Lead Time

A third report that helps indicate the health of change management is a counting of changes in each of your lead time categories. You will probably have urgent changes, emergency changes, and standard changes. You may also have long-running changes for planning releases and other major projects. The balance of activity in each of these categories is important.

The changes by lead time report normally is a simple summary showing the number of changes over the reporting period that falls into each category. From this information, you can make some significant assumptions about how people are working.

If you see too many emergency or urgent changes, you know that your environment is further out of control than you would like. Of course, we will never do away with emergencies in IT, but one of the major benefits of adhering to ITIL best practices is that the emergencies become fewer, and operations can focus on avoiding emergencies rather than reacting to them. If you find too many emergency changes, it is either because someone is abusing the emergency change procedures or because you have not matured in the incident and problem management disciplines. Urgent changes tell a different story. These are changes that need to be accomplished without the normal CAB lead time, so they are approved outside the CAB. If you see lots of urgent changes, the most likely cause is people misunderstanding the CAB and its schedule. You should look closely at who is submitting urgent changes. If you find a pattern, you may need to educate people again on when urgent changes are valid and when they are not.

A healthy, mature environment should see 80 percent of its changes in the standard or long-running category and only 20 percent in the emergency or urgent category. Some organizations actually get down to 5 percent or less of their changes having a shorter-than-desired planning horizon. You should use the changes by lead time report to improve your team and your process until you are comfortable with the balance for your situation.

This is a very good executive measurement to show the overall health of the IT organization. If you have more than 20 percent emergencies or urgent changes, the organization as a whole is most likely reactive or chaotic. On the other hand, if the numbers are 10 percent or even 5 percent, the organization is most likely in a proactive or service-oriented state.

Reports About Releases

When people first hear about ITIL and they learn that release management is one of its disciplines, the common misconception is that release management is just an ITIL name for project management. Hopefully you have learned that this isn't true, but even ITIL veterans realize that there are many similarities between release management and project management.

Because of these similarities, it should not surprise you to find that many of the reports that you produce about releases will be the same as the reports you currently produce under the heading of project management.

Figure 16.4 summarizes the operational release management reports.

Operational Release Reports

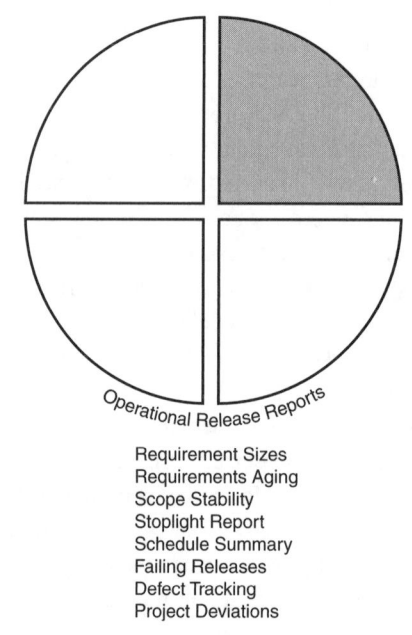

Requirement Sizes
Requirements Aging
Scope Stability
Stoplight Report
Schedule Summary
Failing Releases
Defect Tracking
Project Deviations

Figure 16.4 Operational release management reports are very similar to project management reports.

System Engineering Reports

Standard system engineering reports include those concerned with requirements and scope. Each release has a set of requirements and a specific scope. These should be managed through your standard requirements management process, as described in Chapter 2, "Discovering and Managing Requirements."

One interesting release management report can compare the number of requirements and the sizes of those requirements going into each release. This report gives you a great indication of the size of project that is likely to be successful in your environment. Some organizations do better with small projects that are of short duration and have relatively few new requirements. Other organizations succeed with larger projects that have more content but that release into the environment less frequently. Looking at the number and sizes of requirements can show you which type of project works best in your environment.

Another systems engineering report can show how long requirements take to be satisfied. Each of your release packages should be gathering and keeping requirements constantly. When it is time to create a new release, some of those requirements will be included, and others will be deferred to the next release. Requirements that are either very low in priority or very expensive to implement may wait several releases or may never be implemented. By looking at the age of requirements before they get implemented, you can get a good understanding of whether your releases are satisfying the needs of your organization.

Another useful report measures the changes to scope for each release. After a release has been finalized by creation of a baseline plan, changes often happen. By looking at the number and impact of those changes, you can assess how well the scope was defined in the first place, and by inference find out whether your release planning is effective.

Project Management Reports

Because each release is managed as a project, your organization probably already has standard reports that you will expect the release manager to produce. These reports help immensely when a release begins to go off course and needs additional resources or attention to get back to its plan.

The most fundamental report for each release is the release status report, also known as the project status report. Typically this report shows status against the projected schedule, the allocated resources, and the project's defined quality measurements. For each of these dimensions, a release status report uses red to indicate that something is seriously wrong, yellow to indicate that something is trending in the wrong direction, and green to indicate that everything is working out well. For this reason, the report is often called a stoplight report. You can create a single chart showing the stoplight report for each currently running release to form a good weekly project status deck. This deck can be a great way for IT management to touch base with each project without necessarily diving into the details of all of them.

To get a bigger picture across releases, you will probably want to create a summary schedule report. Created either monthly or quarterly, this report shows the number of projects that are running and is grouped by the project phase. Seeing how many projects are still in the definition phase versus how many are being tested or deployed is a great way to understand the times when certain resources might become scarce. If too many projects are in the test phase, you might run out of testers, whereas too many projects in the definition phase might put a strain on your supply of architects. Seeing these activities coming in advance gives you an opportunity to take action before the problem occurs.

Another very useful report is the failed or failing releases report. Although nobody wants his or her project to be labeled as failing, it is very useful for the organization to know which projects are not meeting their goals. If you establish clear criteria for success, you will be able to show which releases are not meeting those criteria. For example, you might want to declare a project as successful if the total number of days required to complete the project is within 10 percent of the planned days and the actual budget for the project is within 10 percent of the allocated budget. While the project is still ongoing, you can use these criteria to understand whether it will be successful. The failed and failing releases report can be used to allocate additional resources to projects, to focus your "lessons learned" activities, or to determine which kinds of projects are more likely to succeed. It should not be used as a tool to evaluate and punish release managers or release architects, because not all releases are created equal.

Quality Management Reports

When running releases as projects, you should pay attention to the quality of each release. Quality measurements and reports are important both in rescuing releases that are currently in trouble and in planning future releases that will have a higher probability of success.

One basic quality report tracks the number of defects found in each phase of a release project. Many studies have proven that the earlier a defect is found, the easier and cheaper it is to fix. Although some organizations may not be accustomed to thinking about defects in requirements or designs, we all know intuitively that not all requirements and designs are good. If your organization has matured to the point that tracking defects in the early phases of a release project is possible, you should certainly use that information in your defect tracking report. If you are not yet at that level of maturity, start by simply tracking the defects found in testing versus the defects found after deployment. Either way, a defect tracking report is a great way to see whether your reviews, inspections, and tests are successfully producing high-quality releases.

In addition to defect tracking, the quality of a release can be measured by how many times the project must deviate from normal processes and standards. A project deviation report shows whether the release project adheres to corporate standards in areas such as architecture, design, and project management. There may be perfectly good reasons not to use the standards, but a project that strays too far from the standard project and architecture practices probably will run into trouble.

Reports About the Release Management Process

It is important that you have some measurements in place to evaluate the effectiveness of every IT process, and release management is no exception. Especially if release management is a relatively new discipline for your organization, it will be helpful to know if the process is maturing and you are achieving the expected benefits from it. This section describes a set of reports you can use to evaluate the release management process.

Figure 16.5 shows release management metrics.

Release Metrics Reports

DML Tracking Report
Failed Change Report
Deployment Velocity Report
Customer Satisfaction Survey
Plan versus Actual Reports

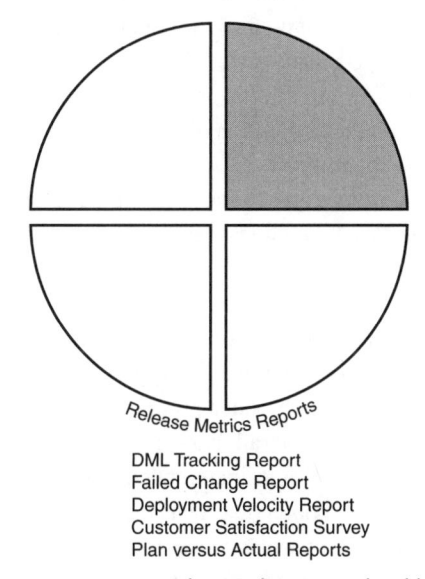

Figure 16.5 Release management metrics track process health.

Deployment Reports

Tracking the deployment component of release management is relatively easy. You can use a variety of good metrics, and you will most likely be able to think of many more. Actually, the difficult part is sorting out useful reports from all the reports you can create.

One extremely useful report is a definitive media library tracking report. It shows how many times software from the library is used. This is a good indication that your deployment activity is gaining the consistency and speed that are made possible with the DML. If the definitive media library is not being used much, even though you know that software is being deployed frequently, you might have a process breakage that could cause random versions of software to be deployed, resulting in significant configuration management issues.

The failed change report is also a good way to measure your deployment maturity. Because deployment is a release management activity, you should look at the failed change report as a way to measure the quality of your execution. Of course, not all failures are failures of execution, which is why you should also look at the failed change report to understand where your release management planning can be improved.

Another good way to understand whether your deployment capability is maturing is by looking at how quickly you can deploy a package across dozens, hundreds, or even thousands of machines. A deployment velocity report shows the number of deployments of a release by week, or by month for a larger deployment. Of course, the data is relevant only for releases that are built and tested once and then deployed many times. Examples might include an operating system patch that must be installed on all your servers, or a desktop office suite that is being rolled out to every user. When you find this kind of situation, the deployment velocity report tells you a great deal about your deployment capability. If you cannot role out the next version of your e-mail client faster than you rolled out the current version, you need to spend some time and energy improving the deployment aspect of your release management service.

Planning Reports

Although managing an individual release is a lot like managing any other project, managing a release package and planning across releases are very much like managing an IT portfolio. The service manager must look out for the broader program by making sure that each release has value on its own and builds toward the overall value of the release package. The service architect must imagine the end technology and find incremental ways to add some technology to each release to achieve that final vision. Reports that focus on the planning aspects of release management measure the effectiveness of the service manager and service architect.

Customer satisfaction is a key measurement of release planning. All service managers should identify the customer set they expect their releases to serve and survey a sampling of them regularly. These surveys measure whether the releases are really providing the expected value to your organization and whether the customers are happy with the frequency and content of the releases. Most organizations find a customer satisfaction survey to be an extremely useful tool, and release management is another place they can be used.

Any release management reports that show plans versus actual attainment can also be used to understand the health of your release planning process. If you find that releases consistently overrun their budget, for example, you may have service managers and service architects who don't understand the real costs of projects. Project overruns are a very frustrating situation for both IT and business management, because they usually result in requests for "emergency" or unplanned requests for additional funding.

If your releases frequently miss their quality goals, perhaps the schedule is too limited and people are sacrificing quality to make dates. You can infer many useful things from comparing actual project results to the original plans for those projects.

Looking Ahead

Reporting is a favorite topic among many IT managers because reports are extremely useful. They can help you analyze the efficiency of the operational environment or help you determine the maturity of an entire process. In this chapter, you have seen how reports can be used to improve your change and release management processes. In the next chapter, you will see that linking processes creates even more opportunities for process improvement and maturity.

CHAPTER 17

Linking to Other Processes

Perhaps the most significant benefit you will gain from implementing ITIL is the close linkages of processes to one another. If this doesn't sound very intriguing, especially if you don't see how this will help your financial bottom line, read on!

Linking processes makes IT more efficient. Linking processes provides cohesion and direction that turn your IT cost center into a set of unified and logical services that your organization needs. Linking processes even helps eliminate problems before they occur, improving the productivity of everyone in your organization who relies on IT.

This chapter describes the many linkages between change management, release management, and other ITIL processes. Along with understanding how each linkage can be made, you will learn how making the linkage benefits your organization.

The danger of talking about process linkage is that some assumptions about the processes are necessary. For the sake of this chapter, the basic working assumption is that you are in the process of implementing the full suite of processes in the ITIL framework and that you are aligning those processes with the best practices defined by ITIL.

If you need to link to processes that are not aligned with ITIL, at best you will be able to modify those processes to at least have the interface points described in this chapter. Integrating ITIL change and release management with other processes that are not aligned with the ITIL framework may be difficult. A good first step is to make those other process look as much like ITIL aligned processes as you can.

Some Other Connections to Consider

Many ITIL practitioners cannot decide whether configuration management or change management should sit at the center of the ITIL universe. More than anything else, this is because the linkage between change management and configuration management is so close that it is very difficult to imagine one without the other. Throughout this book, you have seen hints about the relationship between these two critical processes, but here you will see how to make that relationship real for your organization.

Process Linkage

This book has pointed out the process links between change management and configuration management. Each time you make a change in the IT environment, you either change some tangible thing such as hardware, software, or documentation, or you are changing some intangible thing such as a service, process, or organization. Whether tangible or not, the thing you are changing is a configuration item. Most organizations seeking to implement ITIL quickly document a policy that no configuration item can be changed without a corresponding change record.

The link between change management and configuration management is bidirectional, as shown in Figure 17.1. Each process depends on the other, or it cannot operate. It would be very difficult to request, review, approve, or implement a change without knowing what would change. It is also impossible to maintain accurate configuration information without some way to understand the changes to the environment.

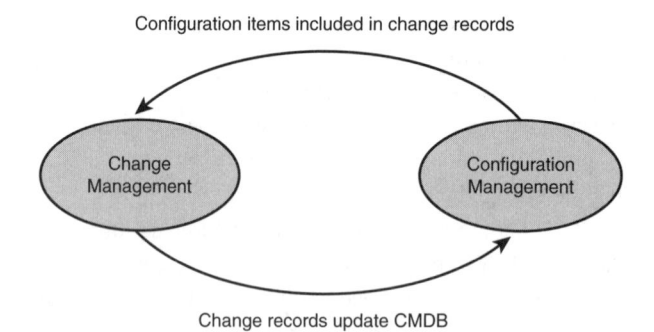

Figure 17.1 Change management and configuration management support one another.

Because of this great dependency of the processes on one another, forming the link between them is somewhat challenging. If you have implemented change management but do not yet have a CMDB, you probably will not have a solid way to associate that tangible or intangible item to a change record. In this case, you are forced to use another database, such as the IT asset repository, or to describe the thing that is changing in a text description inside the change record.

Populating the CMDB can take some number of weeks or even months. During this time, you need to gradually transition your change management process to using configuration items in place of whatever substitute was devised. One way to do that is to seed the CMDB with one row for every kind of CI you will ever create. You enter one server, one application software package, one router, one document, one process, one service, and so on. Because you are simply entering one row for each type, this can be accomplished very quickly. But because you have one valid row for each type, you can have change management users begin tying the appropriate records to their changes.

Of course, you still have to describe in the text change record which item of the given category will be changed until the specific items are populated. In other words, you need to choose "Server" as the configuration item to associate with the change, but in the text of the change, you can enter the actual server name. As your CMDB population project moves along, you can remind users to start entering the actual row instead of the "dummy" row that you seeded initially. When the population of a specific category of configuration items is complete, you can even remove the initial dummy row as long as you're willing to update all the change records that used it to have valid values.

Data Linkage

The data links between configuration management and change management are clear. Each change record must have at least one configuration item associated with it to point to what is being changed. Each configuration item should be tied to each of the change records that modified it so that you can get an accurate history of what happened to that item.

Fortunately, most available integrated service management suites handle this data integration for you. If you are not using an integrated suite, you may have to build this integration yourself. If so, the crucial data elements are the configuration ID and the change record number. These elements must exist in both the configuration management system and the change management tool and must use the same naming convention in both places for the data to integrate well.

When considering the data and tools that will tie together configuration and change management, it is important to think about how that data will be used. Be sure your change management tool has a search capability that can find the appropriate configuration item while the user is creating a change record. If the user needs to leave the change record and go look up a configuration item number in another tool, there is a high probability that she will put only the one required configuration item into the change record instead of really thinking through all the different items that are being changed. Tools that are too difficult to use cause people to take shortcuts, hurting the quality of the processes you are trying to integrate.

Benefits of Integration

You can gain several benefits from integrating change management and configuration management. Configuration management seeks to understand your complete IT environment, whereas change management controls the pace and scope of the changes made in your environment. Together, configuration and change management can offer a very good basis for controlling the entire environment.

When each change record indicates precisely what is being changed and each change record results in an update to the CMDB, you can have great confidence that the CMDB reflects the actual state of your environment rather than the state that existed when you first populated the CMDB. Change control keeps the CMDB updated throughout the normal operational cycles that every environment goes through. Without change control, the CMDB would never be accurate.

Adding the configuration management disciplines of spot checking and data auditing will allow you to understand instances in which change control is not being followed. This is crucial, because change management alone is solid only as long as everyone follows the process. By including configuration management, you can tell when people are not following the process and thus make your change control even stronger.

Linking Changes to Incident Management

Although change management and configuration management form the heart of ITIL, it is change management and incident management that are at the core of IT operations. Long before ITIL was imagined, every IT organization in the world had to define a way to deal with fixing problems and making changes. In the long-ago days when mainframe computers dominated the landscape, most organizations ran IBM's Information Management (InfoMan) product. It featured the ability to record and manage incidents (or problems, as they were called in those days) and changes. With this much history, it should come as no surprise that incident management and change management are very closely related, with many well-developed interfaces between them.

Process Linkage

The incident management process and the change management process have two key relationships between them. These relationships have matured over the years, and most organizations have implemented them to some extent. With the introduction of ITIL change management, you have a great opportunity to revisit the relationship with incident management and optimize any integration you may already have in place.

The first relationship between change management and incident management is that many incidents are resolved by making changes. For example, if a server is running slowly, an incident record is opened. Through the incident management procedures of isolation and determination, you might discover that a network card has failed, causing the operating system to respond very slowly to requests, thus slowing the entire server. At this point, the incident management team invokes change management to schedule a time to replace the card. The incident is resolved with the implementation of the change.

The second relationship between change and incident is that changes occasionally spawn incidents. When a change implementation fails and the backout plan cannot be successfully executed, a service disruption occurs. By definition, every disruption of service is an incident, so the failed change has effectively created an incident. Although this kind of incident should be avoided, it would be naïve not to prepare for it.

Linking the change management process with the incident management process integrates the two components of operations, as shown in Figure 17.2. IT operation consists of the active process of changing the environment (change management) and the passive process of resolving issues as they occur (incident management). These two halves are linked when change management and incident management are integrated.

Linking Changes to Incident Management

Incidents get resolved by changes

Change Management → **Incident Management**

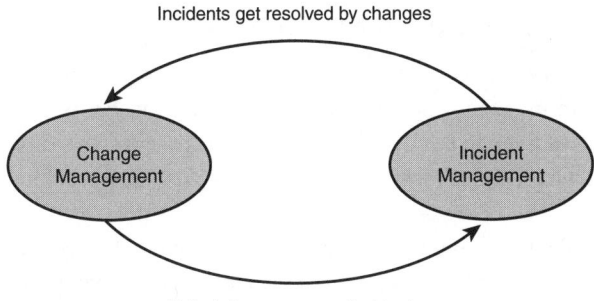

Failed changes cause incidents

Figure 17.2 Change management and incident management are key operational disciplines.

Data Linkage

From the perspective of data, incident management and change management are relatively easy to integrate. Both the change management system and the incident ticketing system have record numbers. You can use the incident identifier within the change system and the change identifier within the incident system to connect the data records.

It is also relatively easy to transition to an integrated change and incident management system. Assuming that you already have an incident system in place when you begin tracking change records, you only need to modify that system to allow association of change records with an incident. Of course, your new change management system will be created to accommodate incident record numbers.

Benefits of Integration

Many technical team members fail to see the benefits of integrating incident and problem management processes. They reason that fixing an incident immediately must be faster than waiting for the change management process to review and approve the proposed fix. In addition, most technical people will not want to announce their failed change.

At a management level, however, this integration has significant benefits. It allows better tracking of incident resolutions, because the change records record details that normally are left out of the incident record, such as an implementation plan and backout plan. Creating a change record to resolve an incident causes people outside of the immediate incident resolution team to get involved. This is helpful because new points of view can often help define a solution that is faster to implement or that will resolve an ongoing problem.

Not all failed changes will result in incidents, because most of the time the change will be backed out successfully. When the environment cannot be recovered, however, creating an incident record has benefits. New points of view can help here as well, because a technician who has an ongoing issue all through the change implementation window may be out of ideas about how to fix it. The incident resolution team can bring new ideas and hopefully get the situation resolved. Also, the incident management process is specifically optimized to resolve incidents quickly. Opening the incident record ensures that the situation spurred by the change gets resolved as quickly as possible.

Linking Changes to Problem Management

Problem management is an area of ITIL that confuses many newcomers. Actually, it is the difference between problem management and incident management that is confusing, because most organizations are accustomed to treating these as the same process. In simplistic ITIL terms, incident management is what happens when something is broken, and problem management is what you do to make sure it doesn't break again.

Given this simple definition, the linkage between change management and problem management is extremely important. When problem management uncovers actions that can stop outages from occurring, it usually implements those actions through change management. This section explores the linkage between problem and change management.

Process Linkage

As just mentioned, the change management process is used to take actions that spring from problem investigations. Imagine that an application in your environment locks up occasionally, with users unable to log in via the web page, but already authenticated users continuing to work. Each time this has happened, the incident management team has rebooted the web server and found that the issue was resolved, but it keeps happening. It is time to move past mere incident management into problem management.

You convene a team to investigate what is causing this application to continue to have issues, and that team determines that the root cause is a faulty memory chip in the web server. The problem management discipline documents the root cause and then documents an action item to replace the memory in the server. This is where change management comes in. The problem management team records a request for change (RFC), and the change management process takes over to review and authorize the change needed to resolve the problem. When the change is implemented successfully and all other action items are completed, the original problem record can be closed. This integration between the change and problem management processes is illustrated in Figure 17.3.

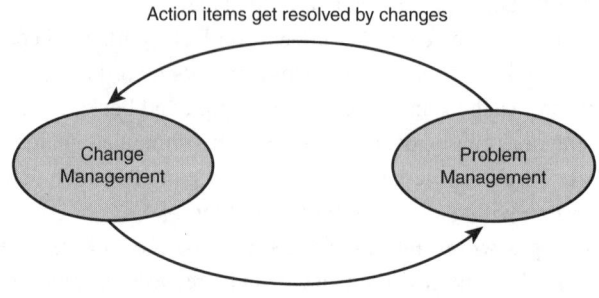

Figure 17.3 Change management is used to resolve action items in the problem management process.

Data Linkage

From a data perspective, the linkage between change management and problem management is not as straightforward as the links from change to configuration and incident management. It would not make sense to put a change record number into a problem record directly, because the problem may have multiple root causes, and each root cause might have multiple corrective actions.

Instead, the change record is put into the corrective action item directly. Unfortunately, not all popular problem management tools or IT service management suites can track action items as records separate from the problem record. If yours does, this integration is fairly easy. If not, you should probably institute some mechanism for tracking action items, such as a spreadsheet or a separate table in your configuration management system. Your integration would then be to that separate tool, not to the problem records themselves.

On the reverse side, you can do one of two things. It might make sense to put the problem record number into the change ticket to indicate which problem is being repaired by the change. On the other hand, you can get more granular and put the identifier of the specific action item into the change record to allow more detailed tracking.

Benefits of Integration

Integrating change management with problem management makes sense only if you are implementing all the ITIL processes. If your definition of problem management encompasses both fixing the issue and making sure it doesn't reoccur (the definition used by many organizations for years), the integration between change management and incident management will suffice.

However, if you plan to fully deploy ITIL problem management as a way to see trends, understand root causes, and stop issues from happening, it makes sense to integrate your action items with change management. When you create this integration point, action items get reviewed and tracked to closure, and failed closures can be highlighted. In short, all the things that are good about the change management process do not need to be duplicated in problem management to deal with action items.

A weakness of many problem management implementations is that root causes get defined but nothing is ever done to fix them. Or perhaps the action items to fix root causes are defined, but then ignored. By integrating problem management with change management, you make these action items much more difficult to ignore.

Linking Release Management and Capacity Management

Lest you think that change management is the only process integrated with the rest of ITIL, this section explores the linkage between release and deployment management and the ITIL discipline of capacity management. Capacity management is the ITIL process of ensuring that resources are available when needed and that you don't have too many resources sitting idle at any time. As it turns out, capacity planning and release management are closely related.

Process Linkage

When planning a release, you must consider many things. Each release should have a set of requirements defined, both for what it will do and for what it will be. The requirements for what a release must do are called functional requirements, and those for what it must be are nonfunctional requirements. Typically nonfunctional requirements cover all the "-ilities," such as availability, reliability, manageability, and so forth. One of the nonfunctional requirements that should be included in each release plan is the capacity that the release must support.

If you have followed the advice given in Chapter 13, "Defining Release Packages," you will have release packages for all your major business applications. The same scope is perfect for a capacity plan. Although a server's amount of disk space or CPU horsepower may be interesting to IT, the business people care about how many transactions their retail store application can process or how many design drawings their CAD system can hold. So each major business application should have a capacity plan in which capacity is measured in terms of the units of business work that can be accomplished.

So the linkage between release management and capacity management comes in the planning phase, where the release plan should specify exactly what it will do to the application's capacity plan. Without appropriate planning, it is common for a later release to actually have less capacity than the earlier release because of a phenomenon known as "code bloat." The new features and functions add more code, which slows down the servers that host the application, making the overall system capable of less processing than it could handle previously. By explicitly defining the capacity needs of the overall application as part of your release planning efforts, you can avoid subtracting capacity when you roll out a new release.

Release deployment is also linked to capacity management in the testing stage. Because you have defined capacity requirements, you should test the business capacity of the new release. This testing is sometimes done through stressing the system by simulating lots of users, or it can be done through modeling tools that estimate capacity based on how the system runs. Either way, your testing activity within release management should be integrated with capacity management to ensure that the deployed system will have at least as much capacity as the one it is replacing. Figure 17.4 shows the interplay between release management and capacity management.

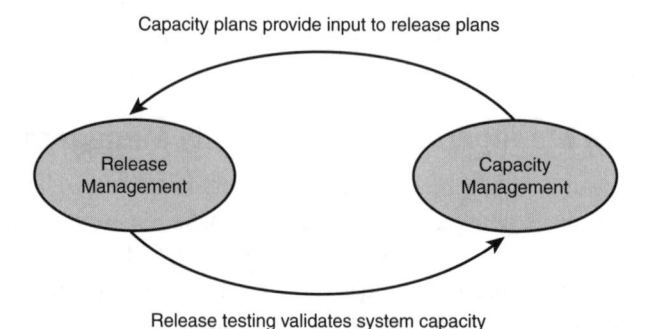

Figure 17.4 Capacity should be taken into account in both planning and testing a release.

Benefits of Integration

Capacity management alone can help your IT organization go from chaotic to highly functional. When coupled with release management, capacity management can virtually eliminate the nasty surprises that often happen with new releases.

By establishing a capacity plan for each of your business applications, and then looking out for the plan during release planning, you can guarantee that your users will not see slowdowns or blockages when the new release goes live. Instead of chasing capacity problems after the system has gone into full production, you can shake them out during testing and find ways to eliminate them. Building this kind of foresight into your release plans will make your "go live" events much less eventful.

Some Other Connections to Consider

This chapter has given some examples of the benefits you can get from integrating change and release management with your other IT processes. One of the strongest aspects of ITIL is the integration of all its individual parts. It is truly a framework of interdependent pieces rather than a mere collection of parts. Rather than create a complete catalog of all integrations, this section simply highlights a few other possible linkages that you can implement as your change and release management processes mature.

You can link change management to service-level management. In ITIL, service-level management is about controlling the quality of service to your non-IT organizations. As part of business and technical impact analysis, you can indicate which service levels are likely to be different as the result of an implemented change. This linkage will help you manage expectations as you work to improve service levels or as you are forced to take steps that will degrade them!

It is possible to tie release management to availability management in much the same way it can be linked with capacity management. In addition to a capacity plan, each of your business applications should have an availability plan. It should show not only the hours the application is scheduled to be available, but also what contingency measures can be put in place should the service suddenly be unavailable. Just like the capacity plan, this availability plan should be updated when planning a new release and validated when testing a release.

Release management can also be tied to service continuity management, the ITIL discipline of planning for the completely unexpected. Your service continuity plan should indicate how and with what priority each service will be restored in the event of a major disrupting factor. Like capacity plans and availability plans, these service continuity plans should be updated with every new release plan. Service continuity tests should also include some of the test cases used to test the latest releases of applications.

Another significant process area in ITIL is financial management, which includes understanding and allocating the costs of IT. Change management plays a significant part in driving IT costs, so linking change management to financial management makes perfect sense. A part of the change review should be estimating the impact of the change on the cost of the particular service that is changing. The work needed to accomplish changes can be allocated back to the department or business unit requesting that change.

Security management is a critical process for every organization today. Each change to the IT environment has the potential to introduce new security vulnerabilities, close out known vulnerabilities, or perhaps both. The change management process should be tightly coupled with security management processes both to screen for potential vulnerabilities that might be introduced and to help close as many gaps as possible in the IT environment.

Looking Ahead

Hopefully this smattering of integration possibilities has helped you understand that change and release management have a key role to play in managing your IT services. They link with virtually every other process, and these linkages create significant benefits that change and release management cannot deliver alone.

Although they are often seen as utilitarian processes, change and release management are the primary controlling processes in the ITIL framework. A weak implementation of these two processes will cause grief, because the environment will slowly drift toward anarchy. A solid implementation, however, can be the cornerstone of a revitalized IT function that will demonstrate its value to the organization many times over. Fortunately, you have now learned everything you need to implement these two key processes on a very solid foundation indeed.

Index

A

accessing legacy data, 86-87
acquiring software, tracking versions in DML, 148
adding
    data tasks to data migration plans, 58
    value to new fields, legacy data, 87-88
administrative changes, work flows, 45
agendas, process workshops, 98-99
allocating requirements to projects, 23-24
alternatives, evaluating (choosing tools based on trade studies), 81
analyzing requirements, 52
application software, software stacks (release packages), 154-155
approval processes, change management, 35-36
architecture, features of change and release management tools, 78-79
archiving aged data 90
assembling FSC, 139
    automating FSC creation process, 140
    multilevel FSC for multilevel CABs, 140-141
asset reuse repositories, 74
assigning requirements proper roles, 52
audit posture, improving with DML, 151
audit programs, building, 171
auditing, 169-171
authorization, processes (change management), 35-36
authorization decisions, business impact analysis and CABs, 183
availability management, 207

B

balancing, requirements, 25
benefits of implementing change and release management, 9-10
    collaboration, 11-12
    confidence, 12
    consistency, 11
    control, 10-11
best practices for deploying new IT processes, 105
    certifying key staff, 105-106
    evaluation and adjustments, 107
    measurements, 106-107
bundled changes, processes (release management), 38-39
business impact analysis, 175
    business impacts, 176-177
    CABs, 182
        authorization decisions, 183
        project decisions, 183

scheduling decisions, 182-183
determining business impact, 177-179
technical impacts, 176
business impacts
business impact analysis, 176-177
determining, 177-179
recording in change records, 179-181
business organization based pilot programs, 113
business requirements, 16

C

CAB (change advisory board) meetings, 12
CABs (change advisory boards), 135
business impact analysis, 182-183
capacity management, linking to release management, 205
benefits of integration, 207
process links, 206
certifying staff for deployment of new IT processes, 105-106
change advisory board (CAB) meetings, 12
change advisory boards. *See* CABs
change aging reports, 190
change and release data, merging, 93-95
change and release management tools
data integration points, 75-76
features to look for, 77
architecture, 78-79
data models, 79

integration, 80
user interfaces, 77-78
work flow, 79-80
ideal tools, 76
process integration points, 74-75
tool integration points, 76
change approvers, 101
change categories
data center changes, 42
data changes, 44
documentation or administrative changes, 45
work flows, 41
workstation changes, 43
change detection and compliance tools, 69-70
change evaluators, 101
change implementers, 101
change management, 6-9
control points, 166-168
integrating schedules with release management, 141-142
measurements, 124-127
optimizing with DML, 149
consistency of deployment, 150
helping the sunset problem, 150-151
improving audit posture, 151
processes, 31-32
approval and authorization, 35-36
documenting request for change (RFC), 34-35
policies, 33-34
post-implementation review, 36-37
reviews and impact assessment, 35

release management and, 6-7
business benefits of, 9-12
tools for, 67-68
change detection and compliance tools, 69-70
dedicated change management tools, 69
integrated service management tools, 68
work flows. *See* work flows
change management process, reports, 189
change aging reports, 190
changes by lead time, 191-192
failed change reports, 190-191
change management roles, 101
change managers, 101
change records, 126
FSC, 138
recording business impact, 179
impact assessments and relationships, 181
impact assessments as data fields, 180-181
impact assessments as text, 180
change reports, 186
change statistics, 188-189
changes by components, 188
changes by implementer, 187
changes by requesters, 187-188
change requesters, 101

Index

change reviewers, 125
change urgency, work flows, 45
   emergency changes, 45-46
   long, complex changes, 47-48
   normal changes, 47
   urgent changes, 47
changes
   linking to configuration management, 199
      benefits of integration, 201-202
      data links, 201
      linking processes, 200-201
   linking to incident management, 202
      benefits of integration, 203
      data links, 203
      process links, 202-203
   linking to problem management, 204-205
changes by lead time report, 191-192
choosing pilot programs, 112-114
choosing tools based on trade studies, 80-82
CI (configuration item), 176
CMDB (configuration management database), 34, 69, 176
collaboration, benefits of implementing change and release management, 11-12
comma-separated value (CSV) files, 87
complex changes, work flows, 47-48
compliance documentation, 167-168
compliance management, 70
component requirements, 17
components, change reports, 188
confidence, benefits of implementing change and release management, 12
configuration items (CI), 34, 127, 176
configuration management, linking changes to, 199
   benefits of integration, 201-202
   data links, 201
   linking processes, 200-201
configuration management database (CMDB), 34, 69, 176
consistency, benefits of implementing change and release management, 11
consistency of deployment, optimizing change management with DML, 150
consolidating data, 90-91
   forming new data records, 93
   identifying common keys, 91
   reconciling data values, 92
   tasks for, 58
contents of DML, 146
control, benefits of implementing change and release management, 10-11
control points, 164-165
   controlling changes, 166-168
   guidelines for, 165-166
   implementing, 165
controlling changes across control points, 166-168
converting data values, legacy data, 88
CSV (comma-separated value) files, 87
customer satisfaction, release planning, 196

D

data
   change and release data, merging, 93-95
   consolidating, 90-91
      forming new data records, 93
      identifying common keys, 91
      reconciling data values, 92
data audits, 170
data center changes, work flows, 42
data changes, work flows, 44
data fields, impact assessments as, 180-181
data integration points, change and release management tools, 75-76
data links
   linking changes to configuration management, 201
   linking changes to incident management, 203
   linking changes to problem management, 205
data migration, planning, 56
   adding data tasks, 58
   tasks for, 56-57
   tasks for data consolidation, 58
data models, features of change and release management tools, 79
data records, forming new, 93

data retention policies, 89
  archiving aged data, 90
data values
  converting, legacy data, 88
  reconciling, 92
dedicated change management tools, 69
defining requirement priorities, 22-23
Definitive Media Library. *See* DML
dependencies, building, 53-55
deploying new IT processes, best practices for, 105-107
deploying new IT products, implementation axis
  geographic implementation, 123
  organizational implementation, 121-122
  technology implementation, 123-124
deployment reports, release management process, 195-196
derived requirements, 19
deriving requirements, 19-21
designing release packages, 158-160
discovering requirements, 17-19
  interviews, 18
  legacy projects, 19
  requirements workshops, 17-18
distributed DMLs, building, 144-145
DML (Definitive Media Library), 143
  building distributed DMLs, 144-145
  contents of, 146
  logical aspects of, 144
  optimizing change management, 149-151
  physical aspects of, 144
  purpose of, 146
  tracking versions
    acquiring new software, 148
    lending software, 149
    replacing lost media, 149
    retiring software packages, 148-149
  using, 147
documentation, defining processes, 30
documentation changes, work flows, 45
documenting request for change (RFC), change management, 34-35

E

elicited requirements, 19
emergency changes, work flows, 45-46
end-of-life cycle, processes (release management), 39
establishing weighting, 81
  choosing tools based on trade studies, 81
estimating task sizes, requirements, 53
evaluating
  alternatives, choosing tools based on trade studies, 81
  pilot programs, 116-117
external audits, 171

F

failed change reports, 190-191
failure of pilot programs, 117-118
features of change and release management tools, 77
  architecture, 78-79
  data models, 79
  integration, 80
  user interfaces, 77-78
  work flow, 79-80
fields, adding new values to (legacy data), 87-88
financial management, 207
forming new data records, 93
FSC (forward schedule of change), 135
  assembling, 139
    automating FSC creation processes, 140
    multilevel FSC for multilevel CABs, 140-141
  change records, 138
  determining what information to include in each change, 137-138
  determining which changes to include, 135-137
  versus release road maps, 142
  timing issues, 138-139

G

geographic implementation, implementation axis, 123
geographically based pilot programs, 112-113
guidelines
  for control points, 165-166
  for release package designs, 158-160

Index

H

hardware, software stacks (release packages), 157-158

I

ideal tools, change and release management tools, 76
identifying policies, defining processes, 29
IMAC (Install, Move, Add, and Change), 43
impact assessment, processes (change management), 35
impact on business. *See* business impact analysis
implementation axis, 121
　geographic implementation, 123
　organizational implementation, 121-122
　technology implementation, 123-124
implementation problems, 130-131
implementers, changes by, 187
implementing
　control points, 165
　tools, 59-61
improving audit posture (optimizing change management with DML), 151
incident management, linking changes to, 202
　benefits of integration, 203
　data links, 203
　process links, 202-203
incident records, 126
Information Technology Infrastructure Library. *See* ITIL
infrastructure release flow, 49

Install, Move, Add, and Change (IMAC), 43
integrated service management tools, 68
integrating change and release management schedules, 141-142
integrating operations
　data integration points, 75-76
　ideal tool, 76
　process integration points, 74-75
　tool integration points, 76
integration
　benefits of
　　linking changes to configuration management, 201-202
　　linking changes to incident management, 203
　　linking changes to problem management, 205
　　linking release management to capacity management, 207
　features of change and release management tools, 80
integration points
　data integration points, 75-76
　ideal tools, 76
　process integration points, 74-75
　tool integration points, 76
integration project release, 50
internal audits, 171
interviews, discovering requirements, 18

ITIL (Information Technology Infrastructure Library), 3
　overview of, 3-4
　service management life cycle, 4-5
　service operations, 6
　service transitions, 5-6
ITIL volume, service management life cycle, 5

J

judging, choosing tools based on trade studies, 82

K

keys, consolidating data, 91

L

legacy data, accessing, 86-87
legacy projects, discovering requirements, 19
legacy systems, migrating, 85
　accessing legacy data, 86-87
　adding values to new fields, 87-88
　converting data values, 88
　unclosed records, 88-89
lending software, tracking versions in DML, 149
license management systems, DML, 147
linking
　changes to configuration management, 199
　　benefits of integration, 201-202
　　data links, 201
　　linking processes, 200-201

changes to incident management, 202-203
changes to problem management, 204-205
processes, 199
release management and capacity management, 205-207
logical aspects of DML, 144

M

managing requirements, 13, 21
   allocating to projects, 23-24
   defining priorities, 22-23
   requirements documents, creating, 21-22
mapping tables, 92
measurements, 124, 129
   change management measurements, 124-127
   for deployment of new IT processes, 106-107
   release management measurements, 127-128
   timing and productivity measurements, 128-129
measuring pilot programs, 114-115
media, replacing lost media (tracking versions in DML), 149
merging change and release data, 93
   configuration items, 94-95
middleware, software stacks (release packages), 155-156
migrating legacy systems, 85
   accessing legacy data, 86-87
   adding values to new fields, 87-88
   converting data values, 88
   unclosed records, 88-89

N

normal changes, work flows, 47

O

operating systems, software stacks (release packages), 156-157
optimizing change management with DML, 149-151
organizational implementation, implementation axis, 121-122
organizations, 100
   change management roles, 101
   release management roles, 101-102
   staffing roles, 102-103
   training, 103
      delivering training, 104-105
      preparing training materials, 103-104

P

parsers, accessing legacy data, 86
participation, process workshops, 98
patch management tools, 73
physical aspects of DML, 144
pilot programs, 109-110
   choosing, 112-114
      business organizations, 113
      geography, 112-113
      technology, 113
   dealing with failure of, 117-118
   evaluating, 116-117
   measuring, 114-115
   reasons for using, 110-112
   running, 115-116
planning
   projects. *See* project planning
   reports, release management process, 196
policies
   data retention, 89
      archiving aged data, 90
   defining processes, 29
   processes, change management, 33-34
post-implementation review, processes (change management), 36-37
prioritizing requirements, 21
   allocating requirements to projects, 23-24
   defining priorities, 22-23
   requirements documents, creating, 21-22
problem management, linking changes to, 204
   benefits of integration, 205
   data links, 205
   process links, 204
problems with implementation, 130-131
procedures, defining processes, 30
process audits, 169-170
process flow, defining processes, 28-29
process integration points, change and release management tools, 74-75

Index

process links
  linking changes to
    configuration management, 200-201
    incident management, 202-203
    problem management, 204
  linking release management to capacity management, 206
process requirements, 16
process workshops, 97
  agendas and purpose of, 98-99
  expected workshop outcomes, 100
  participation, 98
processes
  change management, 31-32
    approval and authorization, 35-36
    documenting request for change (RFC), 34-35
    policies, 33-34
    post-implementation review, 36-37
    reviews and impact assessment, 35
  defining, 27
    documenting work instructions, 30
    identifying needed policies, 29
    procedures, creating, 30
    process flow, 28-29
  linking, 199
  release and deployment management, 32-33
  release management, 37
    release policies, 38
    release unit identification, 37-38
    releases or bundled changes, 38-39
    support and the end-of-life cycle, 39
  subprocesses, 29
productivity measurements, 129
project decisions, business impact analysis and CABs, 183
project management reports, 193-194
project planning, 51
  building complete project plans, 62-63
  building dependencies, 53-55
  completing the first draft, 54-55
  data migration, 56
    tasks for, 56-57
    tasks for data consolidation, 58
  estimating task sizes, 53
  requirements, turning into tasks, 51-53
promotion and deployment tools, 72-73
provisioning tools, 72

Q

quality management reports, 194

R

reconciling data values, 92
recording business impact in change records, 179
  impact assessments and relationships, 181
  impact assessments as data fields, 180-181
  impact assessments as text, 180
records, unclosed records (legacy data), 88-89
regulations, release management, 168-169
relationships, impact assessments and, 181
release and deployment management, processes, 32-33
release engineers, 102
release management, 6-8
  change management and, 6-7
  business benefits of, 9-12
  integrating schedules with change management, 141-142
  linking to capacity management, 205
    benefits of integration, 207
    process links, 206
  measurements, 127-128
  processes, 37
    release policies, 38
    release unit identification, 37-38
    releases or bundled changes, 38-39
    support and end-of-life cycle, 39
  regulations, 168-169

tools for, 70
  asset reuse
    repositories, 74
  patch management
    tools, 73
  promotion and deployment tools, 72-73
  software control
    tools, 72
  work flow tools, 71
work flows, 48
  infrastructure release
    flow, 49
  integration project
    release, 50
  software development
    flow, 48-49
release management process,
  reports, 195
  deployment reports,
    195-196
  planning reports, 196
release management roles,
  101-102
release managers, 102
release packages, 74
  guidelines for design,
    158-160
  software stacks, 153-154
    application software,
      154-155
    hardware, 157-158
    middleware, 155-156
    operating systems,
      156-157
  using, 161
release policies, processes
  (release management), 38
release reports, 192
  project management
    reports, 193-194
  quality management
    reports, 194

system engineering
  reports, 193
release road maps, versus
  FSC, 142
release unit identification,
  processes (release management), 37-38
releases, processes (release
  management), 38-39
replacing lost media, tracking
  versions in DML, 149
reports
  change management
    process, 189
    change aging
      reports, 190
    changes by lead time,
      191-192
    failed change reports,
      190-191
  change reports, 186
    change statistics,
      188-189
    changes by components, 188
    changes by implementer, 187
    changes by requesters,
      187-188
  release management
    process, 195
    deployment reports,
      195-196
    planning reports, 196
  release reports, 192
    project management
      reports, 193-194
    quality management
      reports, 194
    system engineering
      reports, 193

request for change (RFC),
  processes (change management), 34-35
requesters, changes by,
  187-188
requirements, 13, 51
  allocating to projects,
    23-24
  analyzing, 52
  balancing, 25
  choosing tools based on
    trade studies, 81
  derived requirements, 19
  deriving, 19-21
  discovering, 17-19
    interviews, 18
    legacy projects, 19
    requirements workshops, 17-18
  elicited requirements, 19
  estimating task sizes, 53
  prioritizing and
    managing, 21
    allocating requirements
      to projects, 23-24
    defining priorities,
      22-23
    requirements documents, creating, 21-22
  reasons for having, 13-14
  turning into tasks, 51-53
  types of, 15
    business
      requirements, 16
    component requirements, 17
    process
      requirements, 16
    system requirements,
      16-17
requirements documents,
  creating, 21-22

Index

requirements workshops, 17-18
retiring software
   optimizing change management with DML, 150-151
   tracking versions in DML, 148-149
reviews, processes (change management), 35-37
RFC (request for change), documenting (change management), 34-35
roles
   change management roles, 101
   release management roles, 101-102
   staffing roles, 102-103
running pilot programs, 115-116

S

schedules
   integrating change and release management, 141-142
   vendor release schedules, 160
scheduling decisions, business impact analysis and CABs, 182-183
scoring, choosing tools based on trade studies, 82
security management, 208
service architects, 102
service continuity management, 207
service design volume, service management life cycle, 4
service-level management, 207
service management life cycle, ITIL, 4-5
service management suites, 68
service managers, 102
service operation volume, service management life cycle, 4
service operations, ITIL, 6
service strategy volume, service management life cycle, 4
service transition volume, service management life cycle, 4
service transitions, 7
   ITIL, 5-6
software, tracking versions in DML
   acquiring new software, 148
   lending software, 149
   retiring software packages, 148-149
software configuration management systems, 146
software control tools, 72
software development flow, 48-49
software stacks, release packages, 153-154
   application software, 154-155
   hardware, 157-158
   middleware, 155-156
   operating systems, 156-157
staffing roles, 102-103
statistics, change reports, 188-189
subprocesses, 29
support, processes (release management), 39
system engineering reports, 193
system requirements, 16-17

T

tasks
   for acquisition, implementing tools, 59-60
   for customization, implementing tools, 60-61
   for data consolidation, 58
   for data migration, 56-57
   data tasks, adding to data migration plan, 58
   estimating task sizes, requirements for, 53
   for planning, implementing tools, 59
   for training, implementing tools, 61
   turning requirements into, 51-53
teams. *See* organizations
technical impacts, business impact analysis, 176
technology-based pilot programs, 113
technology implementation, implementation axis, 123-124
testing release package designs, 159-160
text, impact assessments as, 180
timing and productivity measurements, 128-129
timing issues, FSC, 138-139
tool integration points, change and release management tools, 76

tools
  asset reuse repositories, 74
  change detection and compliance tools, 69-70
  for change management, 67-70
  choosing based on trade studies, 80-82
  implementing, 59
    tasks for acquisition, 59-60
    tasks for customization, 60-61
    tasks for planning, 59
    tasks for training, 61
  integrated service management tools, 68-69
  patch management tools, 73
  promotion and deployment tools, 72-73
  provisioning tools, 72
  for release management, 70
    asset reuse repositories, 74
    patch management tools, 73
    promotion and deployment tools, 72-73
    software control tools, 72
    work flow tools, 71
  software control tools, 72
  work flow tools, 71
traceability, 23
tracking versions in DML
  acquiring new software, 148
  lending software, 149
  replacing lost media, 149
  retiring software packages, 148-149

training materials, preparing, 103-104
training organizations, 103
  delivering training, 104-105
  preparing training materials, 103-104

U

unclosed records, legacy data, 88-89
urgent changes, work flows, 47
user interfaces, features of change and release management tools, 77-78

V

vendor release schedules, release package designs, 160

W

weighting, establishing, 81
work flow tools, 71
work flows, 41
  change categories, 41
    data center changes, 42
    data changes, 44
    documentation or administrative changes, 45
    workstation changes, 43
  change urgency, 45
    emergency changes, 45-46
    long, complex changes, 47-48
    normal changes, 47
    urgent changes, 47

features of change and release management tools, 79-80
release management, 48
  infrastructure release flow, 49
  integration project release, 50
  software development flow, 48-49
work instructions, defining processes, 30
workshops, process workshops. *See* process workshops
workstation changes, work flows, 43

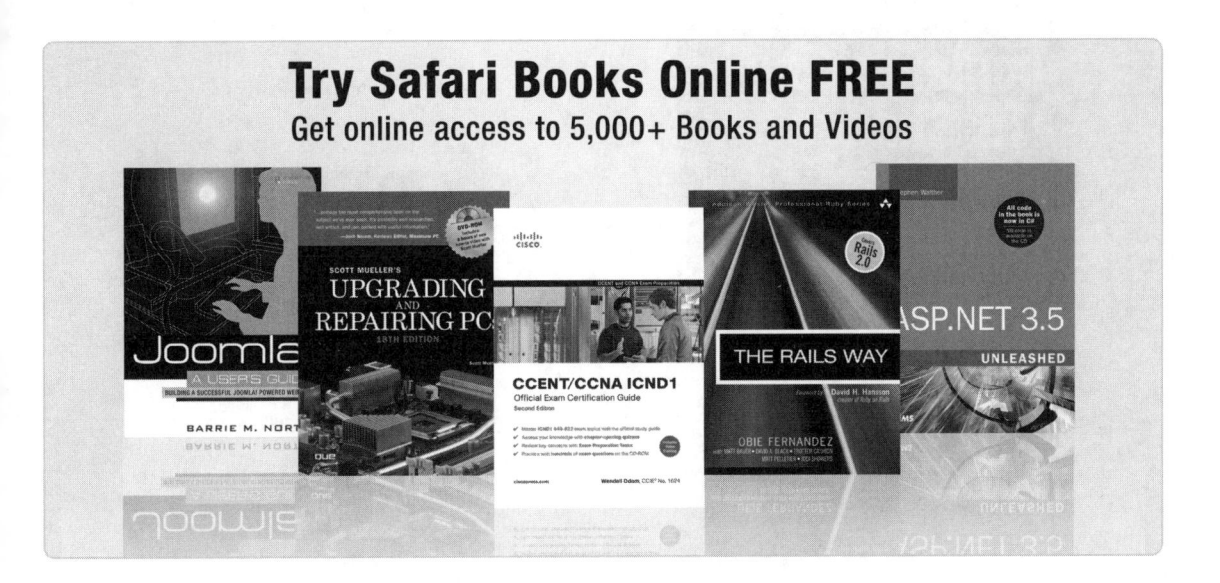

Try Safari Books Online FREE
Get online access to 5,000+ Books and Videos

Safari Books Online

FREE TRIAL—GET STARTED TODAY!
www.informit.com/safaritrial

Find trusted answers, fast
Only Safari lets you search across thousands of best-selling books from the top technology publishers, including Addison-Wesley Professional, Cisco Press, O'Reilly, Prentice Hall, Que, and Sams.

Master the latest tools and techniques
In addition to gaining access to an incredible inventory of technical books, Safari's extensive collection of video tutorials lets you learn from the leading video training experts.

WAIT, THERE'S MORE!

Keep your competitive edge
With Rough Cuts, get access to the developing manuscript and be among the first to learn the newest technologies.

Stay current with emerging technologies
Short Cuts and Quick Reference Sheets are short, concise, focused content created to get you up-to-speed quickly on new and cutting-edge technologies.

FREE Online Edition

Your purchase of **Implementing ITIL Change and Release Management** includes access to a free online edition for 45 days through the Safari Books Online subscription service. Nearly every IBM Press book is available online through Safari Books Online, along with more than 5,000 other technical books and videos from publishers such as Addison-Wesley Professional, Cisco Press, Exam Cram, O'Reilly, Prentice Hall, Que, and Sams.

SAFARI BOOKS ONLINE allows you to search for a specific answer, cut and paste code, download chapters, and stay current with emerging technologies.

Activate your FREE Online Edition at www.informit.com/safarifree

> **STEP 1:** Enter the coupon code: IIGL-5UYF-1UBJ-PFFQ-SCMM.

> **STEP 2:** New Safari users, complete the brief registration form. Safari subscribers, just log in.

If you have difficulty registering on Safari or accessing the online edition, please e-mail customer-service@safaribooksonline.com